CAERPHILLY COUNTY BOROUGH

3 8030

D0590520

ᴐ∩ᴅ Risc
75 T

Game

Eight Weeks That

Published by Accent Press Ltd 2018

www.accentpress.co.uk

Copyright © Steve Howell 2018

The right of Steve Howell to be identified as the author of
this work has been asserted by the author in accordance
with the Copyright, Designs and Patents Act 1988.

Although every effort has been made to ensure the
accuracy of the information contained in this book,
neither the author nor the publisher assumes responsibility
for errors, omissions, or contrary interpretations of the
subject matter herein.

All rights reserved. No part of this book may be
reproduced, stored in a retrieval system, or transmitted in
any form or by any means, electronic, electrostatic,
magnetic tape, mechanical, photocopying, recording or
otherwise, without the written permission of
Accent Press Ltd.

ISBN 9781786155863
eISBN 9781786155870

Printed and bound in Great Britain by
Clays Ltd, St Ives plc

For those who died in the Grenfell Tower fire on Wednesday 14 June 2017 and for their families and those who survived, now fighting for justice.

"There is a crime here that goes beyond denunciation. There is a sorrow here that weeping cannot symbolise. There is a failure here that topples all our success."

John Steinbeck, *The Grapes of Wrath*

Contents

Contents

1 – The Day of Reckoning

"Stand ye calm and resolute,
Like a forest close and mute."
Shelley, *The Masque of Anarchy*

It was 9.50pm, Thursday June 8, 2017. In ten minutes, polls would close in one of the most dramatic and unpredictable general elections of modern times. Jeremy Corbyn's tightly-knit communications team had assembled on the eighth floor at Southside, Labour's head office near Victoria, ready for an all-night media operation. Supplies of biscuits, crisps and chocolate brownies were scattered across the large table we were gathered around. But most of it was untouched. No one was eating – even for comfort – as we waited for the exit poll. Would Theresa May get her landslide, as some polling companies were still predicting? Or did we dare to believe that Labour had closed the gap? Was it possible that we had come from so far behind to deny the Tories a parliamentary majority and possibly see Jeremy form a government?

Never before in a general election had there been so much variation in the polls. The final batch before Election Day differed by nearly 12 percentage points. *Survation* was saying the vote shares would be 41 per cent for the Tories and 40 per cent for Labour – in polling terms, a dead heat. At the other end of spectrum, *BMG* – Labour's own agency – was predicting a 46 per cent to 33

1

per cent Tory victory.[1]

Meetings with *BMG* before and during the campaign had been grim. They were like a parallel world where all the energy and brightness we were seeing across the country was replaced by gloom and paralysing pessimism. The data was abundant, presented in one doom-laden slide after another, but it was completely at odds with the huge crowds turning out to hear Jeremy speak and the response we were getting on social media. But were we kidding ourselves? Were the rallies 'preaching to the converted', as some detractors claimed? Was social media an echo chamber or were the millions of views of our material winning hearts and minds? Younger voters were the nub of this conundrum. We knew we had a huge lead among people under 35, but had they registered in large enough numbers and would they turn out on the day?

What we did know was that we could increase the Labour vote substantially from the 30.4 per cent achieved under Ed Miliband in 2015 and yet still lose seats because of the way an expected collapse in the UKIP vote could boost the Tories in some Labour-held constituencies. In order to deny the Tories a majority, we would have to increase the Labour share of the vote to a level not seen since 1997, which some experts had ridiculed us for even thinking possible.

Conventional wisdom has it that you don't shift opinion in a general election campaign by more than two or three percentage points. The gap we had to close, based on the average of the polls immediately prior to May calling the election on April 18, was 16 points. In the

---

[1] UK Polling Report.

first poll after that, *YouGov* had us a staggering 48 to 24 per cent behind. Even *Survation*, the pollster that ended up calling it correctly, had us trailing 40 to 29 per cent in its first poll on April 22.

Among those directing the campaign, everyone thought we had done well. But there were different views on how well. The formidable operational head of Jeremy's office, Karie Murphy, would not hear talk of anything less than Labour forming a government. Early in the campaign, Jeremy, Jon Trickett, the shadow minister for the cabinet office, and Seumas Milne, the director of strategy and communications[2] in the leader's office, had met the head of the civil service and cabinet secretary, Sir Jeremy Heywood, for an initial briefing. With the polls narrowing, Jon, Karie, Seumas and Andrew Fisher, Jeremy's policy director, met Sir Jeremy again a week before polling to discuss foreign visits and a possible legislative timetable in the event of Jeremy becoming prime minister. Then Karie and Andrew went back again in the final week to talk about Downing Street staffing and the details of what would happen on the day after the election if Labour was the largest party.

Until the final weekend before polling day, my expectations had been much the same as Karie's. I had delayed a trip to California to see my son and his family so that I would be around to help if Jeremy was called upon to form a government. But the Tories had intensified their attacks on us, feeding smears to their friends in the national press and running a shockingly dishonest social media campaign. The day before polling,

---

[2] I was Seumas' deputy and based in the Leader of the Opposition's offices (LOTO) in the House of Commons.

the *Daily Mail* ran a front page editorial under the headline "Apologists for terror" accusing Jeremy, John McDonnell and Diane Abbott of "befriending Britain's enemies." The *Sun*'s offering the same day was another spurious story headlined "Jezza's Jihadi comrades." The *Telegraph*, *Times* and *Express* peddled similar attacks.

These slurs and slanders had been relentless throughout the campaign, but it was hard to tell if this final burst – exploiting real and raw fears of terrorism after the Manchester and London Bridge attacks – would sway some voters at the last minute. I had braced myself for this suppressing our vote, in the way the *Sun* claimed credit for doing in 1992 with its infamous front page: "If Kinnock wins today, will the last person to leave Britain please turn out the lights."[3]

Like it or not, our post-election planning had to straddle all the scenarios. We had sketched out several possibilities. At the top of the range was a Labour government and the implementation of the Downing Street organogram on Karie's desk. At the other extreme was the possibility that the increase in the Labour vote would not be big enough to prevent the loss of some seats, possibly triggering calls for Jeremy to resign. In between there was a hung Parliament, a very narrow Tory majority and something close to the status quo in

---

[3] The paper boasted of its influence afterwards with a headline: 'It's the Sun wot won it.' These days the Sun's circulation is much lower, and social media has provided a direct route to voters. But, as well as having the support of most newspapers, the Tories were spending millions on attack ads on Facebook and other digital platforms, and we couldn't be sure what effect it was having (see chapters 12 and 13).

terms of seats. All our planning anticipated an increase in our vote – the question was how big it would be.

As we waited for the exit poll that night, I was numb from exhaustion and beyond even thinking about the different scenarios. The eight weeks of the campaign had been relentless for everyone working inside the national machine. Labour staffers, temporary recruits, and the teams from Jeremy and John McDonnell's offices – about two hundred of us – had spent just about every waking hour focusing on the most extraordinary election battle anyone, even those of us at the upper end of the age range, could remember.

At any one time, some of the communications and events staff would be out on the road, either with Jeremy or as part of the 'advance' team, sent out to recce the next set of visits and rallies. The rest of us were packed into two floors of the characterless concrete and glass Southside building, living mostly on caffeine, adrenalin and far too much sugary stuff from the convenience store across the road.

I have been involved in some big and memorable campaigns, but never have I seen so many people work so intensively and creatively for so many weeks without a proper break.

And that was just at Southside. At Labour's offices in the regions and nations, in every constituency, and through the unions and campaign groups such as Momentum, tens of thousands of people had been active in the election battle in one way or another. Labour had run a people's campaign, fuelled in equal measure by more than 200,000 small donations and financial support from affiliated trade unions, raised from millions of

5

political levy-paying members. The Tories, on the other hand, had been awash with cash from super-rich donors from the outset, but could turn out only a few dozen people whenever Theresa May appeared anywhere.[4]

On Election Day, however, Labour's national campaign was in limbo. There was nothing more we could do. Jeremy was at home in Islington preparing for election night, having given a final rousing speech to local supporters the night before. All our online advertising – to get the vote out and help people find their polling station – was up and running. Most of the head office staff were either out in key constituencies campaigning on the doorstep or catching up on sleep ready for the night ahead.

I had been to Hendon that afternoon for a trip down memory lane in the part of London I grew up in. The constituency campaign office was in a building that once housed the GP's surgery where I'd had vaccinations and treatment for assorted childhood ailments. Opposite was the Methodist church where my parents were married. The road alongside it, Egerton Gardens, was where my grandmother, Winnie, had lived and in 1969 persuaded my school-friend, Peter Mandelson, and me that we should set up a branch of the Labour Party Young

---

[4] Parties have to report donations of £1,500 or more to the Electoral Commission every quarter. In the second quarter of 2017, a total of £24.9m was raised by the Tories from just 1,192 donors, an average donation of more than £20,000. Labour reported 694 large donations totalling £10.3m, mostly from trade unions. In addition, Labour's national fund-raising campaign for the election raised nearly £5m in personal donations at an average value of about £20.

6

Socialists.[5] Not long afterwards, at the nearby local grammar school, we had led a revolt against the privileges given to prefects by an elitist headteacher, hastening his retirement and smoothing the path for the introduction of comprehensive education in a borough that was one of the last bastions of selection.[6] Neither of us – as politically precocious teenagers – would have imagined that nearly fifty years later we would be so completely at loggerheads over who should be leader of the Labour Party.

Hendon's place in the political world has changed radically since then, too. We lived in Hendon South, which incorporated Golders Green and Hampstead Garden Suburb, where Tory baronet Sir Hugh Vere Huntly Duff Lucas-Tooth had enjoyed a comfortable majority in every election since 1945. Hendon North stretched to Edgware and had been held since 1950 by another Tory baronet, Sir Charles Ian Orr-Ewing, albeit with his majority cut to 600 in 1966 when Labour under Harold Wilson's leadership won a 96-seat majority in Parliament.

Today, the single Hendon constituency is demographically very different. Boundary changes have re-allocated some of the leafier areas to neighbouring constituencies and a 1970s redevelopment of the former Hendon aerodrome has added to the working class vote and introduced greater ethnic diversity. The seat was held by Labour from 1997 to 2010, but it wasn't won back in 2015. Our 2017 candidate, Mike Katz, was battling to overturn a 3,724 Tory majority.

---

[5] Peter Mandelson, 'The Third Man,' HarperPress, 2010, p48.
[6] Donald Macintyre, 'Mandelson – The Biography,' Harper Collins, 1999, p15.

I went with a carload of supporters to the redeveloped aerodrome, now known as the Grahame Park estate, to 'knock up' residents of the low-rise flats who had told canvassers they would vote Labour. It proved exactly the fillip I needed to take my mind off the waiting game. These were not the grudgingly loyal Labour voters I had often encountered in previous elections. Almost everyone showed real enthusiasm. People were proud to say they had already voted or pleased to be reminded. The estate was tatty and neglected, and the sky was grey, but hope was in the air.

As I arrived back at Southside, a WhatsApp message came through from my 24-year-old son, Josh, who lives in Liverpool. This was the first general election in which he had been involved in campaigning: "Just been out door knocking, making sure people are getting out to vote in West Wirral. A mix of big houses and social housing, so you can see why it's a marginal. A lot of people on the ground."

That seemed to be the case everywhere. All day messages had been flooding in to the Labour WhatsApp feeds from supporters in constituencies around the country. One said that 1,900 extra people had registered to vote in Peterborough. At a Lincoln polling station, another message reported, turnout was higher in the first hour and a half than in the whole of 2015. One of our staff had been talking to a friendly but demoralised Tory activist whose two sons had joined the Labour party. From everywhere, it seemed, people were posting photographs of enthusiastic Labour campaigners getting the vote out.

At Southside, the second floor meeting rooms had

been set up for staff to have refreshments while watching the results. Only people who were on duty could access the eighth floor. Jeremy's communications team was on a 48-hour rota that ran continuously from the start of Election Day through to late Friday night. Everyone knew the jobs they had to do. Everyone had some sleeping time allocated and could use the hotel rooms we had booked nearby.

The team met at 9pm that evening to check that everything was in hand for the night ahead. Several upbeat pieces had been drafted for the next day's media, which would be topped and tailed to reflect the actual results. All the shadow cabinet members who were going out to bat for us on the overnight election programmes had been briefed. There was nothing more we could do.

As those final minutes to the close of polling ticked away, the staff who were on duty on the eighth floor began to edge closer to the TV screen just above where I was sitting. Andrew Fisher was standing behind me. To my left was David Prescott, the communications manager for the shadow cabinet, and son of the former deputy prime minister. By the time Big Ben started chiming, everyone was silent.

On screen, David Dimbleby was facing a giant graphic with the exit poll's projected number of seats for each party. It was predicting the Tories would win 314 against 266 for Labour, 34 for the SNP, 14 for the Lib Dems and 22 for other parties. There was a collective gasp as he said "they (the Conservatives) don't have an overall majority." David Prescott, pointing at the Labour total, shouted: "We've gone up forty" (his arithmetic slightly exaggerated). Andrew, understated as ever, calmly said:

9

"Please let it be right." My phone pinged with a text from Kevin Maguire, associate editor of the *Daily Mirror*, saying: "Fantastic. I hope this isn't false hope."

Exit polls, though usually far more accurate than any others, have been known to be wrong. Even a small variance can make a significant difference, as happened in 2015 when the Conservatives won a narrow overall majority after the exit poll had predicted they would fall short. With the actual results not starting to come in for nearly an hour, we needed to temper our elation – it was too early to celebrate denying the Tories a majority, never mind the possibility that Jeremy could be called on to form a government.

Seumas had gone to Islington with Karie to be on hand to advise Jeremy on how he should react to the drama that was about to unfold. In an e-mail, he cautioned against "reacting to the poll directly until we have more evidence or know the percentages."

The first actual result – from Newcastle upon Tyne Central – did little to clarify things. We had held the seat with our share of the vote up nearly ten percentage points, but the Tory vote had also increased by six points. The two per cent swing to Labour was below the exit poll's projection of a seven per cent swing.

Minutes later, Houghton & Sunderland South was even less helpful. We held the seat, but the Tory share of the vote was up by more than ours, boosted by a mass defection from UKIP. This was technically a swing to the Tories that, if repeated everywhere, would give them a majority.

From the next two results – Newcastle East and Sunderland Central – all we learned was that we were doing better on the Tyne than on the Wear. Both were held by Labour but with very different swings.[7] And we were barely any the wiser just before midnight when the Tories held Swindon North despite a four-point swing to us.

It was time, I thought, to visit our own number crunchers in a nearby meeting room, who were not only collating the actual results, but also gathering feedback ahead of the declarations from Labour supporters scrutinising the counts around the country. Patrick Heneghan, the party's long-standing elections director, walked me round the white boards being used to post both results and projections. The latter were encouraging: he said we were on course to gain Rutherglen & Hamilton West, Coatbridge, and East Lothian from the SNP, Leeds North West from the Liberal Democrats, and Battersea, Vale of Clwyd, Cardiff North and Bury North from the Tories. And that was for starters.

Back with the communications team, I watched those gains starting to flow in – Rutherglen & Hamilton West followed by Vale of Clwyd and Battersea – and listened to the pundits trying to talk their way out of their previous derision of our chances. "No one expected Corbyn to be such a good campaigner," said the *BBC*'s Andrew Marr at one point. Really? No one? Where had he been for the past two years?

By 2am, it was clear the exit poll would be more or

---

[7] In Newcastle East, the swing was in line with the exit poll. But in Sunderland Central, though Labour's share of the vote went up, there was a bigger increase in the Tory share, giving a small swing to them.

11

less accurate. Declarations at Stockton South and Bury North had taken our gains to five with swings close to the poll figure. The *BBC*'s political editor, Laura Kuenssberg, was calling it "one of the biggest political upsets in many, many years." At 2.40am, the trend was confirmed when Boris Johnson saw his majority slashed in half after a 6.5 per cent swing to Labour. The Tory foreign secretary was, for once, subdued.

Then, just after 3am, came Jeremy's own result. He had won Islington North by comfortable margins on eight occasions since first being elected in 1983. It would surely be hard to improve on the 60 per cent share of the vote and majority of 21,194 he had achieved in 2015, particularly as he had been on the road for eight weeks with virtually no time for his own contest. The declaration when it came was therefore an extraordinary vote of confidence from his own backyard: Labour's share of the vote had climbed 13 points to 73 per cent, taking his majority up 12,021 to 33,215. The turnout was the highest for the constituency since 1951, and would prove to be one of the highest for the whole country in 2017.

In typically earnest style, he told the crowd at the Sobell Leisure Centre in Islington:

"I'm very, very honoured and humbled by the size of the vote that has been cast for me tonight as the Labour candidate."

But it wasn't just the unprecedented majority that made this unlike any of the other eight acceptance speeches he had given as a winning candidate. Now, as the leader of a resurgent party with the outcome of the election still hanging in the balance, every word would matter to the millions of people watching on live television.

In what was widely interpreted as a victory speech, at least in the sense that Labour had beaten expectations and was on course to deny the Tories a majority, he took the opportunity to reflect on the game-changing nature of the campaign:

"I've travelled the whole country; I've spoken at events and rallies all over the country. And you know what? Politics has changed, and politics isn't going back into the box where it was before. What's happened is people have said they've had quite enough of austerity politics; they've had quite enough of cuts to public expenditure, under-funding our health service, under-funding our schools and our education service, and not giving our young people the chance they deserve in our society, and I'm very, very proud of the campaign that my party has run — our manifesto for the many, not the few. And I'm very proud of the results that are coming in all over the country tonight, of people voting for hope, voting for hope for the future and turning their backs on austerity."

And then came the part the pundits weren't expecting:

"The Prime Minister called the election because she wanted a mandate. Well the mandate she's got is lost Conservative seats, lost votes, lost support and lost confidence. I would have thought that's enough to go, actually, and make way for a government that will be truly representative of the people of this country."

It was a measure of how massively we had defied

expectations that, even though it was clear we would not win more seats than the Tories, few were surprised to hear Jeremy call for May to resign. Not long after he had finished, Laura Kuenssberg texted me: "Amazing result for you guys." It certainly was. The gains were flowing thick and fast by then. Not only were we winning narrowly-held Tory marginals, such as Gower and Derby North, we were also stunning the political world by taking seats, such as Canterbury and Portsmouth South, that had never been Labour and had not been on anyone's radar except ours.

At 6am, it was confirmed there would be a hung Parliament. My final job of the night was to edit an article drafted by Jeremy's adviser for Scotland, Tommy Kane, for the *Daily Record*. Before heading to my hotel for a few hours' sleep, it was a pleasure to be able to sign off a piece saying Labour had increased its share of the vote "by more than in any election since Clement Attlee's historic victory in 1945."

As I walked the empty dawn-lit streets to a hotel in Pimlico, I could not quite believe we had actually done it – and I was far too tired to analyse how – but I knew that Jeremy was right, that politics would never be the same again. Against the odds, and defying almost every rule in the book, the campaign had been a game changer.

2 – Coups and Copeland

"It is getting harder to see how Corbyn can survive."
John Rentoul, the *Independent*[1]

My first conversation about taking a full-time role in Jeremy Corbyn's team came as his leadership was facing a new crisis. It was mid-January 2017. Tristram Hunt had just resigned as Labour MP for Stoke-on-Trent Central. Only three weeks earlier, Jamie Reed, the Labour MP for Copeland, had also handed in his notice. Both were strident Corbyn critics and their resignation letters fuelled a further frenzy of negative media coverage.

There would now be two by-elections at a point where the party's position in the polls had not recovered from the attempt to bring the Labour leader down during the previous summer. Jeremy may have comfortably won that second leadership contest, which was triggered by Shadow Cabinet resignations immediately after the EU referendum, but he faced a bigger challenge in restoring the party's standing among the wider public.

By attempting to oust Jeremy only ten months after he had first been elected, the instigators of the attempted coup had made Labour look a shambles. Like many members following events from a distance, I had been shocked by the way in which – on the Sunday after the referendum – resignations had been orchestrated to

[1] John Rentoul, 'Tristram Hunt's resignation is a sign of things to come for Labour,' the Independent, 13.1.2017.

coincide with hourly news bulletins to have maximum destabilising effect. That's why, when Owen Smith phoned me a week or so later to ask if I would work with him if he stood against Jeremy, I had had no hesitation in urging him to think again.

Owen is a friend and former *BBC* colleague, whom I knew well from moving in the same political circles in Wales. But I told him I could not support him if he went ahead because the issue, for me, was now the principle of democracy being respected, rather than anyone's personal or political qualities as a potential leader. I had voted for Jeremy in the first leadership election, and I supported his strong anti-austerity approach[2], but I had never met him, and could not know what had been going on behind the scenes or whether specific criticisms of his leadership raised by Owen were right or wrong. What I did know was that Jeremy was overwhelmingly elected in a fair process agreed by the party, and that supporting any challenger would imply endorsing the behaviour of a self-serving group that had put itself above the membership.

The attempted coup – and the divisive leadership

---

[2] Throughout the book, I have tried to be consistent in the use of terms. I have used 'neo-liberalism' as a broad heading for an approach to managing capitalism based on the premise that markets are always efficient and the state's role is to keep them as 'free' for profit-making as possible. I have used the word 'austerity' as short-hand for the application of a neo-liberal approach to Britain's crisis since 2010 by the Coalition and Tory governments, characterised mainly by public spending cuts, further privatisation or outsourcing, and tax giveaways to big business and the wealthy.

battle it triggered – undid the progress the party had been making in winning public support. On March 13, 2016, Labour had hit its highest point in the opinion polls for nearly a year when *ICM* had us neck and neck with the Tories on 36 per cent. A week later a *YouGov* poll put us ahead of the Tories for the first time since Jeremy was elected leader. Throughout that spring, we continued to poll consistently above the 30.4 per cent share of the vote Labour achieved in the 2015 general election and within three points of the Tories.[3]

In my view, these polls were in themselves good enough to justify Jeremy being given more time to get his message across. However, the actual position was arguably even better than the polls were suggesting because most pollsters had over-corrected for generational variations in turnout after their failure to predict the 2015 general election accurately. This is not hindsight. It was already obvious that Jeremy was enthusing young people and could reverse the long-term decline in their participation in elections. Many of us also pointed out – often to ridicule from some quarters – that the four parliamentary by-elections in Jeremy's first year saw the Labour vote share increase by an average of 5.4 per cent, a far better performance than the polling figures.

But none of this was good enough for Jeremy's critics. An opposition party should, they insisted, be well ahead of the governing party if it's going to go on to win at the next election. Some compared Jeremy's polling figures unfairly with the sky-high ones of Tony Blair in the months leading up to the 1997 general election when,

---

[3] See UK Polling Report.

after four defeats, Labour was finally poised for victory over a Tory government that was on its knees.

That election is probably responsible for more myths than Ancient Greece – and one of them is the idea that an election outcome is pre-determined by the pattern of polling several years prior to it. In reality, things are much more complex, not least because events[4] have a habit of intervening. David Cameron, for example, got off to a poor start in the polls after being elected Tory leader in 2005, but went on to do well enough to form a government in 2010 – aided largely by the 2008 financial crash and its effect on perceptions of Labour's economic competence. Conversely, Michael Foot lost in 1983 after Labour's seemingly unassailable position in 1980-81 was eroded by the SDP breakaway and then drowned by a tidal wave of jingoism following the Falklands War.

Neil Kinnock's performance in the polls after his election as Labour leader in 1983 is the nearest to a match with Jeremy's. Building from a similarly low base, Labour trailed the Tories in every poll until February 13, 1984, when *Marplan* put us one point ahead. Three weeks later, a *MORI* poll had Labour three points in front. But those polls were to be the only good news for some time: from then until mid-June, Labour trailed the Tories by an average of three points – exactly as we did in the same period of 2016.[5]

Kinnock went on to be given nine years and two

---

[4] I've refrained from using the 'events, dear boy, events' quote often attributed to Harold Macmillan after reading Robert Harris fulminating on the subject: 'As MacMillan never said: that's enough quotations,' the Daily Telegraph, 4.6.2002.

[5] See UK Polling Report.

general elections to prove himself as an electable leader. He was – as far as I know – never criticised by his predecessors for failing to win power, yet he chose to discard any such courtesies when it came to Jeremy, branding him several times during the second leadership contest as "unelectable," and accusing him of being "vain" for not bowing to pressure to stand down.[6]

Many Labour members were genuine in their belief that a leader from the left would suffer the same fate as Michael Foot in 1983. However, the group who had imposed a summer of chaos on the party were very widely seen as having forfeited any legitimacy on that point. The coup had increased the risk that we would not be able to succeed electorally – it had become a potentially self-fulfilling argument because we were bound to emerge from such a bruising and divisive contest with the wider electorate wondering if we were fit to form a government, whatever their view of Jeremy.

This was all the more of concern because of the way the Tories had swiftly filled the leadership role vacated by David Cameron after the EU referendum. In typical Tory style, there were a few betrayals and tantrums, but arm-twisting behind the scenes quickly led to a closing of ranks behind Theresa May without their members having to be troubled with an election. In the short term, the coronation of May – standing in stark contrast to Labour's blood-letting – proved popular with the electorate, especially as it was accompanied by populist rhetoric from the new leader about "a country that works for everyone" and how life for ordinary working

---

[6] Decca Aitkenhead interview with Neil Kinnock, the Guardian, 9.7.2016.

class families "is much harder than many people in Westminster realise."[7]

In the general election ten months later, the contrast between this fine talk and an out-of-touch May trying to sell the dementia tax would of course be plain to see. But it was smart tactics to step onto Labour's political turf at a time when we were in such disarray and many working class voters in our heartlands were at odds with our Remain stance in the EU referendum.

The polls immediately after Jeremy had defeated Owen[8] in a bruising contest gave an indication of the damage the summer had done to Labour: the eight in October 2016 had the Tories leading by an average of 15 percentage points – a gap five times greater than prior to the attempted coup. We had slumped to an average of 27.5 per cent, our worst position since 1983.[9]

Even if those polls did understate our support among young people, three by-elections in Tory-held seats provided inescapable evidence of the magnitude of the challenge we faced. In better times, none of the contests would have been especially significant – nor would any have been seen as winnable – but our vote share was down by an average of six points. And, with party unity in such a fragile state, we did not need the humiliation of slipping from second to third place in Witney (vacated by Cameron), of plummeting from second to fourth in Sleaford and North Hykeham, or of losing our deposit in a

---

[7] Theresa May, first statement as Prime Minister, Downing Street, 13.7.16.

[8] Second Labour leadership election result: Jeremy Corbyn 313,209 (61.8%), Owen Smith 193,229 (38.2%), 24.9.2016.

[9] UK Polling Report.

high-profile contest in Richmond Park, where the Liberal Democrats ousted the Tory-turned-Independent Zac Goldsmith.

By January 2017, the last thing the party leadership would have wanted was two more by-elections and both of them in Labour-held seats which, on the basis of the polls, we looked likely to lose. It was hardly a promising time to be discussing working full-time for Jeremy but, when Seumas phoned me to talk about a possible role as his deputy, I was nevertheless excited at the prospect of being involved in a project that I still believed had the potential to be a political game changer.

The movement supporting Jeremy Corbyn is a product of our times. The 2008 bank crash and the great recession it triggered were events of such a magnitude that politics was bound to change fundamentally. From 2008 to 2012, the banks repossessed 198,600 homes.[10] Official unemployment rose 68 per cent to 2.71 million[11] and many more millions were driven into the precariat, living on meagre and uncertain freelance and part-time work, often on zero hour contracts. Company insolvencies soared as banks bailed out by the taxpayer drove tens of thousands of small businesses to the wall.[12]

---

[10] Two and a half times as many as in the previous five years (78,100). Source: Council of Mortgage Lenders.

[11] According to the Labour Force Survey, seasonally adjusted unemployment rose from 1.61m in Oct-Dec 2007 to 2.71m by Sept-Nov 2011. It was above 2m for nearly six years from Oct 2008 to July 2014. See **www.ons.gov.uk**.

[12] Insolvency Service figures show company insolvencies rising more than 50% in 2008-09 to well over 6,000 per quarter.

Everywhere you turned it was economic carnage.

In his final year in office, Gordon Brown resisted pressure to make draconian cuts and pursued a more active industrial strategy that mitigated some of the worst effects of the crash. But, after the 2010 election, the Tory-Liberal Democrat Coalition resorted to austerity: slashing budgets for public services, introducing a public sector pay cap, cutting welfare benefits and trebling tuition fees. At the same time, in textbook neo-liberal style, they cut taxes on big business profits by 39 per cent and dished out a succession of new tax breaks for the wealthy[13], claiming they would boost investment, which they didn't.

The other measure that was supposed to stimulate the economy was 'quantitative easing' (QE) by the Bank of England, which simply created £445 billion[14] in digital money to buy assets from pension funds and banks thus, in turn, inflating share prices. It sounds like a scam for the wealthy, and it was, but don't take my word for it. The UK's leading investment fund manager, Neil Woodford, said after five years of QE:

> "Policy makers had hoped that by increasing asset prices, they could engineer some sort of 'trickle-down' effect, whereby increasing wealth would lead to increased spending, creation of jobs, and rising business investment, and that a virtuous

---

[13] George Osborne cut the rate of corporation tax for bigger companies from 28% in 2010 to 17% by 2020-21. Other tax giveaways included cuts in capital gains tax, a twenty-fold increase in the allowances for entrepreneurs' relief and its extension to wealthy investors, and a cut in inheritance tax.

[14] Quantitative Easing, Bank of England website.

cycle would ensue. This hasn't happened, primarily because the assets that have increased in value are not broadly held by all members of the economy. The asset-rich have got richer but the asset-poor have not."[15]

During the first Labour leadership election in 2015, Jeremy turned this around by proposing 'people's QE' in which the Bank of England would invest its digital cash in building houses and infrastructure. It was a neat idea, but neo-liberalism had become such a dogma that any new thinking was scorned. One of the rival candidates, Liz Kendall, said:

"His plans for so-called 'people's quantitative easing' risk destabilising our currency and pushing up inflation, harming the living standards of millions of people in this country, particularly the poor and low paid."[16]

This was asserted without irony, and yet Liz's criticism was being made after the Bank of England – set free by Brown in 1997 to act on its own – had spent five years pumping up the wealth of the already 'asset-rich' without any dark warnings from Labour's front bench about currency destabilisation.

Neo-liberalism has since the early 1970s pursued an agenda of privatisation, de-regulation, and globalisation – the free movement internationally of capital, goods, services, and (sometimes) labour. Neo-liberals – from Chile's General Pinochet to most of today's Tory party –

---

[15] Neil Woodford, quoted in 'Woodford Worries,' the Investors Chronicle, 8.8.2014.
[16] Quoted by Patrick Wintour and Rowena Mason, 'Voting closes in Labour leadership election,' the Guardian, 10.9.2015.

23

would prefer to see the state withdraw from almost everything except prosecuting wars and preventing trade unions and others from impeding the pursuit of maximum profit. They see health as a target for profit-making and education largely as a means of producing cogs for a commercial machine (robots preferred).

When I was at school in the 1960s, the teachers spoke of the welfare state with pride. But the election of Margaret Thatcher as prime minister in 1979 marked the beginning of a relentless drive to trash the word 'welfare' itself and roll-back the social democratic capitalist model on every front. In an interview with the *Sunday Times*, after two years in office, Thatcher said:

> "What's irritated me about the whole direction of politics in the last 30 years is that it's always been towards the collectivist society. People have forgotten about the personal society."[17]

What she meant by 'the personal society' is now abundantly clear and would be better described as the everyone-for-themselves, dog-eat-dog society. By the end of her era, neo-liberalism was so pervasive that some Labour figures thought there was no hope of winning an election without adopting most of its central propositions. Thus, when Tony Blair led the party to victory in 1997, it did not seem odd that he would continue the privatising and outsourcing that began under Thatcher, or fund capital spending in the public sector through John Major's private finance initiative (PFI).

---

[17] Interview with Robert Butt, 'Mrs Thatcher: the first two years,' the Sunday Times, 3.5.1981.
See **www.margaretthatcher.org**.

Jeremy is well known for his opposition to regime-change wars, which were a natural corollary of Washington-led economic globalisation, but he was also an early critic of Labour's use of PFI. In 1998, he asked Alan Milburn, the then Labour minister of state for health:

"What estimates he has made of the long-term costs of private finance compared with government borrowing on hospital expansion programmes?"

Milburn replied:

"To be approved, a PFI contract must offer better or comparable value for money to the publicly funded alternative."[18]

We now know that the correct answer would have been that PFI funding is often more than *twice* as expensive as government borrowing.[19]

In 2007, as the neo-liberal economic model was beginning to buckle under mountains of debt, Seumas predicted that the political consequences would be far-reaching. In a *Guardian* column, he wrote:

"If the credit squeeze does indeed trigger a wider economic meltdown, that will certainly mean the end of the neo-liberal consensus that has

---

[18] Hansard, 24.3.1998.

[19] A report by the National Audit Office, published on 18.1.2018, have as an illustration: 'paying off a debt of £100m over 30 years with interest of 2% costs £34m in interest; at 4% this more than doubles to £73m.' See 'PFI1 and PFI2', NAO report, p14.

dominated politics for almost a generation."[20]
Nine months later, Lehman Brothers filed for bankruptcy, triggering a worldwide financial crisis. It would take several years for the political consequences of that cataclysmic event to mature. The varied struggles that developed in response to austerity – from the Occupy Now movement and the WASPI women's campaign, to battles over tuition fees and public sector pay – all helped produce a qualitative shift in the political mood in and around the labour movement. By 2015, Labour members were ready to demonstrate a desire to break decisively with the neo-liberal consensus by electing Jeremy. The question, in early 2017, was whether or not his election would prove to be a game changer in terms of the battle for political power at Westminster.

I had first met Seumas in the early 1980s through a mutual journalist friend, Andrew Murray,[21] who was working for the *Morning Star* at the time. Some years later, after Seumas had become the *Guardian*'s labour correspondent, I helped him arrange an interview with the miners' leader, Arthur Scargill, who was based in Sheffield where I had lived since studying there in 1973. Throughout the 1980s, I devoted most of my spare time to the Sheffield Campaign Against Racism, which the trade unions in the area had been instrumental in

---

[20] Seumas Milne, 'The crisis spells the end of the free-market consensus,' the Guardian, 13.12.2007. This column is among those included in Seumas' book, 'The revenge of history,' Verso, 2012, p145.
[21] Andrew Murray is now chief of staff of Unite and was seconded to work on Labour's general election campaign in May 2017.

forming, and I knew several people at the NUM well enough to set up a meeting. Those interviews were the starting point of Seumas' meticulous research for a book on the 1984-85 miners' strike, *The Enemy Within*,[22] which would come to be regarded as the definitive account of their struggle. Seumas and I kept in touch but rarely saw each other.

In 1986, I became Sheffield City Council's international officer and secretary of British Local Authorities Against Apartheid. After Nelson Mandela was released, and happily the post became redundant, I found my way into journalism and moved to Wales – where my wife, Kim, was from – to work first for the *South Wales Argus* and then *BBC Wales*. When I left the *BBC* in 1997 to become a freelance PR consultant, I had no entrepreneurial aspirations, but I soon found I had more clients than I could handle, and the business that is now called Freshwater grew to employ, at the last count, 55 people in London and Cardiff.

Although as a company Freshwater has no political affiliations, my deputy as chief executive, John Underwood, and the managing director, Angharad Neagle, are both Labour Party members. John had been Labour's director of communication and campaigns

---

[22] Author Naomi Klein described 'The Enemy Within' as: 'The definitive account of the strike - the best book on the Thatcher era' (quoted by Verso). Huw Beynon, reviewing the book for Red Pepper, said: 'Through Seumas Milne's unique reporting into the dark side of the miners' strike, we can find roots of the repression that Britain continues to struggle with.' 15.7.2014.

27

under Neil Kinnock in the early 1990s[23] and was keen when Jeremy was first elected – despite not having voted for him – that we should offer our personal help. In the autumn of 2015, he went into the House of Commons to see John McDonnell, the shadow chancellor, to discuss what assistance we could give on a pro bono basis. This led to occasional exchanges between me and members of John's team, who often provided background material for my monthly business columns for the *Western Mail*, but did not go any further.

By the time Seumas called me in January 2017, I was beginning to wind down my role in Freshwater and had half an eye on retirement. Kim and I were empty-nesters living quietly in Cardiff with thoughts mainly of travelling and grandparenting. I was also midway through writing a second novel. Working for Jeremy in London would, I knew, leave me barely enough time to brush my teeth, never mind do any of the things on my bucket list. But I could not ignore Seumas' frequently-repeated point that politics is not a spectator sport. If I could help, I knew I had no choice politically, and I was lucky that Kim agreed.

While those discussions were going on, a further challenge was brewing for Jeremy on the issue of how to vote on the triggering of Article 50 of the Treaty of the European Union, the first step in the formal Brexit process. Labour had accepted the result of the referendum. The logic of that was that our MPs would vote to fire the starting gun. Whether for personal conviction or because of pressure from their constituents, or both, this was a step too far for some

---

[23] See Philip Gould, 'The Unfinished Revolution,' Abacus, 1998, p101.

shadow cabinet members. By the second week of February, Jeremy had been hit by four resignations, all of them from people who had been loyal to his leadership. The mini-crisis this created was practical as well as political: with most MPs still refusing to serve under Jeremy, losing four more from his team meant more doubling up in jobs and more pressure on the remaining loyalist MPs.

Meanwhile, with polling day on February 23, four days before I was due to start my new job, the by-election campaigns in Copeland and Stoke were proceeding painfully for Labour.

In Copeland, the Tories were looking to over-turn a Labour majority of 2,564. In normal times, that would have been an impossible task for a governing party. But – even leaving aside the abnormality of Labour's position – the Tories had two reasons to be optimistic: firstly, Jeremy's past opposition to nuclear power was as toxic as radioactive sludge in a constituency where the livelihoods of thousands of voters are linked to nuclear reprocessing at Sellafield; secondly, the Tories could play the Brexit card to win over the 6,148 voters who had supported UKIP in the 2015 general election.

In Stoke, the threat to Labour was coming from UKIP itself. With the party leader Paul Nuttall as their candidate, UKIP were treating it as a bridgehead to their conquest of the Labour heartlands. In a Brexit-leaning seat they were facing a Labour candidate, Gareth Snell, who had referred to Brexit as "a massive pile of shit."[24] But their campaign was floundering as Nuttall dug

---

[24] Gareth Snell tweet, 29.9.2016, reported in the Independent, 1.2.2017.

himself into deeper and deeper holes after falsely claiming he had a home in the constituency and "a close friend" who died at Hillsborough.[25]

The results reflected the way the campaigns had gone. The Tories won Copeland with an increase in their vote share – 8.5 percentage points – that was almost identical to the collapse in the UKIP vote. Labour saw off the UKIP threat in Stoke on a poor turnout and with the voting pattern not markedly unchanged from 2015. Labour's share of the vote was down two points in Stoke and five points in Copeland. The Stoke result would, in the longer term, prove the more significant of the two in signaling that the UKIP threat could be seen off. But the Copeland defeat prompted another round of bad headlines for Labour and put more pressure on Jeremy. Though most Labour MPs kept a disciplined silence, Richard Angell of the Blairite pressure group Progress said:

> "The Tory gain in Copeland makes the message clear. A hard-left Momentum-led Labour party is more repugnant to the voters than a Tory government closing a local maternity unit and urgent care centre. It is a disaster."[26]

Not surprisingly, my old friend Peter Mandelson was taken aback when I told him I would be starting work for Jeremy the following week. Just before the by-elections, he had told the *Jewish Chronicle* that he would not "walk away and pass the title deeds" of Labour to "someone like Jeremy Corbyn." He continued:

---

[25] UKIP later blamed the 'close friend' claim on one of its press officers, see the Guardian 14.2.17.
[26] Quoted by Jessica Elgot, the Guardian, 24.2.17

"I don't want to, I resent it, and I work every single day in some small way to bring forward the end of his tenure in office. I work every day — an e-mail, a phone call, a meeting with Labour MPs. I try to galvanise them. Every day I do something to rescue the Labour Party from his leadership."[27]

Peter didn't, however, try to 'rescue' me when I e-mailed him about my new job the day before I started. Knowing my support for Jeremy was solid from our previous exchanges, he simply said:

"I am afraid that, like most of the world, I am not on the Leader's wavelength. It pains me more than I can say that you should be making such a sacrifice but it's your life!"

---

[27] Peter Mandelson speaking at a JC Editor's Choice event, the Jewish Chronicle, 20.2.17.

3 – Under Siege, In More Ways Than One

*"Whatever regard you may hold for me personally, you
are addressing the office of the Vice President."*
John Hoynes to C J Cregg, *West Wing*[1]

Turning the clock forward for a digression: it's Friday,
May 26, the height of the general election battle.
Campaigning has just resumed after the Manchester
terrorist bombing. That morning, Jeremy delivers a
difficult speech responding to the attack. He faces fierce
criticism in the media for daring to say regime-change
wars have made Britain less secure. That afternoon, he
disappears to a hideaway to prepare for what is sure to
be a tough television interview with Andrew Neil.
Probably nothing is further from his thoughts than his
68th birthday. But Labour's digital team hasn't forgotten
it. One of them suggests videoing everyone singing
'Happy Birthday' and sending it to him. An hour or so
later, about sixty staff from all departments gather in the
kitchen area on the eighth floor at Southside to give it
their best musical shot.

It was a heart-warming display of unity and a far cry
from the situation I found three months earlier when I
arrived from Cardiff to start work for Jeremy. The
divisions then were as deep as ever. Labour's Copeland
by-election defeat had triggered another round of
rumours and speculation about a challenge to Jeremy's

---

[1] Season 1, Episode 8, *West Wing*.

leadership. Relations between the two parts of the Labour machine – the staff working for Jeremy in Parliament and those based at the party's head office half a mile away – were not easy, to say the least.

The Leader of the Opposition's offices are known by the acronym LOTO. They are tucked away on the second floor of the Norman Shaw Building, a late Victorian, red-brick edifice on the Embankment. For people of my generation, it will probably be remembered as the original New Scotland Yard. Until 1967, it was the home of the Metropolitan Police and often appeared in movies with its iron gates open and Black Marias coming and going.

Apart from some Labour posters on the walls, I suspect it hasn't changed much since those days. The furniture would lower the tone of an office clearance sale, and you can see the dust rising from the dark green carpet when the sun shines. Co-habiting with a few mice, LOTO's 30 or so staff occupy half a dozen rooms. My desk was one of 16 in a large room overlooking the Thames. With Jeremy's office beyond, it was often a gathering place for shadow cabinet members waiting to see him or special advisers bending ears for their bosses.

Jeremy himself seemed unperturbed by the relentless attacks on him – or perhaps he made a better job of hiding his feelings than most of us would. When we met for the first time he was cheery and welcoming, if slightly surprised – in an appreciative way – that someone would give up another job to work for him. Somehow, even though we shared several common political roots, our paths had never crossed. By the time my Labour activist parents moved from Hendon to Islington, I was at university in Sheffield. When I arranged for British Local Authorities Against Apartheid to hold one of its regular meetings at Islington town hall in the 1980s, it was the then council leader, Margaret Hodge, who gave the welcome.

But there was no time to compare notes on all that. Jeremy was buried from Monday to Thursday in Westminster business – LOTO meetings, shadow cabinet, prime minister's questions (PMQs) – and would then spend Friday in his constituency and the weekend campaigning. My priority was to get my bearings in the Byzantine world of Labour internal politics as it was on Monday, February 27, 2017.

The political rift in the party had produced a staffing structure that was almost unfathomable. At the top of Labour's organisational tree were six senior people – the general secretary, Iain McNicol, and five executive directors – split equally between the two centres of power. Based with Iain at Southside were Emilie Oldknow, who was responsible for governance, membership, and party services, and Patrick Heneghan, who directed elections, organisation, and campaigns. LOTO, meanwhile, had three people designated as executive directors: Seumas for strategy and communications, Karie for operational management, and Andrew for policy.

This parity between the two parts of the national Labour machine was established after Jeremy won the second leadership contest to give LOTO more say in the day to day running of the party. But underneath the top layer were all sorts of anomalies. Southside had its own policy team run by a director, Simon Jackson, who had sign-off powers on press releases even though – not being an *executive* director – he was junior to both Andrew and Seumas. Meanwhile, some Labour communications functions, such as digital and creative, came under Patrick while others, such as the Labour press office, nominally reported to Seumas. LOTO was also in the process of establishing its own campaign team under Niall Sookoo[2] that would operate alongside Patrick's staff.

LOTO had rightly fought hard for greater influence to reflect Jeremy's renewed mandate, but parity at senior level and these parallel structures sometimes led to paralyse in decision-making. Even a simple thing like sending out a press release could be delayed for hours as the people who had to approve it wrangled over the wording. The shadow chancellor, John McDonnell, who had chaired Jeremy's leadership campaigns, was becoming increasingly alarmed at the effect this was having. Political and media critics had found a new line of attack by casting doubt on Jeremy's competence, and supporters around the country were telling him that they wanted to see more 'visible leadership' from us.

It was hard, as a newcomer, to see instantly how a path through the paralysis could be plotted, especially when the attacks on us added an unpleasant distraction. Jeremy bore the brunt of this, but anyone who worked for him was also fair game in the eyes of some of the media. My own arrival at LOTO was marked by the right-wing blogsite, *Guido Fawkes*, with publication of some

---

[2] Niall Sookoo joined the LOTO communications team about 12 months before me, having previously worked for Unite and as a journalist on BBC Newsnight.

colourful sex scenes from my novel, *Over The Line*. That was swiftly followed by a nasty piece in the *Times* by David Aaronovitch, whom I had known in the 1970s student movement. Without troubling himself with the basic rule that journalists ought to try to speak to their subjects – at least at some point in the previous forty years – David described me as an extremist and, his memory muddled, claimed I had once tried to provoke a fight with him.[3]

The Budget on March 8 gave some respite from Labour's troubles, courtesy of a political gift from Philip Hammond on self-employed National Insurance Contributions (NIC). The Chancellor announced that the NIC rates paid by the self-employed would rise from 9 per cent to 10 per cent in 2018, and 11 per cent in 2019, breaking the 'tax lock' commitments in the 2015 Tory manifesto. Within a week, he had to back down, leaving a £2 billion hole in his fiscal plans and confusion over whether or not May knew about the announcement beforehand. It would prove to be a foretaste of U-turns to come, but at that stage she still appeared to be unassailable, and the spotlight soon returned to Labour.

A shadow cabinet away-day had been planned for March 20 which, it was hoped, would focus on policy and prepare the ground for the local elections on May 4. But someone had other ideas when they gave the *Observer* a recording of a local Momentum meeting at which Jon Lansman, the founder of the Corbyn-supporting grassroots group, had said Unite would affiliate to Momentum if Len McCluskey was re-elected as general

---

[3] Published in the Times on 2.3.2017. The Times subsequently published a correction

secretary of the union in a ballot the following month. The paper led with the story the day before the shadow cabinet meeting, hyping it as "a plot to seize control of Labour." They said it would:

> "Alarm many Labour MPs who sought to oust Corbyn in a coup last summer, and who now worry that leftwing activists and some Unite insiders are laying plans to deselect them in a mass purge before the next election."

Labour's deputy leader, Tom Watson, was quoted in the report, claiming it was "a private agreement to fund a political faction that is apparently planning to take control of the Labour party" and evidence of the kind of "entryism" he had warned about during the second leadership election.[4]

By the morning of the shadow cabinet, Tom was touring the radio and TV studios pushing that line, and the scene was set for another fraught meeting. As everyone gathered at Unison's headquarters in Euston, hurrying past door-stepping journalists, there was only one thing on most people's minds – and it wasn't policy or the local elections. Despite Jeremy's efforts to stick to the pre-agreed agenda, anger about Tom's claims soon surfaced, with Jon Trickett and shadow foreign secretary Emily Thornberry among those arguing there had been no need for him to escalate the story.

In the lunch break, Shami Chakrabarti, the shadow attorney general, canvassed the idea of a joint statement from Jeremy and Tom to defuse the row. I worked on it with her and acted as the go-between with Tom. After a

---

[4] 'Secret tape reveals Momentum plot to seize control of Labour,' Toby Helms, the Observer, 19.3.2017.

couple of hours of to-ing and fro-ing in the corridors of the Unison building, a statement was finalised. Crucially, it recognised "the right of groups across the spectrum of Labour's broad church to discuss their views and try to influence the party so long as they operate within the rules." This, in my view, was a clear acceptance that Momentum has as much right to exist as other pressure groups in the party, such as Progress. There was nothing in what Jon Lansman was quoted as saying that broke any party rules.

When that statement was issued in the middle of the afternoon, it temporarily threw some of the political journalists off their stride. They weren't expecting a show of unity and had probably already written their split stories for the next day. But normal service was soon resumed with various leaks feeding reports of the tense exchanges in the meeting itself.

Having hurried back to LOTO for some late afternoon meetings, I was oblivious to the renewed media storm until I arrived at the evening's Parliamentary Labour Party (PLP) meeting. It was my first encounter with the PLP. Though I did not expect it to be an easy meeting for Jeremy, who was attending for the first time since the Copeland defeat, I was not prepared for how openly hostile some of the MPs would be.

The dark neo-Gothic environment of Committee Room 14 did not help. It made it feel like a gathering of angry medieval barons. Imagine the unruliest heckling you have seen in the main chamber of the House of Commons taking place in a packed, gloomy room – then double it. When Jeremy tried to speak, you could hardly hear him. The interruptions may have come from only a small minority, but they were so loud and relentless they made any chance of a meaningful meeting impossible.

Afterwards, it was obvious the journalists in the corridor outside had loved it. Peter Mandelson was heading towards them with a mischievous grin. "Once a spin doctor, always a spin doctor," he said, as he passed, "I shall tell them about the huge ovation Tom got from the PLP." And we were set for more debilitating coverage of Labour splits.

Drinking with a friend in the Strangers' Bar afterwards, I vented about the meeting and said I was shocked at the way Jeremy had been treated.

"But respect has to be earned," my friend said.

"Not always," I replied. "Sometimes respect derives from the office someone holds. Jeremy is the elected leader. Disrespect him, and you are disrespecting the party and the members."

Two days later, I was taken aback to find myself the target of fictitious allegations from one of the MPs who had been heckling Jeremy. Neil Coyle, who represents Bermondsey and Old Southwark, had given the *Evening Standard* a copy of a letter he had sent to the PLP secretary complaining that MPs were "audibly groaned and hissed at" by members of the leader's "entourage." I was named as having "accosted" him in a way that was "aggressive in nature."

As soon as I heard the *Standard* might be running a piece, I phoned their newsdesk to tell them the story was baseless and the reporter who had written it had not directly contacted me. The journalist on the desk said someone would call me back. When they didn't, I asked Carter-Ruck, the media lawyers, to send the editor a letter challenging the allegations and warning they were defamatory. That prompted them to remove any reference to me from the online version, though it was too late to stop it appearing in the printed paper.[5]

It was a Wednesday, which meant almost everyone at Westminster was preoccupied with the ritual confrontation of PMQs. That week, Jeremy took on the Tories for cutting the schools budget while simultaneously reducing corporation tax and the banking levy. May was on the back foot, claiming the new schools funding formula was only a proposal and subject to consultation. But Jeremy pressed his point well by reading a letter from a voter saying teachers were having to purchase pens, pencils, glue-sticks and other necessities from their own pockets.

PMQs is followed by what's aptly described as the 'huddle' for political journalists, who gather in the reception area behind the Commons press gallery to give Downing Street and LOTO spokespeople a weekly grilling. It reminded me – as an ex sports writer – of the chaotic post-match press conferences football managers used to give, often in a corridor, before the *Sky* era of proper staging with the sponsors' brands in view. Just as football reporters rarely wanted to talk about the match, huddle questions are usually unrelated to PMQs and often centre on the Westminster equivalent of transfers and injuries.

Political journalists are officially called the 'lobby'. There are nearly 500 of them altogether, though only a

---

[5] I had never met Coyle then, nor have I since, but he has walked past me several times without the slightest hint of recognition.

tenth of that number would normally come along to the huddle.[6] The broadcasters are based mainly off-site, but the newspaper journalists inhabit a labyrinth of offices within the Parliament building.

The lobby's culture is shaped by a curious blend of gossip and conformism. Journalists love tittle-tattle, knowing some of it will have enough substance to earn them newsdesk brownie points. But they are also surprisingly risk averse. Like football reporters, they collaborate far more than their bosses or readers realise. Fearful of being out of step on a story, they will compare notes and – perhaps unconsciously – reach a consensus on how to frame it. As Jasper Jackson put it in the *New Statesman*:

> "Lobby journalists spend a lot of time with each other, and while they still compete viciously, the set-up is prone to groupthink. The practice of discussing what the 'best line' is from any announcement or speech often leads to homogenised news coverage. It's less conspiracy and more seeking safety in numbers. After all, if everyone else has the same story, then yours can't be wrong."[7]

This is not a new problem. Andrew Marr, at the time the *BBC*'s political editor, made much the same point in his book *My Trade* in 2004. After giving two examples, he said:

> "It is easy to see how independent-spirited

---

[6] For full list, see Register of Journalists' Interests, **www.parliament.uk**

[7] Jasper Jackson, 'Why not let the Canary into the Westminster lobby. It could do with a shake-up,' the New Statesman, 1.8.17.

> journalists who had arrived in the Commons hoping to hold power to account felt stifled by the lobby and quickly came to resent it."[8]

The tendency towards 'groupthink' suits most of the owners of mainstream media when it comes to political coverage. Rupert Murdoch, Lord Rothermere and the others do not mind forfeiting competition and running very similar stories for the greater good of assassinating the character of someone they see as a threat to the natural order of things. Nor do they have to interfere in day to day editorial decisions to get the outcome they want. They set the political direction, employ like-minded loyalists for top jobs to enforce it, and let 'groupthink' and fear of having a very short career do the rest. Of course, media owners like exclusives now and again, but their over-arching concern is to contain debate within the neo-liberal framework so that – whatever the colours of the politicians in power – nothing much changes, unless it is something they want. That system comes under strain when the elite are themselves deeply divided, as we have been seeing with Brexit, but it kicks into gear when there is a perceived existential threat.

Jeremy Corbyn represents such a threat. The very idea of a government 'for the many, not the few' poses a challenge to their interests. No wonder, then, that he has faced near-unanimous hostility from mainstream media and the continual peddling of a host of negative narratives: he's an unelectable hard-left extremist, his policies are unrealistic and would bankrupt the country, he's a bungler who can't run his own party, he's an apologist for terror, and so on.

---

[8] Andrew Marr, 'My Trade,' Pan Macmillan, 2005 edition, p167.

The LOTO communications team was conscious it was spending far too much time trying to counter negative stories emanating from the lobby, but you cannot let them go unchallenged either. My relatively minor tussle with the *Evening Standard* meant I did not go to PMQs that day, but Seumas texted me from the gallery to ask if I thought he should do the huddle. I didn't hesitate to say "no." Not only had a lobby correspondent written a defamatory piece about me without asking for a comment, others had quoted Seumas in their reports of the PLP meeting, breaching their own lobby etiquette on naming sources. I suggested to Seumas he should tell them we won't be briefing until we have some assurances they will play by the rules. He didn't do the huddle, and the only story the lobby had from us at the start of the afternoon was Jeremy's positive performance on school budget cuts.

John McDonnell arrived back from PMQs in upbeat mood. I was working in a small LOTO meeting room used by Seumas as an office when he appeared and settled into an armchair to read the *Guardian*'s report on Jeremy's performance aloud, relishing phrases like "he held his ground well" and "one of his best for a long time."[9] As John read, it struck me how daunting it must be to have your every word scrutinised as Jeremy now did. During his years on the backbenches, he had made some fine speeches that went completely unreported. As leader, he could be crucified for a few 'lacklustre' phrases or failure to 'land a punch'. And he had had to adapt to this without the honeymoon period that is customary for

[9] Andrew Sparrow, PMQs Verdict, the Guardian website, 22.3.2017.

a politician favoured by the media.

Not surprisingly, Jeremy seemed cheerful when I joined him to run through a speech he was due to make the next day at the annual conference of Federation of Small Businesses (FSB) in Torquay. Andrew Fisher was there, too. I had not met Andrew before starting at LOTO, but we had been working together on the speech, and I soon found that his understated, easy-going manner belied a sharp and industrious political operator. Andrew has been a policy advisor for more than 15 years, working first for John when he was a backbench MP, and then for the Public and Commercial Services Union (PCS). His book, *The Failed Experiment*[10], which was published in 2014, unpicked the neo-liberal orthodoxy that produced the banking crisis and offered alternative economic policies that would become central to what we now call Corbynism.

The run-through was in the main LOTO meeting room, which is on the corner of the Norman Shaw Building and has a 180-degree view along the Embankment to the left, and across Westminster Bridge to the right. Jeremy read the speech to us from a lectern, using autocue. It was the best way to test whether the language was clear, and to give Jeremy a chance to make changes.

The speech was important. The FSB conference was a good opportunity to move on from the internal blood-letting and get some momentum back into Jeremy's leadership. A speech about business issues might also wrong-foot the Tories. They had attacked Jeremy for being 'anti-business', but their own credentials were

---

[10] Andrew Fisher, 'The Failed Experiment,' Comerford & Miller, 2014.

tarnished by Hammond's failed attempt to increase NI contribution for the self-employed and an earlier move to make them submit quarterly – instead of annual – tax returns.

Contrary to stereotype, we saw the millions of small business owners and self-employed as a force for growth and innovation, who often had a precarious existence and were being held back in an economy dominated by big business. In the speech, Jeremy was going to announce that a Labour government would "declare war on late payment," an issue that I knew sent the blood pressure of FSB members soaring. Whenever I had attacked the government for not doing anything to enforce 30-day payment in the monthly business column I wrote for the *Western Mail*[11], I would get support from angry business people of all political persuasions.

At the time Andrew and I were working on the speech, an estimated £26 billion was being withheld from suppliers in late payments. This causes thousands of businesses to go bust every year and starves thousands more of vital cash needed for investment. To make matters worse, many big businesses now charge companies to be on their supplier list or demand a 'rebate' from them when their products sell well – a kind of penalty for success. For the economy as a whole, late payment kills jobs and holds back growth.

The Tories only pay lip service to the issue because doing something about it means taking on big businesses.

---

[11] See, for example, my column 'If government paid more attention to the needs of small rather than big business, we could have a better economy', the Western Mail, 21.12.2015, see also **www.walesonline.co.uk.**

But Jeremy was set to announce that Labour would ensure that anyone bidding for a public sector contract must pay its own suppliers within 30 days and introduce a tougher regime for the private sector, involving binding arbitration and fines for persistent late payers.

As Jeremy left the room, having made a few of his own changes to the speech, I felt for the first time that we had made progress on something pro-active and worthwhile. I stayed in the room to catch up on some e-mails and was so engrossed it took me a while to notice the screaming and shouting outside. The Embankment can be noisy at any time with traffic and tourists, but these sounds were abnormal. I went to a window and saw crowds retreating to my left. Curious, I opened the doors onto a small balcony and looked down at the pavement below where two or three police officers were waving their arms frantically and shouting to a few remaining people to clear the area. The traffic on the Embankment was gridlocked. I turned to look across to Westminster Bridge to my right. It was empty apart from a stationary bus, an ambulance – its blue lights flashing – and a white van. People, mostly wearing overalls and yellow helmets, were scurrying around. My view further to the right – and Big Ben – was blocked by Portcullis House.

These impressions were formed in a matter of seconds. I soon realised this was no ordinary incident. Journalistic instincts kicking in, I took two photographs with my phone. As I retreated from the balcony, I turned to see Karie at the door telling me that we had to move out of the rooms facing the river. We went into the LOTO office at the rear of the block. Other staff members were gathering. An office that normally accommodates about 15 people was soon packed with three times that number. Jeremy was at the far end talking to his son, Seb, who works nearby heading up John McDonnell's shadow treasury team.

It was nearly 3pm. Seumas texted me to say he was corralled by police in Portcullis House. All we knew at that stage was that there had been some kind of attack on Westminster Bridge that might have involved more than one perpetrator. The police were saying we would be in lock-down until they had done a search of the entire Palace of Westminster to check whether or not there were any armed terrorists on the loose. Oddly, I thought, there was no police presence in LOTO itself. If someone with a gun had turned up and found us all in a darkened room, we would have been defenceless. The media, meanwhile, knew more than we did about what was going on outside. They were reporting that a car had been driven into dozens of pedestrians walking across Westminster Bridge.

By 4pm, Seumas had found his way back to LOTO, and we got a short statement out saying we understood the incident to be extremely serious and were thinking of the families and friends of the victims. It was clear by then that Jeremy would have to pull out of going to Torquay and stay in Westminster to deal with the fall-out from the attack. When I called the FSB, they were far from surprised.

As the 6pm news bulletins approached, the *BBC* asked us for a video message from Jeremy. Our movements still restricted, we had to improvise. The best location, without going far from the lock-down room, was just outside the nearby toilets where there was a plain white wall. Our equipment was Karie's iPhone. Our script was written on a scrappy piece of paper and brief enough for Jeremy to memorise at short notice. The difficult part was sending it but, after several attempts, the *BBC* confirmed receipt in time for their bulletin.

The next hour or so dragged interminably. The room had become oppressively stuffy and everyone was becoming restless. At one stage, I caught a glimpse of two armed police officers hurrying along the corridor outside, but that was the only visible sign of the seriousness of the events that had been taking place around us. Finally, at 7.30pm, the lock-down was declared over. We were told we could leave, but only via the Black Rod entrance at the southern end of the Palace of Westminster. It was a long walk through the subway under Bridge Street and the maze of passages and courtyards beneath the Parliament buildings, but everyone was eager to escape after nearly five hours confined in one room.

Outside, Westminster was dark and deserted. The police had sealed off the whole area, and I had to loop around their cordon to get to St James' Park tube station. My plan had been to go back to Cardiff and then drive down to the FSB Conference in Torquay the following day. With Jeremy no longer going to Torquay, I would still work from home. Our attempt to move forward politically had been thwarted in the worst of ways – four people killed on the bridge, PC Keith Palmer stabbed by the attacker.

4 – Learning From Bernie, and Finding Our Voice

"This was not going to be a typical campaign. It was not just about electing a candidate. It was the building of a movement."
Bernie Sanders, *Our Revolution*[1]

As Jeremy was campaigning to be Labour leader for the first time in 2015, something unprecedented was happening in the United States: a democratic socialist was emerging as a serious contender for the presidency. Never in US political history had someone labelling themselves with the 'S' word been more than a fringe candidate.[2] Suddenly, and unexpectedly, polls were starting to show that Bernie Sanders, a little-known senator from Vermont, could threaten the 'coronation' of Hillary Clinton as the Democratic party's candidate for the 2016 presidential elections.

---

[1] Bernie Sanders, 'Our Revolution,' Thomas Dunne Books, 2016, p87.

[2] Sanders' hero, Eugene Debs, won 6% of the vote in 1912 and 3.4% in 1920 (while still in prison for opposing US involvement in World War 1). Four years later, Robert La Follette pushed the highwater mark to 16.6% with 4,831,706 votes, coming third as the Progressive Party candidate. 'Fighting Bob' had been Governor of Wisconsin from 1900 to 1906 and represented the state in the US Senate from 1906 until his death in 1925. He had also opposed the war.

When he launched his campaign on May 26, 2015, Sanders only had one other senator backing him, Jeff Merkley, and five members of Congress – Keith Ellison, Tulsi Gabbard, Raul Grijalva, Marcy Kaptur, and Peter Welch. Just after the launch, polls suggested only 10 per cent of registered Democrat voters supported him, compared to 60 per cent or more for Clinton. By August, Sanders' polling figures had hit 30 per cent and Clinton's had dipped below 50.[3]

Clinton had name recognition, huge resources, and the backing of the entire Democrat establishment. However, she had alienated many grassroots Democrat supporters with her backing for regime-change wars and trade deals that had decimated entire industries and destroyed thousands of jobs.

Sanders, on the other hand, had voted against the invasion of Iraq in 2003, and was challenging her with a campaign platform that – like Jeremy's – zeroed-in on growing inequality of wealth. Speaking at his campaign launch, he said:

"There is something profoundly wrong when one family owns more wealth than the bottom 130 million Americans. This grotesque level of inequality is immoral. It is bad economics. It is unsustainable. This type of rigged economy is not what America is supposed to be about. This has got to change, and as your president, together we will change it."[4]

Sanders reiterated that core message in rally after rally

[3] Poll Chart, National Democratic Primary, HuffPost Pollster.

[4] From the speech Sanders made in Burlington, Vermont on 26.5.15 formally announcing he was running for president. Ibid, p120.

across the US through the summer and autumn of 2015. And it soon became clear he was striking a chord with voters. In the city of Minneapolis, he surprised Minnesota's Clinton-supporting senators by attracting 5,000 people to hear him at a venue that held less than half that number.[5] At rallies in the West Coast cities of Seattle, Portland, and Los Angeles, he spoke to more than 70,000 people in three days.[6] On his first visit to the key state of Iowa, he visited the small rural town of Kensett, with a population of 266, and found more than 300 people from the area packed into a community centre waiting for him. The *New York Times* described the crowds at his rallies throughout Iowa on that opening campaign tour as "the first evidence that Mrs. Clinton could face a credible challenge in the Iowa presidential caucuses."[7]

Iowa is always the first state to vote in the nominating process and can be a graveyard for any candidate who does not do well. But, by the time the caucuses were held on February 1, 2016, Sanders was more than credible, and ran Clinton to a virtual dead heat. Then, eight days later, he shocked the political establishment with a landslide win in the next state to vote, New Hampshire, a staggering setback for Clinton in a primary she had won in 2008 when facing a challenge from another outsider, Barack Obama.

Sanders had spoken at 68 meetings in New Hampshire attended by 41,810 people – a big proportion of the 151,584 voters who backed him in the primary had heard first-hand what he stood for. Though his campaign also

---

[5] Bernie Sanders, 'Our Revolution,' p135.

[6] Ibid, p146.

[7] 'Challenging Hillary Clinton, Bernie Sanders gains momentum in Iowa,' the New York Times, 31.5.15.

spent heavily on paid advertising, he believes the excitement and energy generated by those events, and the way his message resonated, were the major reasons for his success.[8]

The Sanders campaign was electrifying the contest, but Clinton was still the frontrunner in national polls and had a formidable political machine that gave her a head start in almost every state. The race would be tight throughout the spring. Clinton won eight of the 12 states voting on March 1, Super Tuesday, and the same again in the 12 mid-March contests. But, later that month and in early April, Sanders bounced back with seven wins in a row.

Going into the New York primary on April 19, the polls had the two candidates neck and neck. The second most populous state was crucial, and the rules governing its primary would prove highly contentious. As in other states, Sanders was attracting huge crowds – 18,000 in South Bronx, 27,000 in Manhattan, and 28,000 in Brooklyn – but many of those attending did not have a vote because New York was a closed primary in which voters had to register as Democrats six months beforehand.[9] Sanders lost by 58 to 42 per cent.

Pressure was now growing for him to stand down. After New York, Clinton was ahead of Sanders by 1,445 to 1,208 among delegates elected by the primaries and caucuses. In media coverage, her lead was inflated by counting pledges from among the 714 super delegates – the party officials and political office-holders who overwhelmingly supported her, but would not actually cast their vote until the Democratic Convention at the end of the nomination

---

[8] Bernie Sanders, 'Our Revolution,' p171.
[9] Bernie Sanders, 'Our Revolution,' p175.

process.[10] Sanders had always said he would take his campaign all the way to the Convention because it was as much about building a movement around his policy platform as it was the nomination. Besides, there were still 1,398 delegates to be elected in 20 primaries and caucuses, including California, the most populous state. Why would Sanders deny millions of Democrats a chance to have their say, especially when there was an outside chance he could still win a majority of the elected delegates? Either way, he believed if he could do well in the remaining contests, he would go into the Convention with momentum and show "who the stronger candidate against Donald Trump was." He decided to "barnstorm" California like "no other presidential candidate had ever done."[11]

In previous years, I have voted in California primaries. My father grew up in Berkeley[12], and I had first registered to vote in US elections in 1972 while I was there during my gap

---

[10] '2016 Delegate Count and Primary Results,' the New York Times website, updated 5.7.2016.

[11] Bernie Sanders, 'Our Revolution,' p179.

[12] My late father, Brandon, was born in New York but grew up mainly in Berkeley. He graduated from UC Berkeley in 1939 and was a founding member of a pioneering San Francisco-based group of architects, planners, and social housing advocates known as 'Telesis'. In the 1940s, he worked in Chile and Puerto Rico before coming to Britain in 1948 to study at the London School of Economics. He married my mother, Cynthia, who was born in Canada but grew up in London, in 1950 and took a lecturing post at Liverpool University. In 1970, he returned to Berkeley as a visiting professor in regional planning, having by then become technical secretary of the Standing Conference on London and South East Regional Planning. He died in 1987.

year. In 2016, I decided to cast my vote as early in the nomination process as I could by participating in the Democrats Abroad primary in March, which backed Sanders heavily. But that was no reason not to also synchronise one of our regular trips to Long Beach to visit our eldest son, Gareth, and his family, with the California primary in June.

The truth is, I wanted to see what it was like to #FeelTheBern. And I was not disappointed. Sanders was tearing up and down the state like someone half his age speaking at two or three rallies a day, all of them attracting thousands of people. The local mainstream media could not ignore it. Social media was saturated with people sharing photographs and videos. Altogether, he spoke to 227,000 people at 40 rallies.

The one I attended – on June 4 on the concourse of the Los Angeles Coliseum – was slickly organised. Staff and volunteers managed the security as more than 13,000 people queued patiently to pass through the barriers. My NUJ press card got me into a media area alongside the stage, which was set up with a sound system that did justice to three hours of music and speeches by Hollywood A listers – among them Rosario Dawson, Shailene Woodley, Max Carver and, my own favourite, 90-year-old Dick Van Dyke "giving a young politician a hand up" by leading a 'we love you, Bernie' sing-along. By the time Sanders made his entrance, the event was all over Twitter and the anticipation was huge. Flanked by his wife, Jane, and his children and grandchildren, he spoke from a lectern, decorated with a US flag and the campaign's 'a future to believe in' strapline, and stuck to a text that embodied the arguments he had been repeating at every single rally for months. There was no message-creep and no need for him to shout – every word would be of broadcast quality for mainstream media and live streaming online.

California was always a long shot for Sanders. The Clintons are consummate political operators and their supporters had a firm grip on California Democratic party apparatus. Both California senators and 37 of the 39 California Democrats in the US House of Representatives had endorsed Clinton before the primary.[13] As grassroots support for Sanders surged at the end of May, Bill Clinton flew out to California to see Jerry Brown, his old adversary in the 1992 presidential primaries, who, as the state's governor, had stayed neutral. Whatever was said, it was enough to persuade Brown to come out for Hillary Clinton in the final days.[14]

Then, on the eve of the poll, came what Sanders would later call "one of the most outrageous moments of the entire campaign."[15] *Associated Press* called the overall Democratic nomination for Clinton, based on telephone calls to super-delegates and a 'projection' of the outcome in California and the other five states voting the next day. Apart from an estimated half a million postal votes, most of which were believed to have gone to Clinton, voting had not yet even started in the biggest state in the union. Yet every media outlet was saying it was a foregone conclusion, Clinton had

---

[13] The two California Democrat members of Congress who did not support Clinton were Alan Lowenthal, Long Beach, and Barbara Lee, Oakland.

[14] 'Why Governor Jerry Brown endorsed Hillary,' the LA Times, 31.5.2016.

[15] Bernie Sanders, 'Our Revolution,' p179.

won the nomination. How much this suppressed the turnout will never be known.

When the California votes were eventually counted, which inexplicably took another four weeks, Sanders had 2,381,714 compared to 2,745,293 for Clinton, with some 2 million registered Democrats staying at home.[16] The 363,579 margin of victory was smaller than the postal vote, which suggests Sanders won a majority of those who voted on the day. That was seen by the campaign's supporters as a moral victory.

More importantly, the overall success of the campaign had given Sanders leverage in the discussions on policy in the lead up to the Democratic Convention in Philadelphia at the end of July. On July 12, Sanders formally endorsed Hillary Clinton having secured "much of what we were fighting for" at a meeting of the Democratic party's platform committee a few days earlier. The key Sanders policies incorporated in the platform included the break-up of too-big-to-fail banks, free tuition at universities and colleges for working families, a minimum wage of $15 an hour, abolition of the death penalty, the closing of loopholes used by corporations to avoid tax, and the creation of millions of jobs through investment in infrastructure.[17]

Clinton's willingness to accommodate Sanders on policy was not, however, matched by a change in her campaign's approach to the election battle with Trump. In the recriminations that followed her defeat, many felt strongly that the Democrats would have won had they either chosen Sanders or heeded his warnings about how

---

[16] 'One month later, California finishes its vote count, and Clinton wins,' the Washington Post, 7.7.2016.

[17] Bernie Sanders, 'Our Revolution,' p181.

angry some working class voters were with the Clinton-Obama establishment. The archaic Electoral College, which was designed in 1787 to make the abolition of slavery harder, meant that Trump's narrow victories in a handful of Midwest states secured his election, even though Clinton won the popular vote. The irony is that Clinton-supporting pundits had argued Sanders should not be the candidate because his appeal was limited to "disaffected Midwest voters," yet those voters abstaining or flipping to Trump proved decisive. The film producer Michael Moore, who supported Sanders but then campaigned in the presidential election for Clinton, argues that the Democrats' neglect of the so-called rustbelt was fatal:

"There were people like me who live in Michigan who were crying out to the Clinton campaign, 'Please come to Michigan, Ohio, Wisconsin'. They decided not to play by the game. It's a bad game. The Electoral College should be changed, but it wasn't gotten rid of, so why were they ignoring these states? It's disgraceful."[18]

As those debates were raging on the other side of the Atlantic, I was not alone among Jeremy's supporters in reflecting on what Labour could learn from the Sanders campaign. Not only was there considerable common ground on policy between Jeremy and Bernie, there was also a strong similarity in the way that they, as 'anti-establishment' politicians, had the authenticity and credibility, on the one hand, to counter the right-wing populism of Trump and Farage and, on the other, to inspire and mobilise young people on a scale not seen for

---

[18] Michael Moore, interview with Variety, 17.1.2017.

a generation.

However, importing ideas from another country, even one with a nominally common language, is a hazardous business. Some ideas do not travel well. Sometimes good ideas are dismissed because of where they have come from.

In the 1980s, people on the left in Britain were enthused by Jesse Jackson's two bids for the presidency, the second garnering nearly 7 million votes. His radical platform and creation of a 'rainbow coalition' carried forward the linkage Martin Luther King Jnr had begun to make between movements for civil rights, economic justice and peace.[19]

When Bill Clinton emerged to win the 1992 presidential election, it was the turn of the Labour modernisers to fall in love with American politics. They saw Clinton's 'new' Democrats, with their focus on appealing to middle class aspiration, as the model for New Labour. Peter Mandelson would later write:

"A major accusation against the modernisers was that we had fallen under the spell of Bill Clinton. This was true. Tony, Gordon and I all visited Washington early in 1993....All three of us came back from meeting members of the Clinton team convinced, as Philip [Gould] had been, that their experience had something to teach us."[20]

But, as New Labour was adopting much of the style and language of the New Democrats, the Clinton presidency

---

[19] See 'Beyond Vietnam' speech by Martin Luther King Jnr at Riverside Church, Upper Manhattan on April 4, 1967, one year before his assassination.

[20] Peter Mandelson, 'The Third Man' HarperPress, 2010, p151.

was floundering. He had focused so much on winning power it seemed he didn't know what to do with it once he was in the White House. In 1994, voters gave their verdict by electing a Republican majority in the House of Representatives for the first time since 1952. And that remained the case to the end of his second term, though it made little practical difference because Clinton and the Republicans had gradually coalesced politically as advocates of the neo-liberal agenda of free trade, bank de-regulation, and regime change in Iraq.[21]

While that political cocktail was also to the taste of New Labour, the one thing they expressly did *not* acquire from Clinton was his liking for campaign rallies. Bill is a charming and engaging orator who loves a big crowd, but New Labour had a strong aversion to political rallies, dismissing them as 'preaching to the converted'. Which is all very well if the media is on your side and giving you plenty of air time, but for politicians challenging the status quo, every opportunity to speak to large numbers of people directly is like gold dust.

Bernie Sanders had made a virtue of necessity in building his campaign around big rallies that were welcoming to people new to politics. Looking back on it afterwards, he wrote:

"A rally of thousands of people standing together...
is something unforgettable and extraordinarily
powerful. It is not something that a television ad

---

[21] Clinton's presidency saw the ratification of the North American Free Trade Agreement, the passing of Gramm-Leach-Bliley Act, allowing the creation of banks that would prove 'too big to fail', and the Iraq Liberation Act, which enshrined the concept of regime change in US law.

can accomplish."[22]

But the Sanders campaign was no one-trick pony. The rallies were like a generator that powered all the other elements, creating virtuous circles of highly-charged activity. Videos of the rallies would be shared far and wide on social media. New volunteers signed up at rallies would be trained to go out canvassing. Contact details collected would be used to disseminate campaign materials and raise money online.

Mass fund-raising from small donors was one of the stand-out features of the Sanders campaign. At the outset, he had decided that "you cannot take on the establishment if you take their money."[23] He was soon rewarded: in the first 24 hours after announcing his candidature, 35,000 donors contributed $1.5 million. That set the pattern. By the end of the campaign, he had raised $232 million from two and a half million people through a total of 8 million donations at an average of just $27.[24]

Sanders was also adept at using social media, despite personally being a novice. When the Republican party held its first debate on August 6, 2015, he was persuaded to tweet his responses as it was happening. His final tweet said:

"It's over. Not one word about income inequality, climate change, Citizens United or student debt.
That's why the Rs are so out of touch."

Retweeted 31,414 times, it was by far the most shared

---

[22] Bernie Sanders, 'Our Revolution,' p91.

[23] Ibid, p51.

[24] Ibid, p114.

tweet of the night.[25] Sanders was hooked. He would later say that social media had given the campaign "the ability to go outside of the corporate interpretation of events, bring our supporters together, and communicate directly with millions of people."[26]

But Sanders was not dismissive of conventional methods. He had used paid-for radio, television and print advertising in numerous previous election campaigns and believed it still played an important role.[27] In his bid for the presidency, as his support grew, he was able to compete with Clinton on paid advertising. By the end, the Sanders campaign had spent more than $100 million[28] on media buying.

What distinguished his use of a conventional medium, however, was the way his ads – in both their imagery and words – were mainly about people and *their* stories. While the Clinton campaign was running traditional candidate messages, focusing on her political record, the Sanders ads were – as marketing agency executives put it – "tapping into what people are feeling"[29] and offering "a deeper sense of idealism."[30] The most well-known is one

---

[25] Ibid, p145.

[26] Ibid, p161.

[27] Ibid, p111.

[28] The non-partisan Center for Responsive Politics estimates that the Sanders campaign spent $118m on media buying, 53% of its total budget. See its website **www.opensecrets.org**

[29] Lenny Stern, co-founder and CEO, SS+K (New York City), which acted as the youth agency for Barack Obama's campaigns in 2008 and 2012, quoted in 'Who's winning the ad battle between Hillary Clinton and Bernie Sanders? Experts weigh in,' AdWeek, 21.2.2016.

[30] Leeann Leahy, CEO, The Via Agency (Portland, Maine), ibid.

that used the Simon & Garfunkel song *America*. But even more groundbreaking was 'It's Not Over', a two-minute video in which Erica Garner talks about her family, her activism, and the death of her father, Eric[31], without mentioning Sanders at all until the final 35 seconds. Kim Getty, the president of Deutsch, a creative agency in Los Angeles, said of it:

"I think that first-person storytelling is very powerful. It's a different approach than the one Hillary is employing, where we see her talking to the camera and giving her perspective on things. It doesn't surprise me at all that this ad is connecting with people. It breaks the norms of political advertising, and I think that there's a lot to be said for that."[32]

In developing its own distinctive style – rooted in its radically different politics – the Sanders campaign nevertheless unashamedly learned from the approach pioneered by Barack Obama in 2008[33]. He too was an insurgent who needed to utilise every conceivable communication channel to beat Hillary Clinton in her first

---

[31] Eric Garner died on July 17, 2014, when a police officer put him in a choke-hold while arresting him on suspicion of selling cigarettes without tax stamps. His death was captured on video, sparking a US-wide protest movement. His daughter, Erica, became a Black Lives Matter activist and supported Bernie Sanders. She died after a heart attack on December 17, 2017.

[32] Kim Getty, president, Deutsch, Los Angeles, ibid.

[33] The Sanders digital strategy was orchestrated by Scott Goodstein, CEO of Revolution Messaging, who was External Online Director for Obama for America in 2008.

bid for the presidency. Never before had a campaign been built around an online platform and made extensive use of social media, then in its infancy. But he blended this with the use of traditional tactics, and took consistency of messaging through all communication channels to new heights.

My daughter, Cerys, was a field worker on the campaign in Philadelphia and wrote an analysis of it, which concluded:

"The Obama campaign's overall success was achieved by its meticulous integration of all its components behind the common key objectives. Everything – from the field programme to the new media strategy – was designed to be mutually reinforcing to create exponential growth in interest and support."[34]

For some supporters on the ground, this level of integration could be frustrating as they had to wait for direction and publicity materials from Obama's campaign headquarters in Chicago. There's a balance to be struck: message and brand discipline should not be so tight that it stifles initiative and creativity. The Sanders campaign seemed to get this right.

At Westminster, as the end of March approached, the inspiring Sanders rally I went to in Los Angeles felt very distant. The local elections were looming. Campaign materials had to be produced within a matter of days, and our plans to get a policy bandwagon rolling had been delayed by the horrific Westminster Bridge attack. In the discussions with Southside during that period, there was

---

[34] Cerys Howell, 'Learning from the Obama campaign,' published by Freshwater, January 2009, p11.

much rolling of ideas when I offered some thoughts on how we should campaign in the local elections. I had half-expected my references to the Sanders campaign to be dismissed, and they were ("he lost," I was told), but I had not bargained for the amusement use of the phrase 'narrative arcs' would cause. The subject has even found its way into a book about the election, *Fall Out*, where the term has somehow mutated into "arc of transformation."[35] This would be funny if it was not so alarming that – even after the election – the party official who spoke to the author, Tim Shipman, still does not appreciate how powerful story-telling is (to adapt Kim Getty's words). It has been used in marketing communications for years simply because it is how most of us talk to each other most of the time[36] – we tell people about things that have happened to us or others and then we might discuss what we feel or think about them. Conversation is mainly story telling. And so is the best political communication[37], which is why some of the Sanders videos were so effective, and why LOTO had already – in late March – arranged to accept a kind offer

---

[35] Tim Shipman, 'Fall Out,' William Collins, 2017, p215. Shipman is the political editor of the Sunday Times.

[36] I am talking here about conversations rather than functional communication about, say, work or household matters.

[37] I'd like to put in a word here for the Freshwater colleagues who produced Invisible Death Row, a video promoting the Welsh Government's organ donor register. Not only did it win awards, it was also a game changer in terms of the discussion on that issue.

from the film director, Ken Loach, to use his skills.[38]

But this goes wider than how you produce a video. The whole campaign needed to tell the same story – an over-arching narrative that voiced people's fears, frustrations and hopes and described a road to a better future. In a dishonest way, the big personalities of neo-liberalism, Ronald Reagan and Margaret Thatcher, were ahead of the curve on this. Their narrative triumphed for a generation because they convinced enough people that public spending and trade unions were to blame for the economic woes that hit capitalism in the 1970s, and that the private sector, set free to operate in de-regulated global markets, would create wealth and affluence. Of course, having nearly every media outlet selling their narrative helped, but that can sustain a story only so far. The neo-liberal narrative took hold at the time because it had a semblance of truth: union action to defend jobs or living standards could be disruptive (and more visible than the under-investment actually causing industrial failure[39]) and Thatcher was, meanwhile, allowing people to buy council houses and shares in privatised industries at bargain basement prices. We now know how it ended up: the rich hoovered up the wealth while the rest of us saw our unions so constrained and weakened that now, for the first time, young people will be

---

[38] Initially we discussed with Ken the possibility of producing some videos for online use. However, when the election was called, we asked him to make three of the five party political broadcasts (see Chapter 6). 'I, Daniel Blake' was BAFTA's 'Outstanding British Film' in 2016.

[39] Under-investment was not entirely invisible: I worked in the steel industry for three years after graduating and one of the cranes I had to use was stamped 'made in 1898'!

worse off than their parents. That is the price we are paying for the success of a neo-liberal narrative which, to paraphrase Robert Peston, conquered all – including the mindset of Tony Blair – by raising the idea that the private sector is superior to the public sector to the status of an eternal truth.[40]

But, if I was ever frustrated by some of those early discussions, one thing that would always lift my spirits was the irrepressible activity of what were known in LOTO as 'Jeremy's outriders.' There were dozens of them on Twitter and Facebook who, day in and day out, were pumping out great material exposing the Tories and putting across many of our arguments. I include in this organised groups such as JeremyCorbyn4PM and Momentum, but mostly they were people acting on their own initiative out of sheer personal commitment. And some of them, such as @Rachael_Swindon and @ScouseGirlMedia, have suffered a fair bit of abuse and harassment for their trouble.

The two outriders I had most contact with were Eoin Clark and Peter Stefanovic. Eoin will be known to many people for his @ToryFibs Twitter feed and its forensic rebuttal of Tory claims and attacks in detailed memes. Peter specialises in hard-hitting videos on the NHS, on the miners' compensation, and in support of the WASPI campaign against the raising of the state pension age for women born in the 1950s.

When I suggested to Jeremy that we should invite Peter in for a chat, he was very enthusiastic. The meeting

---

[40] Robert Peston, 'WTF – What have we done? Why did it happen? How do we take back control?' Hodder & Stoughton, 2017, p261.

was one of the highlights of those early weeks. Peter's passion for what he was doing was inspiring and infectious. He had given up his day job as a lawyer to spend a year campaigning and was eager to persuade the groups he was working with that a Corbyn-led government would address their issues. "That was an incredibly important meeting," he told me recently. "We discussed what might be included in the manifesto and that allowed me to go back to WASPI, the miners, and the junior doctors to tell them what Labour would do."

When the election was called a month or so later, Peter and the other outriders would play a crucial role in mobilising support through social media. The Tories had nothing like it. Since the election, they had produced a 'digital toolkit'[41], but Peter thought it lacked a crucial ingredient:

> "The difference is that we believe *passionately* in what we're doing, in the manifesto, in the principles behind it and how it's going to change the country. You can't manufacture that belief. You're never going to find a Tory who will speak passionately because in their hearts they don't really believe what they stand for is right. They support it because it's the status quo."

Peter is a natural communicator with a knack for finding the right words to make a point or, dare I say it, tell a story. If this was easy, more people would be good at it. But language is a complicated thing. And the Sanders

---

[41] Tory chairperson Brandon Lewis announced plans for a toolkit on 13.1.2018, telling the Daily Telegraph he wanted to see 'people who support us...getting out there in the digital world saying so.'

campaign was not so helpful in this respect. Some of their terms could be imported – a 'rigged' system was one we used – but George Bernard Shaw was right when he said the US and Britain are two countries disunited by a common language. Jeremy could not say he will 'stand up for Main Street against Wall Street' and 'fight for the shrinking middle class' without confusing everyone.

Among British political terms, I felt the phrase 'left behind' presented some problems. In a note to Seumas before I started, I said I thought it was divisive and detracted from the fact that most people had been hit by globalisation and austerity in one way or another. UKIP and far right newspapers such as the *Daily Express* were using 'left behind' to pose predominantly white working class communities against a so-called liberal metropolitan elite. It isn't wrong to try to reclaim a term – I would never concede socialism to 'national socialists' – but in using 'left behind' we were actually reinforcing the false idea that the only people left behind are in Brexit-leaning areas where traditional industries have been decimated. Who is most 'left behind': a young person in Islwyn who can't get a job, or a young person in Islington who can't afford the rent on a bedsitter, never mind buy their own home? Globalisation destroys jobs in some parts of the country and inflates house prices in others. 'Left behind' pits its victims against each other. Which, of course, is why Farage and co use it.

Seumas and I were agreed on this, and he had already started discussing these narrative issues with two consultants, Marc Lopatin and Jem Bendell.[42] In a blog a few months earlier, they had argued that Theresa May had "put her tanks on Labour's lawn" by kicking off her premiership with "a spot of cross-dressing" in her pitch to ordinary working class families. To respond, Labour needed to create a 'permission space' with voters who weren't listening to us because the Tories had been successful in blaming us for the deficit (largely by default because, inexplicably, Ed Balls hadn't put up much of a fight).

Arguing that tactics and language had to be "fit for purpose," they had said:

"And that purpose is securing votes. So, while Corbyn's ultimate vision involves stirring a lost spirit of solidarity and community, Labour must embrace voters as they find them and design conversations accordingly. Because the prize is bigger than re-connecting with former Labour heartlands. When Mrs May references working class families as 'just getting by,' she also knows that millions of families higher up the income ladder identify themselves in the very same terms. They might have a bigger house or God forbid a buy-to-let, but they too are mortgaged to the hilt and are wondering what will happen when the Bank of England starts pushing up interest rates. They too navigate the pickpocket economy and fume at the rising prices of things people never had to pay for from hospital car parking to a university education.

---

[42] Marc Lopatin is a former journalist and a communications consultant and Jem Bendell is professor of sustainability leadership at the University of Cumbria.

"So, when Labour speaks – at the national, regional and local level – it needs to explain how government has been failing families across the board and how this can be fixed. A continued pre-occupation with austerity won't cut it going forwards. Rather, Labour should see this as an irresistible opportunity to unite and resonate with voters…. If Jeremy Corbyn's leadership can lift its gaze beyond the food bank, the government will have a fight on its hands."[43]

I did not see austerity as only being about food banks – or its other extreme manifestations, such as homelessness – but was that the impression we were giving? Marc and Jem were right to alert us to the danger of appearing not to be talking enough about how *most people* were affected – in countless ways – by austerity. We were giving May space to masquerade as a champion of people whose interests she was attacking.

Jon Trickett, meanwhile, had prepared a paper for the LOTO strategy group that overlapped with the discussions Seumas and I were having with Marc and Jem. Jon is one of Jeremy's closest allies and brings to the table not only the insights of an MP from a northern seat – Hemsworth in West Yorkshire – but also a searching political mind that looks beyond what's going on in the trenches. Jon's paper emphasised the need for Labour to create "a majoritarian coalition" around a "transformational" offer rather than use "retail" politics to appeal to different interest groups. When a general election came, we should make it about the kind of

---

[43] Jem Bendell and Marc Lopatin, the Huffington Post, 13.10.2016.

country we wanted to build and why it would serve the interests of the great majority of people, not only those experiencing the most acute symptoms of Tory policies.

Jon's thoughts were echoed in a separate strand of discussion by Greg Philo, professor of communications and social change at the University of Glasgow. Greg was part of a group, which also included Ken Loach and the journalist Paul Mason, discussing these issues in lengthy e-mail trails. Among other things, he said:

"We must address the whole nation – we are seen as defenders of the weak and oppressed – and so we should be! Still, we need to go beyond this – the middle classes are also affected by increasing insecurity, fears over jobs, pensions, health and education. We should talk about the running down of our great public institutions – and the need for a national renewal."

This analysis tallied with my own view that, however the Tories dressed it up, using terms like the 'just about managing' or the 'big society', we had to show that they always act first and foremost in the interests of a tiny elite. This applies on so many fronts. While a pay cap for *everyone* working in the public sector had hit the living standards of millions, the Tories were giving away billions in tax cuts for big business and the richest one per cent. While corporate lawyers were on the fat cat gravy train in the City, the Tories were attacking funding for members of the same profession who preferred to represent people mistreated or injured at work. Even small business owners, who had over the years been the backbone of local Conservative parties, were ignored on an issue like late payment if it meant challenging the big businesses whose cash flows are boosted by it. Looking back on it, we were all inching towards an approach that would gel around 'for the many, not the few' – a suggestion that had not yet surfaced.

But we had taken one step forward: Marc and Jem proposed replacing 'left behind' with 'held back', and we agreed this should be central to our narrative, as anyone who has read Jeremy's foreword to the manifesto will know.[44] 'Held back' could be applied to a whole range of ways in which most people's lives are limited by a society run for the rich. We saw it as majoritarian and unifying – it spoke to both sides of the Brexit divide. More than that, it implies a call to action: whereas 'left behind' encourages people to think of themselves as victims, 'held back' suggests an obstacle to be removed. It prompts questions: what is holding me back, why and how can I do something about it? There was a story emerging here – and, like the best stories, a contradiction that required resolution.

In his book, *WTF*, Robert Peston quotes the following passage from the manifesto foreword:

"Faced with falling living standards, growing job insecurity and shrinking public services, people are under increasing strain. Young people are held back by debt and the cost of housing. Whole families are being held back from the life they have worked towards."

Commenting on it, Peston says that "at a moment when Britons wanted to be understood' Labour had 'described the daily reality for millions of families."[45]

---

[44] See appendix 4.
[45] Robert Peston, 'WTF,' p194.

It is always gratifying to discover later that these seemingly finer points have not gone unnoticed. But, at the end of March 2017, it still seemed we were a long way from putting the rest of the narrative together. 'Held back' was only a starting point for a story that would be resolved by the transformation Labour was advocating. But what words do you use to encapsulate that goal? Jem and Marc had proposed 'a richer Britain'. This was clever in turning the 'cross-dressing' table on the Tories, but there were mixed views about it in the LOTO strategy group – to say the least.

I liked the idea of using the word 'rich' in its non-monetary sense. I was also keen to avoid over-use of traditional language such as 'fairer,' which rightly has a place in the socialist lexicon but can sometimes sound overly worthy and imply we are fighting only for the poorest rather than the great majority. As Jem put it:

"The narrative is intended to make people clear that Labour is speaking to them about their own lives, not asking them to do more emotional work (caring) or to join another person or another group's struggle."

But would 'a richer Britain' do the job? Could it wrong-foot our own supporters? Would it be easy for the media to twist or ridicule what we were saying? As an experiment, in drafting a comment piece for Jeremy for the *Yorkshire Post*, I suggested using the phrase: "Instead of a country run for the rich, we want to see one in which all of us can lead richer lives."[46] This was then quoted in one of several tweets promoting the piece and was

---

[46] Jeremy Corbyn, 'There is an alternative to bargain basement Brexit,' the Yorkshire Post, 30.3.17.

retweeted more times than the others. Though far from being scientific, the experiment did suggest that the words 'rich' and 'richer' could work.

Early in April, we moved to formal focus group testing of the whole narrative. But it proved as inconclusive as our own discussions. While 'held back' went down well, the use of 'a richer Britain' was misinterpreted by some of the participants. Jem and Marc put this down to the methodology, saying the 'richer Britain' frame had been embedded in a statement that implied a commitment to 100 per cent secure employment and 100 per cent home ownership, which were seen as unrealistic. They had a point, but we had run out of time for the local elections, and the campaign co-ordinators, Ian Lavery and Andrew Gwynne, had made it clear they were not on board. So 'held back' made a tentative debut in the local election script, and we deployed 'richer lives' only when posing it against 'a country run for the rich.'

We were still several discussions – and a eureka moment – away from finding the words that would electrify the general election campaign.

5 – Flying Start Sets The Tone

*"Objects in your rearview mirror are closer
than they appear."*
Message to Clinton campaign from Kurt Meyer,
Worth County, Iowa[1]

When Theresa May went walking with her husband, Philip, in the hills above Dolgellau on April 10, 2017, the guidebook she bought said it would give her that moment of clarity you need to make those important decisions. For weeks, her advisers and Tory MPs had been pressing her to call a snap election. They were saying it would "finish off the Labour party for the next twenty years."[2]

But, as the Mays ambled in Wales, Jeremy and John McDonnell were at Luton Town football club to launch Labour's policy of a living wage for all of at least £10 per hour by 2020, which would benefit 5.6 million workers. They had chosen to make the announcement at Kenilworth Road because the club was already

---

[1] Kurt Meyer was chair of the Democratic party in Worth County, Iowa, when Bernie Sanders spoke to a crowd of 300 people in Kensett, a town in the county with a population of 266. The New York Times reported (31.5.15) that afterwards he phoned Troy Price, the Iowa political director for Hillary Clinton, to warn him that Clinton's lead over Sanders might not be as big as the polls were suggesting.

[2] Tim Ross & Tom McTague, 'Betting The House,' Biteback Publishing, 2017, p80.

supporting the Living Wage Foundation and paying its £8.45 an hour rate, rather than the government's £7.50 for the over 25s.

May and her advisers had forgotten a basic rule in politics: metaphorically speaking, when you are about to embark on a difficult journey, *check the rearview mirror*. What the Tories had failed to notice was that on April 6 – with the launch of a policy on free school meals for all primary school children – we had started what the media would dub a 'policy blitz' that gave us momentum just as May was about to call a snap election.

It had been a while coming. Throughout March, Seumas had been pushing for a series of policy interventions that would achieve 'cut through' in the media. The Westminster terrorist attack on March 22 had delayed one of them – an initiative to force big businesses to pay their suppliers on time. When the LOTO strategy group gathered for its last meeting before the Easter recess, the local elections were imminent and time was running out.

There was an abundance of policy – more work had been going on behind the scenes than I had expected – but every commitment had to be fully costed and matched by a revenue source. Which ones were 100 per cent ready to roll out in terms of the fine detail and funding? With our position so fragile politically, we could not afford to make a bad move. And nothing was without risk.

I was sitting next to Diane Abbott. She had been quiet throughout the meeting. Then, with not much time left, she leaned forward and said: "Let's do free school meals." There was silence. No one had mentioned the subject up to that point, though it was on the long list of options. Diane pointed out that the educational and health benefits of free school meals were well established. Labour councils in Islington and Southwark, she said, had funded them for primary school pupils and found improvements in attainment. The cost was relatively modest and could be more than covered by introducing VAT on private school fees – a tax break that epitomised privilege in an era of austerity. A consensus soon emerged that free primary school meals would be the first announcement. With one decision made, the others seemed to fall like dominos. Free school meals would be followed by the £10 minimum wage policy, the delayed declaration of a war on late payment, and a pensioners' pledge. We had the makings of a plan.

Two weeks later, on the Saturday of the Easter weekend, the *Independent* was reporting that "Jeremy Corbyn's policies for a future Labour government have the support of the majority of the British public."[3] The poll it had commissioned from *ComRes* suggested there was 71 per cent support for the raising of the minimum wage and 53 per cent support for funding free primary school meals by charging VAT on private school fees. For good measure (although we had not suggested it), it had also found that 62 per cent supported an increase in the top rate of tax from 45p to 50p. The comment from our spokesperson in the *Independent* would prove prescient:

"The people in Britain have been held back too long but we have the ideas and the will to change the country for the better. There's so much more to come and, as the party comes together to

[3] The Independent website, 15.4.2017.

campaign for these popular polices, we are convinced our support in the polls will increase."

That was on April 15, just three days before the snap election announcement. Did the Tory high command notice what we were doing? Or were they like over-confident premier league high-fliers, so certain of their own invincibility that they had failed to spot the opposing team's recent run of good results?

I had been away for a few days before Easter and was looking forward to the policy blitz continuing, as planned, in the weeks leading up to the local elections. As I travelled to London on the early train from Cardiff on Tuesday April 18, I felt we had turned a corner and begun to break out of the constraints that had thwarted the positive leadership Jeremy wanted to give. The possibility of a general election was not on my mind. There had been some discussion about it at shadow cabinet and senior management meetings. Seumas thought May would call one and wanted us to be ready. But there was no point in dwelling on the 'will she, won't she' question. We had to devote our energy to things within our control, and be prepared for anything. The policy blitz before Easter was part of that.

When I arrived at Westminster, word was already out that May would be making a statement in Downing Street at 11.15am. LOTO was abuzz with speculation. For the best part of two hours, shadow cabinet members and advisers came, went, and came back again. No one seemed to know what to do with themselves. The small TV screen above one of the desks was showing a lectern in Downing Street in front of the firmly shut front door of Number 10. People would stare at it for a while, then shrug and go away. I tried to catch up on some e-mails, but it was impossible to do much else.

When the Prime Minister finally appeared on the TV screen, the silence was instant. No one moved or said anything as she claimed an election was necessary at this moment of "enormous national significance" when "the country needs strong and stable leadership... to see us through Brexit and beyond." She framed it repeatedly as an election about Brexit, which the Tories would deliver in the national interest and the opposition parties would "jeopardise with political game-playing." The middle passage of her statement accused us of trying to bring government to a standstill and fighting Brexit every step of the way. We were, she claimed, endangering the security of millions of working people, weakening the government's negotiating position in Europe and risking Britain's ability to make a success of Brexit.

If you asked people now what they remember about that speech, they would probably say the phrase "strong and stable" – and those words were used four times – but what struck me at the time was how transparently she was trying to capture the whole Brexit vote. At that point, Labour had already demonstrated its acceptance of the referendum result by voting to trigger article 50. But she was raising the spectre of 'sabotage of Brexit' to try to redraw the political map of Britain in the self-interest of the Tories. Their concern was not the national interest: they thought they could wipe Labour out in its heartlands by playing the Brexit card. It was cynical, but it wasn't obvious then that it would prove to be a hopeless political misjudgement: that people may have been divided on Brexit, but they were also angry about austerity and a

81

rigged system that favoured a privileged few. What was clear was that Labour would need to win votes across the EU referendum divide, not by fudging the issues, but by alerting people to the Tory agenda of using Brexit to attack workers' rights and create a low wage tax haven for big business. We knew we had to put Brexit in the context of the kind of country we wanted Britain to be.

Our policy blitz was set to continue that day with the announcement of a pledge to increase the Carers' Allowance. The 800,000 people who look after older, disabled, and seriously ill relatives and friends in their homes save the government billions in care costs. A £10 uplift in their £63.10 a week allowance was not only fair but was also integral to our plan for a National Care Service, which would later be a key part of Labour's manifesto.[4]

Jeremy had arrived at Westminster early for an interview for *The Victoria Derbyshire Show*. Once May had made her announcement, the shadow cabinet was hurriedly convened to agree that Labour would not stand in the way of an election. Under the Fixed Term Parliament Act, the Tories would need our support to get the required two-thirds majority in the House of Commons to trigger an election earlier than 2020 – and no one had any hesitation about giving it.

Jeremy's mood was upbeat, almost gung-ho. It was clear he felt – as we all did – that this was our moment. "We are in the fight of our lives," he told 30 or so LOTO staff when we gathered for a pep talk. We had a responsibility, he said, to the people looking to us to deliver change to do everything we could to win. He was already speaking with the enthusiasm and optimism that

---

[4] Labour Manifesto, 'For The Many Not The Few,' p71.

would characterise his campaigning. We all gave him a cheer, and then he was gone – like a sprinter out of his blocks – to catch a train to Birmingham for, as planned, a visit to a Carers Hub.

For the rest of us, there was no time to lose. The mood was euphoric, but there was – inevitably – devil in the detail. That afternoon, LOTO's senior staff met Iain McNicol and the directors from Southside, who had arrived with a shopping list of questions. Would we have a list of target seats? Which seats would Jeremy visit? Who would negotiate the TV debate arrangements? When would the launch event be? Would we have a campaign bus? Who would sign-off national materials for LOTO? What would our daily meeting cycle be? Most of these could not be resolved on the spot and were left with us to discuss.

It is generally the leader of the party's prerogative to set the strategy for the national campaign – or what's often called the 'air war' – while the party machine, through its organisation in the nations and regions, conducts the 'ground war' at constituency level. But the thorny question of target seats is one that overlaps the two because the constituencies on the list benefit from national spending, and this needed to be settled urgently so that those chosen could plan their campaigns.

On Iain's suggestion, it was agreed that the target list would be discussed later at a separate meeting at Southside involving the national campaign co-ordinators, Ian Lavery and Andrew Gwynne. That meeting approved a target list of 268 contests for some level of support. But, as it included all the Labour seats, this meant only 36 were held by the Tories or other parties – which we referred to as 'offensive seats' – and even these would not get the full financial and direct mail package that would go to seats we were defending. Support for the 36 offensive seats – not enough to win a majority – was limited to inclusion in digital advertising campaigns which, at that stage, had no funding. Given Labour's position in the polls, it was not unreasonable to start by shoring up our defences. But this target list was hastily agreed before any discussion on overall strategy and would soon become a bone of contention as LOTO pressed for the implementation of its 'campaigning to win' approach.

As that meeting was going on, the *Daily Mirror* was pushing to have an Op-Ed from Jeremy for the next morning's paper. It was frantic, but Seumas and I got something drafted and ran it by Jeremy. The campaign would, it said, be about "more than individual policies" and would put forward "our vision for Britain." It warned the Tories were taking "a reckless approach to Brexit" and would use it "to tip the economic scales even further in favour of their super-rich supporters." Giving a foretaste of what would later be in the manifesto, it promised investment in growth and affordable housing, free access to education and training, a living wage of £10 per hour by 2020, and an NHS and care services where people, not privatisation, would come first.

The missing ingredient was a magic phrase to sum up what we were fighting for. That would take a little longer, but it felt like we were off to a flying start. Plans were in place for Jeremy's first outdoor election rally in Croydon the following evening and for a speech at Church House in Westminster the day after. In the five hours after May's announcement, more than 2,500 people joined the party and £150,000 was donated online at an average of £23. Crucially, plans were already being hatched for what would prove to be the most successful voter registration campaign ever seen in Britain.

One of the many things the Tories underestimated was how angry young people felt, and how passionately they would respond to a leader with policies they could believe in – as long as they were certain he believed in them, too. And that was another thing the Tories misjudged: they thought that attacking Jeremy for sticking to views that were outside the mainstream would diminish him, but all it did was emphasise his consistent integrity and willingness to fight a status quo that patently wasn't working for most people, especially the young.

We were confident voters would respond positively to Jeremy's openness and authenticity. While we certainly did not foresee huge crowds chanting 'Oh, Jeremy Corbyn,' we had been looking at the detail behind the polls for weeks and knew he had already improved Labour's standing among young people. The challenge was to mount a campaign that would motivate more of them to register to vote before the May 22 deadline.

The first full day of the campaign was – for Seumas and me – dominated by one issue: the need for a strapline that would be on everything we produced. The pressure to make a decision was intense because leaflets were going to print and artwork was needed for the campaign bus. That afternoon, Labour's national executive committee (NEC) was due to gather for a scheduled meeting and would expect our general election presentation to answer this most basic of questions. The strapline we had used for the local elections – 'standing up for you' – was designed to position candidates as champions of their communities, but it was not applicable to a campaign aiming to win power at Westminster and deliver fundamental change. The idea of people being 'held back' was already built into our narrative, as was juxtaposing 'a society rigged for the rich' against 'one in which people could lead richer lives.' But the two campaign co-ordinators were still deeply unhappy about any other use of 'rich' or 'richer,' and almost everything else we toyed with seemed lame and unoriginal.

As I pressed on with writing the presentation for the NEC, Seumas went to see Andrew Gwynne and Ian Lavery to listen to their concerns and discuss other options. The meeting was inconclusive, but Andrew came back to LOTO to continue the brainstorm with Seumas by running through past Labour straplines and discussing which ones had worked and which hadn't. They agreed the 2005 motto 'Britain forward, not back' was the worst they could remember with the 2015 effort 'better plan for a better future' not very far behind.

As they delved deeper into the past, the words 'the many, not the few' from the party's constitution came up.[5] The phrase was part of a new version of Clause 4 proposed by Tony Blair and adopted at a special

---

[5] Clause 4 of the Labour party constitution reads: 'The Labour party is a democratic socialist party. It believes that by the strength of our common endeavour we achieve more than we achieve alone, so as to create for each of us the means to realise our true potential and for all of us a community in which power, wealth and opportunity are in the hands of *the many, not the few*, where the rights we enjoy reflect the duties we owe, and where we live together, freely, in a spirit of solidarity, tolerance and respect.'

conference in 1995 to replace Labour's long standing commitment to "common ownership of the means of production, distribution and exchange." The dropping of the old Clause 4 was opposed by those of us who saw it as a New Labour move to distance the party from the idea of public ownership. However, the new clause contained phrases that are common ground for everyone in the party, among them the words adapted from Shelley's poem.[6] For Seumas, it felt right to use them again in a different context, and Andrew agreed.

By now it was nearly midday, and my NEC presentation still had a big hole in it. When I scurried into Seumas' room, he said: "What do you think of 'for the many, not the few'?" It was one of those FFS moments when you realise there's a good reason why some things stand the test of time – in this case, nearly 200 years. With the word 'for' added, the phrase encapsulated the idea of a building society that serves the great majority and *not* accepting one that is run by and for a privileged elite. It went beyond modifying the way the country is run by making it 'fairer' or 'better' and implied a transformation to a wholly different way of doing things.

Of course, the fact that Tony Blair had used the words complicated this interpretation. Would some people consider it sullied, given what has happened since? How could the same slogan apply to a "centrist" platform – whose proponents were "intensely relaxed about people

---

[6] From the poem 'Masque of Anarchy,' written by Percy Shelley in 1819 following the Peterloo massacre when cavalry charged into a crowd of tens of thousands of people at St Peter's Field, Manchester who were demanding the right to vote. Fifteen people were killed and hundreds were injured.

getting filthy rich"[7] – as well as our much more radical one? We hardly had any time to debate these doubts, but would the vast majority of voters know or care about them anyway? My instinct was that most people would not be aware of how 'the many, not the few' had been used before and those that did would realise Jeremy – of all people – truly meant the message it embodied, as the policies in the manifesto would show.

Making the presentation at the NEC was like dancing on egg shells. It was only my second NEC meeting and I did not know most of the people in the room. I was conscious that many of them had been – and probably still were – hostile to Jeremy's leadership, and I was keen not to reopen any old wounds at a time when we needed unity for the campaign. The presentation gave an assessment of why the election had been called and outlined how our strategy would be to build on the successful policy blitz, push for head-to-head TV debates, and take the campaign to offensive as well as defensive seats. In marked contrast to the buoyant mood in LOTO, the discussion was subdued and much more preoccupied with threats and difficulties than opportunities.

The liveliest exchange – which was later leaked to the media – centred on a section headed "the Tories are the real extremists." This was not a campaign proposal but one of three slides dealing with the likely nature of the Tory attack on us. It listed some responses that would turn a much abused and ill-defined word around by showing the extreme impact austerity has had on people

---

[7] Peter Mandelson made the comment in 1998 to Lewis Platt, the CEO of Hewlett Packard, with the rider 'as long as they pay their taxes.'

and public services. When some NEC members took it to be a strapline and opposed its use, Seumas made it clear that it was only for rebuttal purposes. However, only two days later, the *Daily Telegraph* portrayed this as a "Labour campaign swerve over Corbyn's terror links." According to its report, unnamed NEC sources had said fears were raised that "it would prompt questions about Mr Corbyn's views on terrorist groups such as Hamas and Hezbollah," though no one had mentioned either organisation.[8]

It was sobering that, even as we entered such a crucial battle, somebody could not resist the temptation to score a point through a hostile Tory newspaper. But the more substantial issue was the difference of opinion it reflected: in LOTO's view, Jeremy's approach to security and international solidarity, as well as his style of leadership, were potential positives and not ground we should concede to the Tories without a fight. Even on a tactical level it would have been folly not to consider some way of counter-attacking to expose the hypocrisy of the Tories.

The *Telegraph* piece highlighted both how difficult it was to have open and honest discussion within the party on strategy, and how unlikely it would be that we would get much positive coverage in the major newspapers. Within LOTO, we had already decided there was no point in making a big investment in relations with the national press, with some honourable exceptions such as the *Mirror* and the *Guardian*.

The broadcast media was a different matter because

---

[8] Kate McCann, 'Labour campaign swerve over Corbyn's terror group links,' the Daily Telegraph, 22.4.2017.

of the requirement for them to give all the parties a fair platform. In the first week of the campaign, Seumas and I met with the *BBC* to discuss their coverage of the campaign and plans for the debates. In the confusing lexicon of journalism, the 'editor, *BBC* political news' and '*BBC* political editor' designate very different roles. The former is Katy Searle, who is a manager running what some insiders call a 'taxi rank of political correspondents', and the latter is Laura Kuenssberg, who is the top taxi driver and gets to choose which journey she wants to take on any given day. We met with them both and talked through the daily campaign routine, what they needed from us and mundane matters such as whether or not there would be a separate bus for the media (the answer to which was they would have to arrange their own travel). When it came to discussing the debates, both were firmly of the view that May would not budge on her decision not to go head-to-head with Jeremy.

A meeting with senior *Mirror* journalists was much more productive than the time invested in handling endless calls from other print media with ever more spurious 'stories', most sounding suspiciously like briefings from Tory headquarters. I would prefer all newspapers to stick solely to reporting the news but, given most of them were acting as Tory campaign instruments, the *Mirror*'s apparent eagerness to work with us was more than welcome. Naturally, they were looking for exclusives and access to Jeremy that their competitors would not get and that would be tailored to the interests of their readers – which positively included Jeremy's allotment and enthusiasm for jam-making and gardening.

While these behind-the-scenes discussions were going on, Jeremy had already clocked up some serious mileage on the campaign trail. By the end of the first week, he had spoken at a major indoor rally at Church House in Westminster and visited Croydon, Swindon, Bristol, Cardiff, Manchester, Warrington, and Crewe. Everything was being organised at breakneck speed and publicised mainly by word-of-mouth, e-mail, and social media, yet the turnouts were surpassing anyone's expectations. This was great, of course, but it presented a huge organisational challenge, epitomised by chaotic scenes in Cardiff where the 700 plus people who gathered on Whitchurch Common could not hear or see Jeremy properly because of an inadequate sound system and no staging. I was following events on Twitter from my flat in Cardiff Bay, where I was buried in campaign planning and copywriting. In a Twitter direct message, Hannah McCoy, a local Labour supporter, told me privately that she thought "it was a shame that some may have not been able to hear what Jeremy had to say." She added that Jeremy "was, as always, wonderful and spoke with passion and fire in his belly" but she urged us to make sure he could be heard and looked "leader-like" at rallies. Others sent me similar comments.

This kind of social media feedback would, as the campaign developed, prove invaluable. Over the eight weeks, a diverse dozen or so people scattered across the country – most of whom I had never met – became an informal personal focus group, offering me their comments on how things were going. They were supportive, but not uncritical and, by chance, were mixed in terms of ethnicity, gender, and age. It was self-selecting and nowhere near scientific, but – as I would be spending nearly all my waking hours in an office block in central London – a channel to the wider world was very welcome.

Hannah and other people's comments on the Cardiff event had underlined the need for a big investment in the campaign tour. We could not afford to give hostile media any opportunities to portray Jeremy as a 'rabble rouser' and Labour as a 'shambles.' I passed on the feedback to LOTO colleagues and the next day was pleased to get a message from Sian Jones, LOTO's head of media, saying: "They did a great job in Crewe today with a quality PA system and much better stewarding."

Those early rallies gave us a feel for the mood. It was clear Jeremy had pulling power that went beyond the converted – in Cardiff, I had people contacting me who had never been to a political meeting. His unassuming ease of manner was also already contrasting nicely with the wooden appearances of May at tightly-controlled events. That first weekend, while campaigning in Dudley, she dodged journalists' questions on tax rises and the 'triple lock' on pensions, before giving a short speech to a hand-picked audience in which her 'strong and stable' mantra featured 12 times.[9] Within the Labour campaign it was becoming a joke, but there was no sign yet of it affecting voting intentions: the polls for the Sunday papers were still dire with us languishing on just over 26 per cent while the Tories averaged nearly 46 per cent. *Survation*, for the *Mail on Sunday*, had the parties'

---

[9] Jon Stone, 'Theresa May refuses to spell out Tory tax policy,' the Independent, 22.4.2017.

closest margin at 40 to 29 per cent. At the other end of the spectrum, *ComRes* in the *Sunday Mirror* was reporting a cataclysmic 50 to 25 per cent Tory margin.[10]

Those polls were in the field before the first weekend's campaigning, and prior to our well-received announcement that Labour would create four new public holidays, marking the patron saints' days of England, Northern Ireland, Scotland and Wales. Nevertheless, the mismatch between voter intentions and the size and enthusiasm of the crowds greeting Jeremy did present a conundrum. Conventional Labour campaign wisdom was that mass rallies are not a route to mass electoral support. Bernie Sanders had shown how they could be – his rallies had been the centrepiece of a campaign that won more than 13 million votes. The key was their inclusiveness and the way they energised and mobilised people for the wider campaigning activities.

The outline campaign plan I drafted that weekend was a first stab at applying that approach. But I had a further nagging worry, which may have been unfounded, but seemed worth flagging. In a note to Seumas with the plan, I said I was concerned about the effect of Labour's split on the campaign and the possibility of us operating in parallel silos. There was a danger of LOTO and Southside defaulting to "their respective campaigning comfort zones" with one re-running the tactics of the successful leadership battles, and the other "stuck in the groove" of "every Labour election campaign of the last three decades." We needed, my e-mail argued, "a step change – something much bigger and more professional – without jettisoning any of the good things we can take

---

[10] UK Polling Report.

93

from both the Southside machine or the Corbyn team's experience."

The outline was a very basic three-page document for discussion at a joint election strategy meeting between LOTO and Southside on Monday, April 24. Two pages consisted of a table setting out the themes, key policy announcements, and events for each week of the campaign. It was prefaced by a front sheet with 12 strategy bullet points, the first of which was simply, 'we are campaigning to win.' The second, with rolling eyes anticipated, said the campaign should have a narrative arc that would go from talking about how people are being held back, to showing them how things could be different. It would be a story of a rigged system, and of a different Britain 'run for the many not the few.' All the policy announcements would be in that context, with the aim of inspiring belief in the transformation Labour was offering and the hope that it could be achieved.

The key practicalities in the plan were that we should target both defensive and offensive seats, run a celebrity-led voter registration campaign on a scale never seen before, invest in reaching older voters, especially through Facebook, and address directly the concerns about security, the economy, and leadership. It said the campaign and manifesto launches would be on May 9 and 16 respectively, and the budget should be "at least £12 million, including the £4 million already agreed" – in total, much the same as had been spent in 2015, but with a shorter period in which to raise it.

On the train to London that Monday morning, I agonised over how we should deal with security and sent an e-mail to the LOTO senior team saying I thought

Jeremy would need 'a Philadelphia moment.' This was a reference to a speech Barack Obama made in 2008 when, while fighting Hillary Clinton for the Democratic party nomination for president, he had been attacked over his links with Rev. Jeremiah Wright, a pastor who had made remarks that were seen as unpatriotic and inflammatory. The conventional expectation was that Obama would disown Wright to pacify white voters. But Obama defied the norm, and chose instead to re-frame the debate by putting Wright's remarks in a broader context. In a calm and measured speech, delivered without departing from his carefully-crafted script, he took an invited audience in Philadelphia through the African-American story in a very personal way. He described Wright as "like family to me," someone who had "strengthened my faith, officiated my wedding, and baptized my children." He said:

"Not once in my conversations with him have I heard him talk about any ethnic group in derogatory terms, or treat whites with whom he interacted with anything but courtesy and respect. He contains within him the contradictions — the good and the bad — of the community that he has served diligently for so many years. I can no more disown him than I can disown the black community. I can no more disown him than I can disown my white grandmother — a woman who helped raise me, a woman who sacrificed again and again for me, a woman who loves me as much as she loves anything in this world, but a woman who once confessed her fear of black men who passed her by on the street, and who on more than one occasion has uttered racial or ethnic stereotypes that made me cringe. These people are a part of me. And they are part of America, this country that I love."[11]

Many people believe that this speech was a pivotal moment that turned the nomination battle Obama's way and ultimately won him the presidency. Once in the White House, some of his actions – not least the use of extra-judicial drone executions and the senseless bombing of Libya – were deeply disappointing, but there is no question that his Philadelphia speech was political communication at its best. It was honest. It dealt with the most sensitive and difficult issue of the campaign in a direct and intelligent way. Even people who did not agree with him respected the integrity he displayed.

My e-mail said that Jeremy would be attacked on security and international policy in much the same way as Obama had been over Wright, and that he should similarly seek to re-frame the question by asking "what happened to the New World Order we were promised when the Berlin Wall came down?" The speech would allow Jeremy to make clear that "being for peace is a strength," and to question whether or not the world is safer, and we are more secure, after the regime-change wars Britain has been involved in. My LOTO colleagues were of much the same mind, and we added the speech to the plan, scheduling it for Friday, May 12, in between the campaign and manifesto launches. It was a good decision in its own right, but it would also prove to be tragically prescient.

The meeting with Southside that afternoon discussed

---

[11] Barack Obama, 'A More Perfect Union,' speech at the National Constitution Center, Philadelphia, 18.3.2008.

what had by then been adopted as LOTO's campaign plan. Some details were added and action points agreed, but the only dissent from the main recommendations was a sceptical comment about an online voter registration campaign from Patrick Heneghan, the executive director for elections at Southside, who said:

"The evidence is you only get people signed up by putting a piece of paper in their hands on the doorstep."

It was hard to argue with the experience of someone who has been at the centre of Labour's election machine for 20 years, but the view in LOTO was that he was underestimating how Jeremy's huge social media presence and support among young people would give an online campaign far more chance of success than in previous elections.

A more unsettling challenge to the viability of a 'campaign to win' strategy came in the next meeting when the party's pollster, Michael Turner of *BMG,* presented some brutally-bad voting intention data. Their weekend poll had the Tories on 47 per cent and us on 28 per cent. That wasn't quite as bad as *ComRes* was projecting in the *Sunday Mirror*, but *BMG*'s felt worse because they translated it into a Labour seat projection that ranged from a worst case of 127 to a best case of 182. Even if what Michael called "aggressive weighting" against young people voting was excessive, our chances of preventing May's landslide seemed slim. In the discussion, Michael could not point to any cracks in the bleak wall we faced:

"UKIP has served as a gateway to the Tories for Labour voters... you lose them and they don't come back... Labour can't beat the Tories on

Brexit...you're in no man's land... most of the public think you're pro-EU, but Remain voters are not the ones you need..."

It was dire. Even the normally irrepressible Ian Lavery looked stunned afterwards.

As if the *BMG* meeting wasn't bad enough, the first news headline I saw just after it predicted the end of Labour in Wales. A *YouGov* poll had found that Wales was, in the words of Cardiff University professor Roger Scully, "on the brink of an electoral earthquake." It put the Tories on 40 per cent of the Welsh vote (up 12 per cent on the equivalent poll three months earlier) and Labour on 30 per cent (down 3 per cent). Scully said: "Labour faces losing a general election in Wales for the first time since 1918," and put it down to "a direct move by many former UKIP supporters into the Conservative ranks."[12] The poll had been in the field immediately after the snap election was called and did not reflect the influence of early campaigning, but it was still another warning of the danger of pro-Brexit voters giving the Tories a landslide. If anything remotely like it came to pass, it would be hard for me to show my face in Cardiff again.

But there was no time to dwell on my fears of a frosty homecoming. The next 48 hours would be crucial in fleshing out a campaign plan that could stop the Tories. No one in LOTO was letting the polls deflect us. Andrew Fisher and his team had been working out when each of the major policy initiatives would be ready to announce. Niall Sookoo, LOTO's campaign co-ordinator, had produced a grid based on the outline campaign plan into

---

[12] Roger Scully, 'Sensational poll suggests Tories could end Labour majority in Wales,' ITV, 24.4.2017.

which all the policy announcements would also be slotted by Andrew and Seumas. Another group had been planning the voter registration campaign, ready for a launch event on Saturday, April 29. Karie was orchestrating the constituency visits. And so, the 'to do' list went on: key messages and a script to finalise, five party political broadcasts to plan, major speeches to draft.

If anyone needed encouragement, there were some portentous fragments of good news. The Electoral Commission reported that more than half a million people had visited their voter registration website since the election was called. And encouraging social media figures were coming through showing 'likes' of the Labour Facebook page rising 13 per cent to over 616,000 in the first week, while the Tories had seen a rise of only 0.5 per cent to 570,000. Jeremy's already sky-high 'likes' on Facebook had gone up 1.3 per cent to 853,000, and videos posted on his page had been viewed in total well over 3 million times.

This was all happening while Parliament was still in session, which meant Jeremy could not get out of Westminster most of that week. But the final PMQs before the dissolution did give him a platform to spell out our campaign messages and go head-to-head with May for possibly the last time before voting. PMQs is a 'damned if you do, damned if you don't' event. Preparation soaks up far more time than a ritual only of interest to hardened politicos warrants, but you know the news will travel much further if it goes badly for Jeremy. And then there are the questions. If Jeremy sticks to one topic he has a better chance of cornering

May, but is open to criticism for his choice of issue. He has tried to humanise PMQs by introducing questions from the public, but pressing May on multiple topics makes it easier for her to evade answering any of them.

On this occasion, the call was made to use questions sent in by the public to show how people were being held back on five of the big issues we would be fighting the election on – housing, school budgets, public sector pay, the NHS, and the raising of the state pension age for women. Anyone watching with an open mind could not but empathise with the stories of people like Andy, whose three adult children couldn't afford their own homes, and Maureen, who had worked for 45 years and then been told she couldn't have the pension that was rightfully hers. May responded by resorting more than once to her 'strong and stable' soundbite. Anticipating this, Jeremy finished with a flourish saying:

"Strong leadership is about standing up for the many, not the few, but the Prime Minister and the Conservatives only look after the richest, not the rest. They are strong against the weak and weak against the strong."

It didn't go unnoticed that the passage used both 'for the many, not the few' from 1997 and a final sentence adapted from Ed Miliband, but why reinvent the wheel?[13] Watching with Seumas from a packed press gallery, I thought it summed up our position nicely and would be shared widely on social media.

Among the instant Twitter reactions, the *Sun*'s verdict was Jeremy had been "savaged," and *Sky*'s political

---

[13] Peter Edwards, 'PMQs verdict: Corbyn channels the spirit of Miliband to disrupt robotic PM,' Labour List, 26.4.2017.

correspondent, Beth Rigby, said he had dealt "no real blows." But the *Times* diarist Patrick Kidd thought Jeremy did "rather well, as he did last week." On May, he added:

"There's much more to being a good PM than PMQs, of course, but May remains quite weak at this. No wonder she's dodging TV debates."[14]

The *Guardian*, meanwhile, gave Jeremy a double-edged verdict that might have been about a relegation-threatened team coming away with a point from the Etihad Stadium. "It did not feel as if anyone secured a great triumph," they said. "But in the circumstances, and with polling organisations pouring humiliation over Corbyn by the hour, that probably amounted to something of a win for the Labour leader."[15]

For Jeremy, it was all water off a duck's back. He was happy to be able to get out on the campaign trail that afternoon by joining an NHS nurses' protest, and the following day by visiting a housing project in Harlow.

The campaign plan, however, was not yet as settled as we thought. A LOTO-Southside strategy meeting the morning after PMQs – Thursday, April 27 – saw a concerted push for a rethink of our 'campaign to win' approach in light of *BMG*'s bleak polling figures. The senior people from Southside argued that "campaigns don't swing an election more than 2-3 per cent," and therefore we had to concentrate on holding the seats we had. Andrew Fisher replied that Labour hadn't previously "offered the things we're offering in this election." The manifesto, he said, would be "transformative" and would

---

[14] See respective Twitter feeds.
[15] Andrew Sparrow, 'PMQs - Snap verdict,' the Guardian website, 26.4.2017.

"inspire people to register and vote." As evidence, I quoted the latest Electoral Commission figures on traffic to their website. But the response was that "visiting doesn't mean registering," non-voters are called non-voters because "they don't vote," and the manifesto would have no effect because "nobody reads them."

It was a tense discussion, and it continued like that for the best part of an hour. Both sides knew how much was at stake politically. The Southside arguments carried the weight of greater experience of running an electoral machine. My roots were in issue-based political campaigning and my involvement in general elections – though stretching back to 1966 – was limited to local activity. Could they be right? Were we in danger of spreading ourselves too thinly and leaving our heartlands exposed to a Tory offensive? They had the evidence of the polling. It was also true that campaigns did not traditionally move opinion much and that the bland manifestos of modern elections were hardly read. But voter turn-out was on the rise: after collapsing from 78 per cent in 1992 to 59 per cent in 2001, it had increased to 66 per cent in 2015. And there was other evidence of interest in politics growing again – not only in Britain but also in the US and Europe – even if some of their choices were misplaced. From a progressive point of view, these stirrings had manifested themselves in the surprise emergence of Jean-Luc Melenchon in France, the Podemos movement in Spain, Sanders in the US and, of course, Jeremy's two successful leadership campaigns.

Organisations tend to breed what I call the certainty syndrome. It's like Dutch Elm disease for bureaucracies. They are necessarily built on what has worked in the past; and, of course, experience is valuable. But then they call this 'best practice,' and it gets ossified into an article of faith. People say things like 'this is the way the PLP expects it to be' or 'you can't say that.' Before you know it, there's a culture of certainty that is blind to contrary evidence, especially when it is first emerging.

We could have continued our esoteric debate for hours. But it was not an argument anyone could 'win'. Ultimately, it was a question of judgement, and mine – I admit – was based on instinct as much as evidence. Firstly, I could not imagine sustaining a purely defensive strategy through a long campaign. To use another football metaphor, teams that try to pack their penalty area for 90 minutes usually collapse under the relentless pressure, while those that defend in their opponent's half often throw seemingly stronger adversaries off their stride. Secondly, and this was my bottom line, we simply owed it to the millions who were pinning their hopes on us for an end to austerity to give winning our best shot.

Iain McNicol closed the discussion by proposing a compromise: we would "try it [LOTO's] way" for a couple of weeks and "see where we get to." That, we clarified, meant reviewing the strategy on May 15, giving us ten days of national campaigning and policy announcements after the local elections to shift the polls in our direction.

6 – Early Surge Meets Reality Check

"I have learned over the years that when one's mind is made up, this diminishes fear; knowing what must be done does away with fear."
Rosa Parks, US civil rights movement leader

It was the last Friday in April. For a couple of days, the LOTO offices had been like a transit camp. Parliament was about to shut up shop for the election. MPs had left for their constituencies to become candidates again. Their staff were in limbo. As there was technically no 'leader of the opposition,' this applied to us. We had to pack our stuff up and move to Labour's Southside head office for the rest of the campaign, joined by shadow cabinet staffers who had been allocated roles by Karie, chief marshal of the troops. Everyone would be on Labour's payroll from the start of May to comply with the rules for what's known as 'Short money,' which provides only for fulfilling 'parliamentary functions.'[1]

The move into Southside made the campaign seem real. It felt like, after a flying start, we were digging in for a long race. For the remaining six weeks, the pace would be relentless.

The Southside building is on Victoria Street in the heart of one of the most affluent parts of London. Westminster city council, which has offices nearby, has never been held by Labour, and you would struggle to find a two-bedroom

---

[1] Named after Edward Short, the Labour minister who introduced funding for opposition parties in 1974.

flat in the area for less than a million pounds.

Southside itself is bright and airy compared to LOTO's offices in the Norman Shaw building. The Labour party occupies two floors – the second and the eighth – both of which are mainly open plan. The second floor was home to the press office, media monitoring unit and policy team. The eighth – and top – floor housed the events, digital, creative, supporter engagement and election teams, among others. Iain McNicol's office-cum-meeting room was also on the eighth, and Jeremy was allocated a nearby meeting room, which was separated from the open-plan area by a frosted glass wall and had panoramic views across Westminster through the other three, clear glass walls. Officially called the north room, it – inevitably – became known as 'the glasshouse'. Jeremy would base himself there on the rare occasions he was not on the road, but the glasshouse was mainly used by Karie, Seumas, and me.[2] Both Iain and Jeremy's rooms jutted out over a flat roof and had exits that led to the fire escape. Iain and Seumas would often pace the parallel gangways – about fifty feet apart – with their phones pressed to their ears, giving the exasperated health and safety officer palpitations.

Having been working for Jeremy for only two months, I didn't know many of the Southside staff. Some seemed intrigued by the invading Corbynistas, as if we had landed from Mars. A few – only a handful – could barely conceal their disdain. My overwhelming impression that day, however, was

---

[2] Jeremy's room would also provide refuge when they were in London to the three northern MPs who did a lot of media interviews for the campaign: Ian Lavery, Andrew Gwynne, and Jon Trickett. Andrew Murray, the chief of staff of Unite, worked from the eighth floor after joining us on May 12. Andrew Fisher usually based himself with his team, which sat alongside the Southside policy team on the second floor.

of people who, whatever their views, were professional and eager to contribute to a successful campaign.

Over the next six weeks, a large part of my time would be spent working with the creative and digital teams under Tom Geldard, and the supporter engagement team directed by Ben Nolan. Within the former, Tom Lavelle orchestrated the digital operation, and Chloe Green was responsible for content for Labour's website and social media feeds. During the election, there were more than thirty communications staff working in that part of the eighth floor, including graphic designers, web developers, copywriters and videographers. All of them came within Patrick Heneghan's department, but I was their go-to person in LOTO for content sign-off and, increasingly as the campaign developed and the budget grew, for decisions on priorities and strategy.

The LOTO communications team, meanwhile, doubled in number for the campaign and was based on the second floor alongside Labour's press office staff. The demands on them were enormous – we needed people not only to prepare outgoing releases, handle incoming inquiries and be on the road with Jeremy, but also to recce the locations for future visits and plan for big announcements and speeches. The two senior people in LOTO communications, Sian Jones and James Schneider, bore the brunt of managing everything, with David Prescott leading on media relations for shadow cabinet members, and the other two LOTO press officers, Angie Williams and Sophie Nazemi, spending a lot of time out with Jeremy. That core team was, by the time we had moved into Southside, supplemented by PCS union press officer Rich Simcox, freelance journalist Lizzie Mistry, former Momentum press officer Georgie Robertson, shadow treasury adviser Joe Ryle, and former *South Wales Argus* editor Steve Hoselitz, my old boss and, at 70, thrilled to be involved. Jeremy's long-standing social media marvel, Jack Bond, sat with the LOTO communications team and was joined by Ben Sellers, who had worked on Jeremy's leadership campaigns.

In the early stages of the campaign, I had met with Carol Linforth, Southside's director of events, to discuss LOTO's ideas for big Sanders-style events. It was good to find we were on the same wavelength about how the campaign and manifesto launches and Jeremy's rallies should be staged. The venues would be big, and there would be no half measures in terms of visual impact. Carol and her team would, throughout the campaign, work closely with Karie and LOTO's own event managers, Kat Fletcher and Marshajane Thompson, to produce 71 events around the country, a staggering achievement in just eight weeks, and one of the stand-out successes of the campaign.

The last weekend in April saw us implement what would be one of our guiding principles: we would turn supposed weaknesses into positives. In the opening 12 days of the campaign, it had become abundantly clear the Tories were pushing the image of Theresa May as a strong leader even to the exclusion of their own brand. Their newspaper adverts were headlined 'Theresa May for Britain' and pictured her looking dynamic and presidential. The word Tory was often not mentioned at all. The party was reduced to being 'Theresa's team.'

The flip side of this was that they would personalise their attack on Labour, principally targeting Jeremy. In the final PMQs, May had said "every vote for him is a vote for a chaotic Brexit... to weaken our economy... [and] for a coalition of chaos." Jeremy would be "a weak leader propped up by the Liberal Democrats and the Scottish nationalists," whereas she would provide "strong and stable leadership in the national interest, building a stronger and more secure future for this country."[3]

The challenge was clear, and we had anticipated it well before May called the election. Our narrative consultant, Marc Lopatin, and I had met Jeremy in March to discuss the idea of him making a speech about his approach to leadership. We wanted it to be a personal statement telling his own story. "The country needs to know more about you," Marc told him. Seumas had warned us Jeremy would be reluctant to speak about himself, but he seemed persuaded, and the speech was pencilled in for late April. Once May had thrown down the gauntlet of an election, what was a good idea in March had become a burning necessity. We firmed up our plans: it would be held on Saturday, April 29 at London Metropolitan University, in the heart of working class Bethnal Green and Bow. Seumas, Marc, and his co-consultant, Jem, took the lead in working on the speech and had two sessions discussing and rehearsing it with Jeremy.[4]

When we released some of the themes of the speech beforehand to the media, most journalists seemed mystified. Some thought, with Jeremy's personal ratings so far behind May's, we were on a suicide mission in tackling what they saw as a Tory ace. With more than a hint of a sneer, the *Telegraph* reported the speech as an attempt by Jeremy to counter Tory attacks on his suitability for office by citing "his arrest when protesting apartheid as proof of

---

[3]Prime Minister's Questions, House of Commons Hansard, 26.4.2017.
[4] Throughout the campaign, speech-writing was a collective effort. Though one or two people would prepare an initial draft, the final version would involve input from other members of the LOTO strategy group and Jeremy himself.

his prime ministerial credentials."[5] It says a lot, of course, about the *Telegraph* that they took it as read that Jeremy's anti-apartheid activism would *not* boost his standing as a leader. But the central point Jeremy would make in his speech was, in any case, subtler than that. He was talking about "how the privilege of being an MP could help achieve... profound and lasting change" not from above but by using their standing and influence to encourage people "to act together to overturn unfairness."

Reflecting on his early years as an MP in the 1980s, he said:

"At the time, young protesters were being shot dead on the streets by the racist apartheid regime in South Africa – Nelson Mandela and hundreds of ANC leaders were in prison. The Conservative government refused to impose sanctions, entertained the leaders of the regime and banned protests outside the South African embassy in London. Being an MP helped bring attention to that ban and the wider cause of South Africa's liberation – and got a group of us arrested. But the space for people in Britain to organise in support of freedom in South Africa was defended and strengthened. And I realised then that political leaders can – if they want to – create and preserve the space for others to organise and transform countries."

In looking at the period since then, Jeremy did not criticise Tony Blair or his other predecessors by name, but he distanced himself from them in saying "the leaders who had come and gone" had not given "a clear invitation" for people to make a sustained attempt to rid this country of

---

[5] Ben Riley-Smith, 'Jeremy Corbyn: Arrest for protesting apartheid shows why I am ready to lead Britain,' the Daily Telegraph website, 29.4.2017.

the rigged economy that holds people back. On the contrary, he said, all the major parties had "bought into Conservative ideas about markets, finance and the economy" that "ultimately left us with no defence against a global financial crisis that had its roots in another country's housing market."

This was said not so much as a vindication of his own stand against neo-liberal economics, but as a warning that if any leader goes unchallenged and stops listening "they can make some of the most damaging mistakes [and] even put our country at risk." There were clear signs, he said, that Theresa May and her closest advisers were slipping into a "presidential bunker mentality," whereas he saw leadership as being about "holding open the space for dissent, new thinking and fit-for-purpose policy." He continued:

"For many years, I couldn't see much beyond how so many political leaders manipulated us while giving in again and again to vested interests. I didn't want to be like that. And it wasn't clear to me there could be another way. But I've learned there is. Whereas insecure leaders want to feel stronger by asking you to give them more power, I recognise strong leadership as equipping *you* with more power.....We are not going to have free thinking shut down by a hostile media or an elite that scoffs at anyone who dares to step out of line. No, each of us has a contribution to make. We have ideas for a better tomorrow and we are going to respond together. We are a party that wants to bring together people and ideas, and harness the thirst for real and lasting change. If you agree our times demand a response from all parts of our society and all corners of our country, then I am proud to be your leader. And if you want someone to hold that space open for you to help change the direction of your life and our country, then I am proud to be your leader."

The speech was covered live on the 24-hour television news channels, streamed online and shared thousands of times on social media. We did not expect most mainstream media outlets to abandon their stereotypes of what a leader should be like, but we were confident the speech would resonate with voters looking for change. And we also used it as a platform for Jeremy to make a call for young people to "step up" and "claim your future." He said:

"You have till May 22. Over 2.4 million young people are missing from the UK's electoral register. Barely 40 per cent of 18 to 24-year olds turn out to vote. The Conservatives are more than happy with this state of affairs. Apathy and resignation will secure them seats on Election Day."

I watched the speech from my friend's house in north London where I had been staying since starting work for Jeremy. My main preoccupation that morning had been with securing some money for digital advertising to support the voter registration campaign. While I was confident the burst of activity on Twitter when we launched it at 3pm that day would ensure it reached far into the audience we were targeting, some media buying would carry it even further and sustain it for longer.

We had some great content. Our creative agency, Krow Communications,[6] had produced a cheeky video blowing raspberries at Donald Trump, Marine Le Pen, and Nigel Farage before saying "voting matters." The Southside

---

[6] Krow Communications were appointed several months before I started and had developed some campaign ideas, which Seumas and I had discussed with them in March, ready for a possible snap election.

creative team had come up with another called "Things you can do in two minutes," showing that voter registration would take only as long as checking your e-mail or making a cup of tea. But, at that stage, no funding for the campaign was available from the main Labour election budget, so I turned to Unite whose executive council had given its recently re-elected general secretary, Len McCluskey, discretion over how to spend money set aside for the campaign. Seeing the importance of voter registration, he had no hesitation in committing some of the Unite budget to it.

That settled, I headed for the Tube to start a journey back to Cardiff for one night at home. It took four times as long as usual due to the rail electrification work going on, but the edge was taken off my frustrations by the messages coming through on WhatsApp about that weekend's polls. On the average of four polls for the Sunday papers, we were up by nearly four points and the Tories were down by two. The gap was still in the teens in three of them, but *ORB* for the *Sunday Telegraph* had the Tories on 42 per cent and us on 31 per cent, our best polling figures since December.[7] That early bounce would prove to be one of the biggest of the campaign – surpassed only by the upward movement in the polls in the seven days after the manifesto was leaked. The latter proved expensive for me personally because I promised to buy everyone in the team a drink when we hit 35 per cent.

After the election, some justified their lack of belief in Labour's chances of closing the gap on the Tories by claiming the so-called 'Corbyn surge' happened very late in the campaign. But the polls – though mostly understating our support – show the upward trend started on day one and continued, with only one week of downward

---

[7] UK Polling Report.

movement, right up to the final week. What I did not realise that weekend was that we were about to hit the one rough patch.

The May Day bank holiday saw us start the week on the front foot with the announcement of a 20-point workers' rights package and new rights for renters that would "call time on bad landlords." The former included our pledges to ban zero hours contracts, introduce a living wage of at least £10 an hour by 2020 and give all workers – whether part-time or full-time, temporary or permanent – equal rights from day one. It also said we would end the public sector pay cap and roll-out a maximum pay ratio of 20:1 in the public sector and for firms bidding for public contracts. The renters' rights policy said a Labour government would set legal minimum standards to ensure properties are fit for human habitation, provide free advice to tenants, and give local councils new powers to licence landlords and impose fines on those who fail to meet the standards.

The response to these policies on Facebook and Twitter was very positive but, with the notable exceptions of the *Mirror, Independent* and *Guardian*, mainstream media coverage was either negative or minimal. From the outset it had been obvious we would have to rely heavily on social media to get our message across, which would mean investing heavily in both content and expanding our reach.

Content is always the starting point with any communications, but that's all the more the case with social media as material can so easily be shared if it goes down well – and that's the big prize. But it is not just a matter of getting the politics right: the words, images and video have to have the impact to hook people instantly and hold their attention. In the noisy and competitive world of social media, if someone reads a post or watches a video for more than 10 seconds you are doing well. Content has to be succinct and incisive but, most of all, it has to have humanity, humour, and hope (in some permutation). The most successful political campaign posts on social media are nearly always those that tell personal stories (like Erica Garner's video for the Sanders campaign)[8], make people laugh (as the actor Rob Delaney did in his Vote Labour video)[9] or inspire belief that a better way is possible (as our final campaign video did so brilliantly using Lily Allen's *Somewhere Only We Know*).[10]

There was never any doubt we had the people with the talent, passion, and politics – across LOTO, Labour and the outriders – to beat the Tories hands down on content. We were also starting from a stronger position: Jeremy had more than twice as many Facebook likes and Twitter followers as Theresa May when the election was called.

But we still had two problems. Firstly, while I was certain our social media reach would grow 'organically' (the increases in likes and followers that come from winning political support and people voluntarily sharing good content), would it expand *rapidly enough* to win the election? Big and growing as Jeremy's social media presence was, even our most successful posts were – in the early weeks – reaching only 5-10 per cent of the UK's 32 million Facebook users and around 10 per cent of the 18 million people on Twitter.[11]

Secondly, even if we could achieve remarkable growth, as we did, would our content be seen by the voters we most needed to reach in the battleground seats we were defending or trying to win? I do not subscribe to the view that social media is an echo chamber. That's ridiculously

---

[8] The Sanders campaign video 'It's Not Over' was discussed in Chapter 4.

[9] See 'Rob Delaney is backing Labour,' YouTube, 3.6.2017.

[10] See Chapter 13 for more about the campaign video.

[11] Source: Statista

simplistic. But it is true that the algorithms tend to put content in front of those likely to be pre-disposed to it, and that people tend to gravitate towards the views they agree with. Which is great for building a movement – and movements are a big part of winning elections – but, with less than six weeks to polling day, we also had to get our content in front of crucial voters who might not go looking for it themselves. And we had to start immediately.

The practical means for doing this were available. Facebook and the other social media giants have a commercial interest in making it as easy as possible for advertisers to target very specific audiences. They have the data – age, gender, location, occupation, education, interests and viewing history – and you can set your criteria. The Labour party had taken this even further by developing its 'Promote' database, which matched Facebook profiles with names and addresses on the electoral register supplied by the credit agency, Experian.[12] Like it or not, your data is their product: credit agencies encourage people to register to vote on the basis that it helps lenders and insurance companies verify your identity and build what's known as your Data Self. This kind of data, lawfully gathered, is now the bedrock of most marketing strategies and of immense value in an election campaign.

So, what's the beef? Quite simply, there was no money. We had the strategy, content, technology and data – but

---

[12] The Experian website says: 'Your Data Self is a version of you that's made up of your credit history and other information – it tells companies how well you've managed your finances in the past. Lenders must ensure they've got a full, accurate picture of your Data Self, so as part of this they need to confirm your identity and address. Being on the electoral roll makes this easier for lenders to do – and it helps protect you from identity theft and fraud too.'

we did not yet have the cash to buy the extra reach[13] into the various social media and other online channels. In traditional direct mail terms, it was like having the address lists and leaflets, but no money for postage. We were hearing that the Tories were going to spend £5 million on Facebook advertising alone – our kitty for all paid digital advertising, at that stage, was barely a hundredth of that.

The campaign budget was one of two main items on the agenda of a LOTO-Southside strategy call on the afternoon of the bank holiday Monday afternoon. The position was pretty grim. Core budget costs – for staffing, defensive seat funding, Jeremy's tour, polling, political broadcasts and other essential costs – had crept up to £6.5 million, and we had only £5 million of it covered. Most of the £5 million had been carried over from the previous year's massive growth in membership. Virtually all the high net worth donors of the Blair years had abandoned Labour, and most of the unions had not yet come through with substantial contributions. That meant even a paltry provision of

---

[13] Digital marketing jargon can be confusing, not least because different platforms have their own terms for very similar things. Twitter uses the term 'impressions' for how many people have seen a tweet, whereas Facebook uses 'reach'. When speaking generally about the extent of our social media audience, I use 'reach'. The key thing, however, is 'engagement'. This includes 'views' of a video (on any digital channel) and all other types of inter-action (on Twitter: likes, retweets and replies; or, on Facebook, likes, shares and comments). Engagement drives reach. High levels of engagement mean that a piece of content is seen beyond those who have chosen to follow you on Twitter or 'like' your Facebook page. For example, Jeremy's post on Twitter (5.6.2017) supporting Sadiq Khan after the London Bridge terrorist attack gained 4.3m impressions – a 'reach' that was three times Jeremy's following. This was achieved 'organically' i.e. without paying to promote the tweet.

£150,000 for digital advertising was hypothetical, and all I had available to spend was the smaller but very welcome contribution Unite had initially pledged.

A more realistic measure of what we needed to invest in digital to win the election was a wish list drawn up by Tom Lavelle. The previous week, when I had expressed concern about the lack of a digital budget, Iain McNicol told me to produce one myself. But it turned out Tom had already done one for Patrick Heneghan, which I discovered when I consulted Tom about digital spending and he gave me the estimate he had produced, which came to £1.74 million. His thinking, at that stage, was that more than half the budget should be spent on Facebook with the rest going mainly on a mixture of Google AdWords, Twitter, and what are known as 'programmatic remarketing' and 'pre-roll' adverts. The latter are, respectively, the ones that follow you around the Internet, and those you have to watch on YouTube before you can see the video you have selected. Other elements – notably Snapchat – would be added to the mix later, but it seemed a pretty good plan to me.

While my main preoccupation was with finding money for digital campaigning, that was not the only item for which funds were lacking: there was no money either for newspaper advertising or a multi-million-pound direct mail campaign that Patrick wanted to run. With the online fund-raising hard to predict at such an early stage, the joint strategy group decided to make a pitch for some serious cash from the unions at a meeting scheduled for later that week – for which Patrick and I would prepare three scenarios showing how we would spend an extra £3 million, £5 million, or £7 million.

The second item on the conference call agenda was grimmer still. Though the campaign had been going well, we faced the brutal fact that most of the local elections being held that Thursday were for seats that were last contested midway through the Coalition government era when Labour was riding high. In England, the benchmark was 2013 when we made a net gain of about 250 seats on the same councils. In Wales, we were up against 2012 results that were the best Labour had achieved since the 22 Welsh unitary authorities were formed in 1999. And, in Scotland, we faced comparison with 2012 results that pre-dated the ascendancy of the SNP and our virtual wipe-out there in the 2015 general election. A paper prepared by Patrick gave losing 450 seats overall as a "reasonable estimate." On top of this, of the six new Metro mayorships, Patrick's forecast suggested we would win only three – Liverpool, Greater Manchester and Tees Valley – with West Midlands going narrowly to the Tories along with the West of England and Cambridgeshire.

For me, there was a personal dimension. I had known Sion Simon, Labour's candidate for West Midlands' mayor, since he worked for Freshwater as a consultant after standing down as an MP in 2010. He had married my daughter, Cerys, a few years later and they had just had a son together. Sion was facing a slick opponent in Andy Street, the former managing director of John Lewis, who – like May – was playing down his Tory politics, yet had the full weight of the party's machine behind him. With only three days until polling, there was no magic wand we could wave to speed up the improvement in our polling. I could only hope that Sion's strong standing in his home base of Birmingham would outweigh the expected high Tory turn-out in leafy Solihull and Dudley.

By this stage, the campaign had established a cycle of daily meetings, the first of which was a short strategy call at 7am to take stock of breaking news and the day ahead. The call on the Tuesday after the bank holiday was dominated by a running story about what May and Jean-

Claude Juncker, the European Commission president, had or had not said to each other over dinner at Downing Street the previous Wednesday. Over the weekend, a German newspaper had published a leaked account of the exchange saying that the talks broke up after May refused to accept EU demands for an exit fee of up to £50 billion. Juncker was reported to have told May that the EU was not "a golf club" the UK could simply walk out of and that he was "ten times as sceptical" as before about the chances of a trade deal. Downing Street had taken the highly unusual step of commenting on the leak. May, while nominally dismissing it as Brussels gossip, said "this also shows that actually these negotiations are at times going to be tough."[14] Whoever was behind the story, it suited the Tories to play up the Brussels bogey and position May as someone who wasn't going to be pushed around. We decided to prepare some lines in anticipation of media questions on the leak, but not to be distracted from our own announcement of a policy to put 10,000 more police on the streets to cut crime.

As the strategy call was coming to an end, news came through that Diane Abbott had got muddled on the cost of the extra police jobs in an interview with Nick Ferrari on *LBC* radio. At first, it did not seem of exceptional concern – interviews sometimes go wrong and you have to move on. But, as the morning progressed and Diane toured the studios talking about the policy, it became clear that she was struggling to recover her composure. As can sometimes happen, one bad interview triggers a downward spiral. Worse still, the rest of the media was running the story and playing clips from the original *LBC*

---

[14] Macer Hall, 'I'll stand up for Britain! May's fury at Brussels' DIRTY TRICKS amid leaked Brexit talks,' the Daily Express, 2.5.2017.

interview over and over again. It all hinged on the fact that, at first, she had said the policy would cost 300 *thousand* pounds when she should have said 300 *million*. It was a human error that anyone could have made.[15] The media — including Nick Ferrari — had been given a briefing on the policy and knew the cost would be £298.8 million annually, once fully implemented, and that this would be amply covered by the £735 million a Labour government would recoup annually by reversing a Tory capital gains tax giveaway. They could easily have made that clear — so that their listeners had the facts — but giving Labour a bashing was much more fun.

This episode established a pattern: for the rest of the campaign, virtually all Labour interviews would include a memory test. It was a game that we were vulnerable to because we had done the right thing and costed every policy we would announce, but there was little equivalent testing of Tory spokespeople. Could they remember, say, how many people with disabilities had lost benefits through their welfare reforms, or how many times George Osborne had changed the target date for eliminating the deficit? And was this trying-to-catch-politicians-out game providing a service to viewers and listeners anyway? No doubt many enjoyed it but, if they were asked what qualities they were looking for in a home secretary, would remembering financial figures be anywhere near the top — higher than their views on security, crime, immigration or, as in this case, the impact of police cuts on communities around the country? Of course, if the Tories or independent experts had evidence challenging our figures, that would be a story and worth discussing — but not with Diane, because the public finance implications of our policies were a matter for John McDonnell and his shadow

---

[15] We would later discover that there was a health reason behind Diane's lapse (see Chapter 13).

treasury team. Besides, the presenters asking these questions *always* had the figures in front of them in the briefing papers we supplied for every policy announcement.

How much we were damaged that week by Diane's lapse is hard to say. Paradoxically, later in the campaign we may have benefited because the constant repetition of her mistake gave our policy of reversing police cuts more coverage than it might otherwise have gained, and meant no one could accuse us of inventing it opportunistically after the Manchester attack when security became such a huge issue.

Spirits at Southside were temporarily dampened, and there would be a post mortem at a longer strategy meeting that afternoon, but I did not let it deter me from going on a rare outing I had promised myself. My routine on most days of the campaign was simple: up at 5am, do a few e-mails, get picked up by a car at 6.30am, join the strategy call at 7am on the way to Westminster and then spend 12 to 14 hours working at Southside before heading back to where I was staying to do some final calls and e-mails. Other members of the campaign team worked similarly long hours, but their roles took them out and about more. My job was bunker based. But, that day, Ken Loach and Sixteen Productions were filming with Jeremy for a party political broadcast (PPB) at the Park Theatre in his constituency. This was one of three PPBs the *I, Daniel Blake* director would be making for us and – following on from the leadership speech – it would be about Jeremy and his values. I could have nominated someone else to go along in case Jeremy was door-stepped by the media but, as the person over-seeing the PPBs, I had a good excuse to see a master of film-making at work.

I wasn't disappointed. When I arrived, Ken and his producer, Rebecca O'Brien, were marshalling a small army of production staff and meticulously checking to ensure everything – setting, sound, lighting – would be just right for the interview. We were in the theatre's large upstairs coffee bar. Jeremy was sitting in a corner, chatting with Karie and his wife, Laura, while having some make-up applied. In another corner, Sixteen's researcher, Izzy Charman, was running through the questions for the interview with five Labour party members who would be conducting it. "We wanted people who were interested in the issues and would tease out of Jeremy the ideas that were driving him," Ken explained.

The number of people involved was a far cry from my days as a *BBC* reporter in the 1990s when research consisted of a quick visit to the cuttings library and you went out on the job with one camera person. When the interview started, it was obvious Izzy and the Labour volunteers had done their homework. Their questions spanned everything from Jeremy's childhood in Shropshire and two years as a youth worker in Jamaica, to what motivated him to get involved in politics and his views on the big issues of the moment. He talked about joining the Labour party as a teenager and being active in the 1966 general election, and he described seeing TV reports of the US dropping napalm on villages in Vietnam,[16] calling it "a formative experience." Asked if he was a pacifist, he said:

"No, but I'm a person of peace. I don't glory in war and I don't think anyone should."

---

[16] In the Vietnam War, the US dropped napalm bombs indiscriminately on towns and villages causing thousands of deaths. Under what's known as the Inhumane Weapons Convention, it is now 'prohibited in all circumstances to make the civilian population as such, individual civilians or civilian objects the object of attack by incendiary weapons' (Article 2, Clause 1, 'Protocol on prohibitions and restrictions on the use of incendiary weapons'). See: **www.unog.ch**

Towards the end, Jeremy made a heartfelt plea for a different way of doing things. He said:

"I love this country, I love the history, the beauty, the diversity of this country. But people are not at ease – there's inequality, there's injustice, there's anger. There's anger because people can't get on, there's anger because people can't get anywhere to live, there's anger because young people are not getting the jobs they want. Let's do it differently – where we work from the principle that the role of government is to give everybody a decent chance."

Hearing that, I knew we had the makings of a great PPB, and left feeling buoyed by working with people who were both at the top of their profession and totally committed to what we were trying to achieve.

My escape from the attacks on us was, however, all too brief. That evening, word reached us that the Tories would be doing a 'Labour tax and debt bombshell' press conference the next morning, the day before the local election vote. An embargoed release, said the Tories, had produced a "damning dossier that lays bare the estimated £45 billion black hole in Jeremy Corbyn's nonsensical tax and spending promises." And it quoted David Davis as saying Jeremy's "irresponsible ideas pose a grave risk to the future of Britain's economy and the finances of every family in the country." In four short paragraphs, Jeremy was named seven times, the strong and stable leadership of Theresa May was mentioned twice, and the words Labour and Tory did not appear at all. That this was a personal attack on Jeremy became even clearer when we saw their poster with his picture over an image of a bomb with the slogan: "No bombs for our army, one big bombshell for your family."[17]

By midnight, the Treasury team had obtained and analysed the dossier, and a release quoting Andrew Gwynne saying it contained "error after error" and "blatant misrepresentations" was ready to go out. The rebuttal answered "10 Tory mistakes amongst many" by explaining, in some cases, exactly how we would fund the policies and, in others, that items in the dossier were not, in fact, Labour policy. We also pointed out that the supposed 'black hole' was calculated by including borrowing for infrastructure investment and mixing it up with spending on services, a deliberate obfuscation that would become a feature of the Tory campaign. The Tories knew that few people would look at the details of the argument – their aim was to create an impression of Jeremy as a spendthrift pacifist who would leave the country defenceless, and most newspapers happily played along with it.

The press conference that Wednesday morning gave the 'bombshell' story enough impetus to take it into the lunchtime bulletins. But the afternoon saw May use her return to Downing Street, after informing the Queen that parliament had been dissolved, to launch a new attack on Jeremy under the guise of warning of a sinister Brussels plot to put him in Number 10. Exploiting all the drama a return from the Buckingham Palace provides, she said:

"In the last few days, we have seen just how tough these talks are likely to be. Britain's negotiating position in Europe has been misrepresented in the continental press. The European commission's negotiating stance has hardened. Threats against Britain have been issued by European politicians and

---

[17] Anushka Asthana, 'Tories lay into Jeremy Corbyn with tax bombshell advert,' the Guardian, 3.5.2017.

officials. All of these acts have been deliberately timed to affect the result of the general election which will take place on 8 June."[18]

This showed, she continued, how "more than ever we need to be led by a prime minister and government that is strong and stable." The alternative of letting "the bureaucrats of Brussels run all over us," which she implied Jeremy would allow, would put "your economic security and prosperity at risk."

It was unprecedented, certainly in modern times, for a British prime minister to be accusing foreign powers of interfering in a British general election. But we were not the only ones to realise that the main target was Jeremy. In an analysis on the *BBC* website, Laura Kuenssberg described it as "an argument with not one, but two bogeymen." She said:

> "It's not surprising that the Tory campaign is going after Jeremy Corbyn in this election. Nor surprising that Theresa May, having chosen to call an election for a Brexit mandate, will use the circumstances to her advantage. But the surprise is that, at this early stage, with such a gap in the polls, the Tory campaign has already hit this note on this scale."[19]

Indeed, it was. And it was important our response avoided falling into the trap she had laid by not looking 'soft' on Brussels, while also pointing out that her tactics were unnecessarily straining relations with the EU for purely party-political gain. We probably surprised the Tories in saying the prime minister was right that there are those in Brussels who don't want a deal, but we added that "that is also true of leading figures in the Tory party, who want to use Brexit to turn Britain into a low

---

[18] Theresa May, statement in Downing Street, 3.5.2017.

[19] Laura Kuenssberg, 'Project Fear 3.0?' BBC website, 3.5.2017.

wage, tax haven." We said "the threat and risk" that comes from the Tories is that they have said "no deal would lead to a different economic model for Britain" which means "wiping out employment rights and consumer protections and giving still more tax breaks to the rich and big corporations."

By the eve of the local elections, we were beginning to feel a little punch drunk. We had undoubtedly had the better of the first two weeks, but the last two days had seen the Tories land some serious blows. The question was, how much damage had they done? And what else were they plotting?

7 – Regaining Momentum

"Don't be fooled by the local election results – the Tories still face an uphill battle in their bid to crush Labour."
Professor John Curtice, the *Independent*[1]

National campaigning took a back seat on Thursday 4 May as Labour activists across the country concentrated on getting the vote out in the local elections. At Southside, however, behind-the-scenes work on the campaign continued unabated – all departments ploughed on with planning events, fine-tuning policies for the manifesto, and producing content for all the communication channels.

Campaign finance was again top of my 'to do' list because we would be making our pitch to the affiliated trade unions, who were coming to Southside for their monthly liaison meeting. Patrick Heneghan and I had finalised the three budget options to present to them after some haggling over the split between digital advertising and direct mail spending. High postal and print costs make direct mail roughly ten times as expensive per item as the average click-through to an online advert, and yet there is no evidence it is proportionately that much more effective. By spending more online, we would reach more voters in more seats. It would also allow us to be nimbler, because online

---

[1] John Curtice, professor of politics at Strathclyde University, see the Independent, 5.5.2017.

adverts can be turned on and off almost instantly. Patrick had agreed to push digital spending up from a quarter to about a third of the total in each of the three scenarios, but direct marketing was still allocated nearly £4 million in the £7 million budget scenario. Nevertheless, we went into the meeting with a common position.

Jeremy attended for the first 20 minutes to give an over-view of the campaign, but he left us to talk about the details and explain how more money would allow us to go beyond the basics of a campaign tour and whatever mainstream and social media coverage we could achieve without paying for it. None of the unions made commitments then and there, but that was expected. However, what emerged from the discussion, worryingly, was that the political funds of most of the unions had not yet recovered from the spending on the 2015 general election.

This meeting would, a few days later, be portrayed in the *Sunday Times* in terms I found unrecognisable. A report by the paper's political editor, Tim Shipman, said I had "demanded £7 million from the trade union barons for a nationwide campaign promoting the leader" and been refused. It quoted an unnamed Labour official as saying "the 'ask' was unhinged" and that "a deal was done later for a more realistic amount."[2] I had never met Shipman, nor was I given a chance to comment. As noted in Chapter 6, the £7 million figure was not my suggestion but the highest of three options agreed by the joint LOTO-Southside strategy group. As for "promoting the leader," the £6.5 million core budget already covered the

---

[2] Tim Shipman, 'Labour tax rise to hit earners on £80,000,' the Sunday Times, 7.5.2017.

cost of Jeremy's campaign bus and all the rallies. The scenarios presented to the unions were for spending beyond that, of which nearly all would be for direct mail and digital advertising focused on policies and issues. Not for the first time – or the last – a major national newspaper was publishing a fictitious version of events from a disloyal source.

That day's strategy meeting took stock of the previous few days. The attacks on us over Brexit and tax had opened the door to fresh questioning of our strategy by Southside directors. We couldn't win, they argued, by "banging on about leadership" or "flogging the dead horse of Brexit." They wanted us to concentrate on the NHS, which polled well for Labour. Yet that was precisely the problem: people trusted us on the NHS, but were nevertheless intending to vote Tory because of Brexit and greater confidence in May to deliver it. We had also only just started to tell our wider story of how the country could be transformed to serve the many, not the few. We were not prepared to abandon it at the first sign of trouble. Niall Sookoo, the LOTO campaign co-ordinator, said quietly, "we have to make Theresa May the leader of the Conservative party." The point was strikingly simple: we could not let her get away with cleansing herself of the Tory brand, which was still toxic in our heartlands. Niall's comment wasn't picked up in the meeting, but LOTO decided soon afterwards to refer to 'Theresa May's Tories' and revive the term 'nasty party' at every opportunity.

The local election results in the early hours of Friday morning were bad, though not quite as bad as Patrick had projected. We held on – against expectations – in my home city of Cardiff, which had been won back by Labour in 2012 after eight years of no overall majority. We also retained control of the councils in the other two South Wales cities of Newport and Swansea. In England, the earlier-than-anticipated declaration of Ros Jones' comfortable re-election as mayor of Doncaster – winning on the first round, unlike four years earlier – gave grounds for optimism. But the results in the strongly Brexit-supporting South Wales valleys were a warning signal: we lost control of the councils in Merthyr Tydfil and Blaenau Gwent, and saw our majority slashed in Rhondda Cynon Taff.

As the day progressed, it was hard to make sense of the cross-currents. It was no surprise Steve Rotheram was elected metro mayor of Liverpool City Region by a thumping margin. But – in an echo of the South Wales valleys – we failed to win the mayorship in strongly Leave-voting Tees Valley. Meanwhile, back in the north-west, Andy Burnham won the Greater Manchester metro mayoral contest by an even bigger margin than Steve's victory on Merseyside. As for the West Midlands, I was hearing from my daughter at the count that things were not going well: Andy Street was ahead on the first ballot and Sion would have to do well on the transfers from the four smaller parties to win on the second. But a text soon afterwards from the *Daily Telegraph*'s Kate McCann said:

> "Second preferences not looking so hot. Our info is that Lib and Green second preferences are going to Street."

We had planned for different scenarios. Jeremy had gone to Liverpool to join Steve's celebrations at 4.30pm but, for obvious reasons, he would only go on to Birmingham if Sion won. When news came through that Street had taken West Midlands by a slender 0.8 per cent margin – just 3,776 votes in a turn-out of more than half a million – we reverted to the alternative of Jeremy speaking at a rally in Manchester at 7pm. The trouble was that Andy Burnham had made other plans. With Jeremy already on his way to Manchester, it emerged that Andy had arranged a meal with family and friends and would not be joining him. We faced a 'damned if you do damned if you don't' dilemma: go ahead with the rally without Andy, or cancel it. Karie had little choice but to make the call that – as an Andy snub story would surface either way – going ahead would energise our supporters and send out a message that Jeremy was back on the campaign trail.

Watching that Manchester rally on television at Southside, it was good to see Jeremy arrive flanked by local MPs and shadow cabinet members Becky Long-Bailey and Andrew Gwynne, and then give a typically upbeat and optimistic speech. But the crowd of a few hundred people, while a good turn-out at short notice, was small by Jeremy's standards, and the event had the slightly chaotic look of the leadership contests. The impression that gave to millions of viewers across the country was not what I thought we wanted with the election only five weeks away.

And yet the local elections results were themselves not quite as disastrous as the media was saying. The loss of 382 council seats was bad for sure, but it was below Patrick Heneghan's forecast 450-plus figure, and the projected general election vote based on the results put the Tories on 38 per cent and Labour 27 per cent, a narrower gap than the 17 point average of the latest polls. When I tweeted that and said "all to play for," a few journalists found it very amusing. But were they still prisoners of their own version of the certainty syndrome and failing to see the fluidity of the situation?

The contrarian-inclined Professor John Curtice had been spelling out in interviews all day that these were not great results for a Tory prime minister who had hung her hat on winning a landslide. In a piece that evening for the *Independent* website, he said that, while they give little reason to anticipate a Labour victory in June, what remains in doubt is just how big a majority the Conservatives might yet secure. He continued:

"Indeed, although a strong advance in the local elections in Scotland gives the (Tory) party good reason to anticipate making some gains north of the border next month, there was little sign of the strong Tory advance in Wales that one recent poll seemed to identify. Meanwhile, despite signal successes for the party in the West Midlands and Tees Valley mayoral races, elsewhere the party struggled to replicate its 2015 performance, let alone improve on it."[3]

However optimistically or pessimistically any of us viewed the results at the time, the local elections had certainly given us some pointers, and one of them was that Brexit was playing havoc with traditional voting patterns. The day after the local elections, another member of my emerging personal focus group messaged me asking why the campaign wasn't saying more about Brexit. Jawwad Mustafa, a Labour member and student

---

[3] John Curtice, the Independent, 5.5.2017.

in Sunderland, said:

> "Brexit happens to be the issue of the day, and the Prime Minister is dominating the conversation on it. Our failure to counteract that will allow the Tories to continue to make the case that they're best placed to negotiate Brexit when that simply isn't the case. I heard today a lady in Wales (saying she) is voting Conservative, and the surprising fact is that she works in a food bank. Many people are focusing on Brexit over domestic issues, and we need to get in on that and make our voice loud and clear."

Jawwad's comments were of particular interest because they came from a heavily Leave-voting area. If we were to stop the Tories disingenuously mopping up working class Leave voters, we had to warn them what a Tory Brexit would be like. But Jawwad had a further point: Labour had failed to spell out that the 2008 financial crash was a global one and "dispel the myth that the Tories are somehow better at managing the economy."

The latter was central to our plans for what we had known from the start of the campaign would be a crucial weekend. We had decided at the outset that Jeremy should go to the Midlands – one of our most difficult battlegrounds – on Saturday. But finding a venue had been problematic because we had to avoid areas where the local election results were in doubt, which most of them were. We settled on Leicester for an early afternoon rally that would give Jeremy a chance to give a measured response to the local elections while pivoting the narrative forward to the battle for power at Westminster. It would be scripted so that we had tight messaging going into the Sunday papers, and it would set the scene for an announcement of our personal tax guarantee in a major speech John McDonnell would give the next day on economic policy. The following week would then see the national campaign launch in Manchester on the Tuesday, a series of big policy announcements, and finish with Jeremy's 'Philadelphia moment' speech on security at Chatham House on the Friday.

It would be a manic seven days for everyone involved in the campaign – and crucial to our chances of closing the gap. My own priorities for the weekend were the speeches for the launch and Chatham House, and a script for the PPB on Brexit.

Seumas had asked me to send him the Chatham House draft by lunchtime on Sunday. Jennifer Larbie, LOTO's foreign policy adviser, had already written a large chunk of it. My job was to frame the policy positions in the wider context of the failure of regime-change wars and the effect they had on our security. The challenge, however, was to find a way into the subject that did not simply follow a well-trodden path or sound like Jeremy saying 'I told you so'. The anniversary of VE Day, which was on the Monday before the speech, provided a topical peg. It would also allow Jeremy to quote General Eisenhower, who was the supreme commander of the Allied forces in Europe, and went on to warn of the dangers of a "military-industrial complex" gaining "unwarranted influence" on foreign policy. His comments, which I knew would be familiar to Jeremy, were made in an emotional final television address in 1961 after serving two terms as President of the United

States. He said:

> "Only an alert and knowledgeable citizenry can compel the proper meshing of the huge industrial and military machinery of defence with our peaceful methods and goals, so that security and liberty may prosper together."

This was a heartfelt warning from a 70-year-old man who had seen first-hand what a war costing 70 million lives was like and who had been at the centre of cold war tensions and conflicts as president. The fact that he was a Republican would illustrate the point that concern about the influence of the arms industry on foreign policy transcends the left-right divide. And it would also – by implication – rightly put Jeremy among the 'alert citizenry' who had questioned the endless interventions that have created more problems than they have solved. The speech reiterated the warning he had made many times that they had not only failed in their own terms, but had also made the world more dangerous and put the security of the British people at risk.

On the wider campaign front, meanwhile, we did seem to be moving forward. Jeremy's speech in Leicester to a big and enthusiastic audience had come across well on TV and social media. Our personal tax pledge – committing to no increase in VAT or National Insurance contributions and no increase in income tax for 95 per cent of earners – had been released to the media on Saturday for the Sunday papers. John McDonnell would be on *The Andrew Marr Show* that morning and would then deliver his keynote speech on the economy at the Museum of London. We also had a social media campaign running to publicise the tax pledge, having anticipated that much of the mainstream media would treat it as a 'bombshell' for higher earners.

The *Sunday Times* front page headline was "Labour tax rise to hit earners on £80,000." Tim Shipman's report, which also included the spurious account of our meeting with the unions, opened by saying "Labour will today propose sweeping tax rises for those earning more than £80,000 a year in a bid to shore up the party's core support." It said John McDonnell's speech that day would announce plans that would mean "high earners would have to fund Labour's spending plans, which the Tories have costed at £45 billion." This, as Shipman well knew, was misleading. We had already announced a range of tax measures to raise money to fund our plans, none of which would touch income earned from working. Income tax rises for the top 5 per cent would, in fact, account for only *13 per cent* of the money we needed to raise. Nearly three-quarters of the cost of new spending would be covered by clamping down on tax avoidance, extending stamp duty to financial derivatives, and partially reversing Tory corporation, inheritance and capital gains tax cuts. In other words, we would invest in the NHS, social care, education and other vital services mainly by taxing *unearned* income and reversing tax giveaways to big companies.

Not content with erroneous reporting on tax and our campaign finances, the same piece also claimed 'senior Labour officials' were saying "Corbyn's team have abandoned hope of winning and are focused on driving up Labour's vote share rather than saving key seats." It said:

"Seumas Milne, Corbyn's most senior aide, and his

deputy Steve Howell will argue Corbyn should keep
his job if he matches the 30.4 per cent Ed Miliband
won at the general election two years ago."

An unnamed campaign official was then quoted as
saying:

"Their entire focus is motivating Labour and
potential Labour voters in safe seats. They have no
interest in targeting winnable seats."

I was dumbfounded. Having spent almost every day since
April 18 pushing reluctant senior Labour officials at
Southside to target offensive seats, I could barely believe
what I was reading. Their argument that we should focus
almost-exclusively on defensive seats had a basis in the
polls and, while strongly disagreeing, I accepted it was
their honest assessment of the situation. But now
someone was feeding Shipman with the exact opposite
of the truth, and he was reporting it as fact without even
checking with either Seumas or me. I was surprised only
because hostile newspapers had generally been coming
to us for a token comment on negative stories that they
would tag on at the end, if only to protect themselves
against libel proceedings.

It soon became clear that the *Sunday Times* piece was
part of a concerted attack on Jeremy from within the
party. Leading the way – or at least serving as a front
person – was Jo Green, a former Labour press officer
from the Blair era. In an article for the *Spectator*, he
claimed that Jeremy had given up Labour's "historic
commitment to forming a government" and was only
interested in "maximising the vote share, not winning
seats." He said:

"Whatever the result, Corbyn and his supporters

will argue millions voted for socialism and the job is not finished. The PLP should not allow this argument to take root. The immediate priority the day after polling day must be to ensure a quick leadership contest. Optimists hope this will see the end of Corbyn and that no hard-left alternative to replace him will be on the ballot. That contest should return to the electoral college system. The three-quid member experiment has been a disaster and surely cannot be repeated. There is also much to be said for only allowing two candidates, rather than indulging fringe candidates. No more 'lending votes'. Let's look serious about picking a PM. We're not a debating society."[4]

Indeed, we were not a debating society. Tens of thousands of members across the country were eyeballs-out trying to oust the Tories from office and open the door to a society for the many, not the few. Since the election was called, Jeremy had visited 22 constituencies, only five of which were Labour held. With the campaign bus hitting the road from Tuesday, the tempo would increase. By the end of the campaign, Jeremy had visited 82 seats of which 44 were Tory, SNPor Liberal Democrat held. Of course, candidates defending Labour majorities needed support too, especially where a collapse in the UKIP vote might add to the Tory threat. Jeremy was utterly determined to get to as many constituencies as he could. As someone who is five years younger than him, I was awestruck at his energy and indefatigable

---

[4] Jo Green, 'How to save the Labour party', the Spectator, 5.5.2017.

commitment to winning. The only people behaving like we were a debating society were Jo Green and the anonymous sources feeding newspapers hostile to Labour.

We did not dignify any of this with a response, but the negative stories did highlight the need to secure more money for the campaign and ensure it was spent – in line with our strategy – on fighting to win. On Monday, May 8, Unite came through with £2.25 million in response to the pitch we had made on local election day. Most of this was earmarked immediately for spending on campaign publicity, but the issue of targeting continued to be a source of tension. While decisions on Jeremy's campaign visits were entirely in the hands of LOTO, the lists for digital advertising, direct mail and newspaper advertising were managed by Southside. I discussed this with Patrick and told him that LOTO wanted the new money from Unite to go on offensive as well as defensive seats.

For much of that week, we haggled over which constituencies would be targeted for different types of publicity. By Thursday, I decided to put my concern that we were still not fully implementing a 'campaign to win' strategy in writing. In an e-mail to Patrick, I said we were not applying "the premise on which we asked the unions for extra money" and pointed out that Jeremy was being publicly attacked on the issue. Patrick, in reply, referred to new polling figures *BMG* had presented the previous day, which suggested the Tory lead was growing in offensive seats. "I'm not sure where the evidence is to suggest that we have improved in a way that now gives us a chance in these seats," he said. But, in my view, this was self-fulfilling: we had not been spending money in

Tory-held seats and even a turbo-charged Jeremy could not visit all of them.

In the end, the deadlock was broken by Andrew Murray, Unite's chief of staff, who had been seconded to the campaign and joined us on Friday, May 12. Andrew was treated by Southside directors with the respect that someone from Labour's largest affiliate should command, and insisted on seeing for himself the data spreadsheets being used for different types of targeting. His pressure produced some concessions, but what really transformed the situation was a step change in our financial position. Not only had the Unite money come in, the flow of small donations from supporters around the country was much greater than expected. As it became clear that we would far exceed the £2 million raised online in 2015, the lists – for direct mail and newspaper advertising as well as digital advertising – were expanded much deeper into Tory territory, helping to deliver some surprise wins.

As well as supporting me on that issue, Andrew's arrival was timely at a point when the capacity of the senior team in LOTO was stretched very thinly across the multiple things we were trying to oversee. It was good to have another experienced person sitting in the glasshouse helping with decision-making, speech writing and checking the huge flow of content being pumped out by the campaign.

While the targeting wrangle was rumbling on in the background, the campaign launch in Manchester that Tuesday had gone superbly and really lifted everyone only five days after the local elections. At Southside, the mood was buoyant as we watched on television the former Coronation Street actor Julie Hesmondhalgh saying the election must lead to a country that "gives a toss about stuff" and introducing Jeremy as "a man who's given his life to giving a toss about other people." Standing in front of the campaign bus, Jeremy invited Andy Burnham on stage to lay to rest the previous Friday's crossed wires and then put some real fire into a speech that laid out what was at stake in the election.

One of the biggest cheers came when Jeremy thanked Rupert Murdoch for publishing the *Sunday Times* Rich List showing that Britain's richest 1,000 people had seen their wealth rise by 14 per cent in the last year to £658 billion – nearly six times the budget of the NHS.

"Imagine the outcry," he said, "if public sector workers decided to put in for a 14 per cent pay rise. But it's no surprise that the richest have got even richer after the tens of billions the Tories have handed them in tax cuts. That's what we mean when we say the system is rigged for the rich."

That evening, we achieved our best social media results of the campaign to date when Jeremy posted a *Daily Mirror* story exposing how a third of the top 100 people on the Rich List were also Tory donors. It was seen by more than 2.9 million on Facebook and 2.3 million on Twitter, with more than 60,000 people on each 'engaging' with it in some way. And, to round off the launch day, our first PPB – presented by actor Maxine Peake – attracted a 6.5 million television audience and racked up 1.1 mllion views on Labour's Facebook page.

The following evening, I walked across St James' Park to get some exercise before catching the Tube back to where I was staying. The day had been tense – Andrew Murray had not arrived at this point to help resolve the targeting issues – and the stroll was helping me clear my head and re-connect with the outside world. It was a fine spring evening and the park was bustling with people. As I passed Horse Guards Parade, my phone started vibrating. It was a text from Kate McCann at the *Daily Telegraph* asking me to phone her. I get on well with Kate, but a call from her is rarely good news. I phoned James Schneider to check what was breaking. Someone had leaked our manifesto to the *Telegraph* and *Daily Mirror*. Seumas was in a meeting, but James had spoken to him and was handling the calls. Both papers had the whole document, and there was not much we could say because it had not yet been endorsed by Labour's NEC, shadow cabinet and union affiliates at what is known as the Clause V meeting. That was due to take place the next day – Thursday, May 11 – and had almost unlimited potential for volatility.

The next 24 hours were fraught. Most of the media was speculating about Labour in-fighting or attacking the manifesto as a left-wing throwback to the 1970s. We had to pull Jeremy out of a poster campaign launch on Thursday morning to avoid him facing a barrage of questions he couldn't answer without pre-judging the Clause V meeting. And to literally add pain to events, the car taking Jeremy to the meeting collided with a *BBC* camera operator, Giles Wooltorton, injuring his foot. Anyone who thinks the leak was a smart double game by Jeremy's team has no idea how concerned we were about the sensitivities around the manifesto and the risk of divisions surfacing at the Clause V meeting.

My own view is that the leak is much more likely to have been instigated by enemies of the Labour party than any of the factions inside it. There was no upside to it from any genuine Labour point of view. But there were plenty of people hostile to the party who could have paid handsomely to disrupt our campaign and pre-empt our launch of the manifesto the following Tuesday. Motive is usually the key to these things.

At Southside, it was an emotional moment when Jeremy emerged from the Clause V meeting to tell the media that the manifesto had been unanimously adopted. He said:

"We've amended a draft document that was put forward in the most informed, interesting, sensible discussion and debate in our party, and we'll present this manifesto to the British people in the next few days. Our manifesto will be an offer – and we believe the policies in it are very popular – an offer that will transform the lives of many people in our society and ensure that we have a government in Britain on 8 June that will work for the many, not the few and give everyone in our society a decent opportunity and a decent chance. So, nobody is ignored, nobody is forgotten and nobody is left behind. The details will be published in the next few days. The details will be set out to you, including the costings of all the pledges and promises that we make."

The Clause V meeting had gone on a long time but only because people had issues to press that were secondary to the core themes. Trident renewal had to be in the manifesto because it is Labour conference policy, but

145

otherwise Jeremy's opponents in the party were briefing privately that "they were content to let him have the manifesto he wants but in return he must take full responsibility if voters find it less appealing than he does."[5]

After the Clause V meeting, Jeremy came directly back to Southside to run through his Chatham House speech with Jennifer Larbie and me. He was in fine spirits. The tensions of the day had evaporated by then, and he instantly turned his attention to the finer points of international affairs. He made a few tweaks to the speech, one of which was the important addition of a reference to the 1969 Nuclear Non-Proliferation Treaty. He was keen to make the link to an achievement of former Labour prime minister Harold Wilson and highlight its relevance now as a basis for preventing the spread of nuclear weapons.

When he took the stage at Chatham House the next morning, you could tell he felt on home turf, talking about a subject that was his life's work – how we could build a more peaceful and just world. The speech was broadcast live on the news channels and Facebook. It did the job we set out to do in presenting an alternative view of the security issue. While it did not prove to be the defining 'Philadelphia moment' I had envisaged, it certainly set us in good stead for those moments when they came.

---

[5] Iain Watson, BBC political correspondent, 'General election 2017: Labour manifesto draft leaked,' BBC, 11.5.2017.

8 – For The Many, Not The Few

"I love Jeremy, but the star of the show was the manifesto."
Emily Thornberry, Shadow Foreign Secretary[1]

The morning after the manifesto leak, two leading Tory papers led on Labour's plans for nationalisation, running virtually identical headlines. The *Telegraph* called it "Corbyn's manifesto to take Britain back to the 1970s," while the *Mail* went with "Labour's manifesto to drag us back to the 1970s."

Their lack of originality was unsurprising, but it did underline just how out of touch they were with the mood of the electorate. Most voters are too young to remember the 1970s. Of those who do, many have changed their minds about public ownership, or were never unhappy in the first place with the way electricity and water were provided, or how the railways were run. Indeed, the Central Electricity Generating Board deserves credit for creating the super grid, on which we still largely rely, and British Rail set world records with the Intercity 125 high speed trains introduced in the 1970s.[2] Water,

---

[1] Interview with Heather Stewart, the Guardian, 1.7.2017.

[2] A less attractive side of the history of Britain's railways under public ownership was the 1963 Beeching Report. Appointed as chair of the British Railways Board by the MacMillan Tory government, Richard Beeching instigated the closure of more than a third of the rail network, deeming lines 'unprofitable' by using commercial criteria that were not applied to the road system.

meanwhile, was run by local authorities until 1973 when 12 Regional Water Authorities were created to give some economies of scale – and, as we now know, neat packages for ease of cheap sale. It would probably be fair to say that agnosticism or apathy were the most common attitudes to the running of these industries – a case of 'you don't know what you've got 'til it's gone.'

But Margaret Thatcher did have her supporters and could brush off criticism that she was squandering public assets to give the public finances a short-term boost – or, as her Tory predecessor, Harold MacMillan, famously put it: "selling off the family silver."[3] For a few years, government campaigns promoting privatisation – such as the 'Tell Sid' adverts for the British Gas sale – proved successful. Share offers to the public lent credibility to the idea that this was people's capitalism. However, those shares were soon mopped up by big investors. While some 'Sids' did make a quick buck, the reality was that the people (or at least their elected representatives) had lost control of entire industries and had to watch them being turned into cash cows for the private sector. That so many of them would also become foreign owned simply added insult to injury.[4]

---

[3] Harold MacMillan, speech to the Tory Reform Group, 8.11.1985.
[4] The Thatcher government sold off British Telecom, British Airways, Rolls-Royce, British Airports Authority, British Gas, British Steel and the water and electricity industries. The privatisation of British Gas in 1986 was promoted by the 'Tell Sid' TV advertising campaign to encourage the public to buy shares. Most of the shares were soon mopped up by institutional investors, and what was British Gas has now been broken up into Centrica, BG Group, and National Grid.

Three decades later, when Ed Miliband announced in 2013 that a Labour government would freeze energy prices, public opinion had turned so strongly against privatisation that he would have had wide support for going the whole hog: a *YouGov* poll at the time found that 68 per cent of those asked wanted to bring the energy companies into public ownership. Only 21 per cent said they should remain private.[5]

By 2017, there really was not any doubt that public opinion strongly supported more public ownership. On the weekend before the official launch of Labour's manifesto, the campaign group *We Own It* published the results of a poll conducted by *Survation* showing that most people supported nationalisation of rail, water, and energy. This applied equally across Leave and Remain voters. A majority of Tory voters were against any more privatisation, and even favoured re-nationalisation of water. The director of *We Own It*, Cat Hobbs, said the results confirmed that "people have had enough of the rip off merchants running our railway and providing basic services like energy and water... We need to rebalance the economy – local and national public ownership can give us real control and improve our lives."[6]

The manifesto specifically pledged to reverse the privatisation of Royal Mail, renationalise the water industry, bring rail back into public ownership as franchises expire, and implement a phased transition to a publicly-owned energy sector. It also said Labour would give more people a stake in the economy by doubling the

---

[5] 'Nationalise energy and rail companies, say public,' YouGov, 4.11.2013.

[6] Survation poll for We Own It, 12.5.2017.

size of the co-operative sector and introducing a 'right to own' that would make employees the 'buyer of first refusal' when the company they work for is being taken over.

In attacking our plans, the Tory media was deluding itself about public opinion and doing us a favour. Their scaremongering about nationalisation, far from making us less popular, helped to achieve the opposite by connecting Jeremy with policies a majority of the public supported. If my theory is correct that the leak is more likely to have come from a Tory-supporting source than a Labour one, it failed spectacularly. The idea that the manifesto would be our Achilles heel was hopelessly wrong. Their tirade gave our policies more publicity than we could have anticipated in our wildest dreams.

Jeremy shrewdly judged the manifesto to be our ace and waved it proudly at virtually every event. Far from not being read, supplies of hard copies ran out within days. Online, more than 2.4 million people visited Labour's website to read it, racking up 6 million page views. It was our single most-viewed piece of content and, as Emily Thornberry later said, very much the star of the show.

We did not know it then, but the weekend of May 13-14 would prove to be the beginning of the second phase of Labour's surge. The Clause V meeting was behind us, having united around the transformational manifesto Jeremy wanted. The Chatham House speech had set out Jeremy's clear alternative to the Tories on the defining issue of security. And the generous support from Unite alongside the donations flooding in online meant we were no longer shackled by a lack of finance.

But there is no denying the first two weeks of May had been difficult and put us all under huge pressure. The Tory 'tax bombshell' attack, the fall-out from the local elections, and the wrangles inside the campaign about spending on offensive seats had all taken their toll as we reached the midpoint between the election being called and polling day. By that Saturday we had been campaigning for 26 days, and we had another 26 days ahead. At the time, far from being obvious that we were on the cusp of a new surge, it felt like we were about to experience the political equivalent of hitting the wall in a marathon. We had made a flying start and seen a four-point advance in the polls by the end of April, but our progress had slowed in early May. The four opinion polls published that weekend showed support for Labour had risen only slightly to an average of just over 31 per cent. The Tories were still leading by 15 to 18 percentage points.[7] As Andrew Murray calculated, at that rate, it would take us until the end of July to catch them up.

The fieldwork for those polls had mostly been done before the manifesto leak and did not give us much idea how people were reacting to it. But there were some encouraging pointers in the detail. All the polls had Labour well ahead of the Tories on the bread and butter issues of the NHS, education and housing. *ComRes* found that most voters did not believe May's claim to want to help people who are "just about managing." In *Opinium*'s survey, Jeremy beat May by 14 points on being "in touch with ordinary people" and by five points as someone who "sticks to his principles."

It was clear that, although Jeremy was still way behind

---

[7] UK Polling Report.

when people were asked who would make the best prime minister, he was striking a chord with voters as a down-to-earth person with integrity. Conversely, many voters were willing to give their support to May, even though they did not believe she would do anything for them. The main issue behind this paradox was undoubtedly Brexit and the feeling among many working class Leave voters that they could rely on the Tories more than Labour to deliver the decision of the referendum.

For us, in various discussions over that weekend, this prompted a honing of our strategy in three ways. Firstly, we decided to escalate our efforts to warn people that 'Theresa's team' was no different from the Tories of old and just as much 'the nasty party' as it had been in 2002 when May herself first used the term. We drafted some key messages spelling out that the Tories had not changed their spots and could not be trusted. We suggested to Jeremy that he should start talking about the 'nasty surprises' in store if the Tories were given another five years. And Jon Trickett wrote a piece for the *Mirror* warning against a "coronation" of May that would put "Theresa's Tories... the nasty party of ruthless NHS cuts" back in power.[8]

Secondly, as a member of my informal focus group had urged a week earlier, we agreed that we needed to do more to win the support of pro-Brexit working class voters, especially in the north of England. Jeremy's speech at the campaign launch had made clear that Labour accepted the result of the referendum and that the question now was "what sort of Brexit do we want?" He said Labour's "jobs-first Brexit" would safeguard the

[8] John Trickett, the Sunday Mirror, 14.5.2017.

future of Britain's vital industries and pave the way to a genuinely fairer society. But we felt we now had to pose the issue in sharper and simpler terms as a Labour Brexit versus a Tory Brexit. The script for a PPB on Brexit, which I drafted that weekend, said:

"There's a choice in this election between a Labour Brexit that would put jobs first, and a Tory Brexit geared to the interests of the City, that would plug Britain into a race to the bottom on wages and public services."

It ended by asking voters who they *trusted* to fight for their future in the Brexit process, Labour or the Tories.

Thirdly, we had to give people more confidence that there was a clear alternative to austerity. If voters did not believe May would help the 'just about managing' yet were still voting for her, it was probably – apart from the Brexit factor – because they did not see how things could be different. In varying degrees, people were aware that austerity was one-sided, that some people were doing well and gaining from tax cuts or stashing their money away in tax havens. But were they aware of the scale of it? And did they feel they could do anything about it? Did they believe things could be different, that a better way was possible?

Looking back on the campaign, one of the things that did not come across strongly enough was how the manifesto was underpinned by a coherent strategy for building an economy that really does work for the overwhelming majority. This was, in part, because of the way the two terrorist attacks disrupted our plans during the three weeks before polling and forced us to focus more on security. It was also because of the need to make the most of the 24-hour news cycle, which meant the manifesto had to be chopped into bite-sized 'stories' for media consumption rather than presented as a package. Inevitably, to a degree, it became a case of announcing 'we're going to do this' and saying 'it'll cost that'.

On the campaign trail, it was different. Jeremy would happily go "off-piste," as he liked to put it, and talk about his vision of an inclusive society built on a collective approach.[9] In some 100 rallies across the country he addressed tens of thousands of people and painted a picture of a more just and equal society. In his final eve-of-poll rally in Islington, he said that the campaign had been about "positively asserting" that "a society that cares for all is better than as society that cares only for the few."[10]

The millions who took the step of reading the manifesto will also have found a coherent programme for moving towards the kind of society Jeremy was talking about. The foreword set out that 'narrative' in an undiluted way. It proceeded from talking about the different ways people are being held back to explaining how – in the fifth richest country in the world – things could be different. Its starting point was a plan for investing in skills, infrastructure and new industries, and ensuring that the wealth created would be spread more equally. The prime vehicles for this would be a National Transformation Fund, utilising government borrowing powers for big projects such as Crossrail for the North,

[9] Note to LOTO strategy group from Jeremy, 15.5.2017.
[10] Jeremy Corbyn, eve-of-poll rally, Union Chapel, Islington, London, 7.6.2017.

and a National Investment Bank that would leverage private capital to provide long-term growth funding for small businesses and co-operatives. Together, they would invest £500 billion over ten years. Alongside this, the public sector's buying power – worth £200 billion annually – would be used to ensure that private sector suppliers pay their taxes, respect workers' rights, protect the environment, provide training, and pay sub-contractors on time.

The attention-grabbing policies in the manifesto were the ones of immediate benefit to millions of people, such as scrapping tuition fees and investing more in the NHS, housing and schools. Those commitments were fully-costed with the source of funding identified in a detailed document that was handed out to journalists at the manifesto launch in Bradford on May 16. The funding was for a parliamentary term, and the tax projections were drawn from official figures based on current economic projections.

Jeremy, John McDonnell and their respective policy teams were well aware, however, that the longer-term sustainability of top quality public services and rising living standards depends on having a strong and growing economy. Their belief that a progressive government could intervene to drive that growth was dubbed "hard left" by much of the media, but it is actually in tune with a wider body of opinion that sees neo-liberal economics – characterised by de-regulation, privatisation, fiscal conservatism and globalisation (free trade and free movement of capital) – as having failed, even in its own terms. This extends from people who consider themselves firm socialists to others who see the by-products of neo-liberalism, such as economic instability and extreme levels of inequality, as undermining a capitalist system they believe in.

In 2014, Christine Lagarde, the managing director of the International Monetary Fund (IMF), referred to Karl Marx's prediction that "capitalism, in its excesses, carried the seeds of its own destruction" in warning that the system had to rebuild trust and tackle inequality. Referring to the banking crisis and subsequent recession, she continued:

"Capitalism has been characterized by 'excess'—in risk-taking, leverage, opacity, complexity, and compensation. It led to massive destruction of value. It has also been associated with high unemployment, rising social tensions, and growing political disillusion."[11]

Two years later, three IMF economists produced a paper arguing that neo-liberalism had been "over-sold" and that "instead of delivering growth, some neo-liberal policies have increased inequality, in turn jeopardising durable expansion." Their paper focused specifically on two aspects of neo-liberalism: fiscal consolidation (austerity) and free movement of capital. On the latter, while they saw benefits in direct foreign investment, they said that short term capital flows contributed little or nothing to growth but created "greater volatility and increased risk of crisis." Of austerity, they thought "the short-run costs in terms of lower output and welfare and

---

[11] Christine Lagarde, Conference on Inclusive Capitalism, 27.5.2014.

higher unemployment have been underplayed."[12]

Under Ed Miliband, Labour began to challenge neo-liberalism and particularly the growing inequality it had produced. Delivering the Hugo Young Lecture in 2014, he said:

"People the world over are beginning to recognise some fundamental facts again. That it offends people's basic sense of fairness when the gaps between those at the top and everyone else just keep getting bigger regardless of contribution. That it holds our economies back when the wages of the majority are squeezed and it weakens our societies when the gaps between the rungs on the ladder of opportunity get wider and wider. And that our nations are less likely to succeed when they lack that vital sense of common life, as they always must when the very richest live in one world and everyone else a very different one. I believe that these insights are at the heart of a new wave of progressive politics. And will be for years to come."[13]

The Tories, meanwhile, enthusiastically pursued the neo-liberal agenda, with George Osborne imposing severe constraints on public spending while rewarding their wealthy backers with sweeping cuts in taxes on profits and capital gains, and through the ongoing programme of privatisation and outsourcing. In successive budgets,

---

[12] 'Neo-liberalism: Oversold?' by Jonathan D. Ostry, Prakash Loungani and Davide Furceri (members of IMF's Research Department), Finance & Development magazine, published by the IMF, June 2016, Vol 53, No 2.

[13] Ed Miliband, Hugo Young Lecture, 10.2.2014.

Osborne cut the corporation tax rate for big companies from 28 per cent in 2010 to 17 per cent by 2020. Capital gains tax, inheritance tax, and the bank levy were also cut. And entrepreneurs' relief, originally introduced by Gordon Brown to incentivise start-ups, was transformed into a tax giveaway for already-rich investors with a staggering £20 million maximum allowance per investor.[14]

Even as deficit reduction targets were being missed, Osborne carried on making tax cuts that cost the public purse tens of billions of pounds in lost revenues. In his final budget speech before being sacked by May, Osborne described corporation tax as "one of the most distortive and unproductive taxes there is."[15] He claimed that letting companies keep more profit would lead to more investment, but that wasn't happening. Instead, big business had simply increased the proportion of net profit after tax distributed in dividends from 44 per cent in 2005 to 64 per cent in 2015. In other words, the tax cuts were being used to line the pockets of shareholders rather than for investment in growth.[16]

Philip Hammond has continued where Osborne left off, despite mounting evidence of the damage being done not only to cash-starved public services but also the productivity of the wider economy. With business investment declining, the British output per head has fallen further and further behind its competitors and has

---

[14] Originally, entrepreneurs' relief applied only to founders who worked in a business and had a limit of a £1m capital gain.
[15] George Osborne, Budget speech, Hansard, 16.3.2016.
[16] Kyle Caldwell, 'The chart that shows UK dividends are reaching breaking point,' the Daily Telegraph, 22.11.2015.

now reached a point where it takes a British worker five days to produce as much as a German worker can in four. This is what comes from being more dogmatically attached to neo-liberalism than virtually any other ruling party in a major developed economy.

However, for the super-rich the weakened state of the British economy is hardly likely to have been much of a worry. Over the seven years since 2010, the aggregate wealth of the richest 1,000 people in Britain has doubled.[17] According to the High Pay Centre, the average pay of FTSE 100 chief executives increased 33 per cent from £4.13 million in 2010 to £5.48 million in 2015. FTSE 100 CEOs earn 147 times as much as the average wage of their employees.[18]

Given the context of the economic challenges facing the country withBrexit looming, you might have expected the general election to produce a serious debate about economic policy. But the Tory mantra from the outset was "Corbyn will bankrupt Britain." At the heart of this was a deliberate attempt to muddy the waters on the difference between spending money on services and investing it in long-term assets that will deliver an ongoing return to the economy.

In a speech to the Welsh Labour Conference a few weeks before the election was called, Jeremy said:

"As every businessperson knows, there is a world of difference between borrowing for capital spending and borrowing to fund the payroll and day-to-day trading or service delivery. And as any home owner who has ever had a mortgage knows,

[17] Rich List 2017, the Sunday Times, 7.5.2017.

[18] Annual survey of FTSE100 CEOs, High Pay Centre, 7.8.2016.

taking on huge debt can save you money in the long run. We should not be afraid of debt or borrowing."

The phrase 'we should not be afraid of debt or borrowing' was a speech-writing lapse on my part. It was far too easy to take out of the context of capital spending – and that's exactly what the Tories did. However, the hypocrisy of this was revealed after the election when, in an interview about the housing crisis on *The Andrew Marr Show* in November 2017, the communities' secretary, Sajid Javid, said:

"I'd make a distinction between the deficit, which needs to keep coming down, [and] investing for the future. Taking advantage of record low interest rates, can be the right thing to do if done sensibly. And that can help not just with the housing itself but one of the big issues is with the infrastructure investment that's needed alongside the housing."[19]

Javid's point is virtually identical to Jeremy's but on the day after our manifesto launch you would have thought the Tories never borrowed money for anything. This even applied to bringing water back into public ownership by swapping government bonds for shares – a simple transaction that would mean the current owners being paid interest instead of dividends.

The details of this probably did not matter much to most voters, but the polling figures and feedback from focus groups did suggest that some of the mud being thrown at us on economic issues was sticking and affecting our support, especially among older voters. In one focus group of Brexit-supporting Labour voters in the

[19] Sajid Javid on The Andrew Marr Show, 22.10.2017.

north of England, there was support for our plans to reverse corporation tax cuts and clampdown on tax evasion, but "scepticism about whether these measures would raise anything like enough."

While older voters were more likely to be influenced by mainstream media, Jeremy's reach on social media was growing so rapidly it was hard to keep up. And a new ingredient gave it a further boost at this point. To be honest, I had never heard of Grime until artists such as Stormzy and Jme signed up for our voter registration campaign. The best moment in my initiation came on the Sunday before the manifesto launch when Jeremy appeared in a video talking politics with Jme. The *Sun* described it as "cringeworthy" and called Jeremy a "hapless leftie," but this was completely out of step with the mood on Twitter where thousands of people were sharing it.

Since the start of the campaign, Jeremy had been gaining about 50,000 new Twitter followers every week, taking him over the million mark by the time of the manifesto launch. On Facebook it was the same story. Through both platforms, the campaign's political messages were being translated into lively content – using graphics and video – that people were keen to share. On Twitter alone, Jeremy's posts racked up a staggering 1.5 million retweets in eight weeks.

One of the highlights of the social media campaign came on the eve of the manifesto launch when Jeremy gate-crashed Theresa May's appearance on *ITV*'s Facebook Live. May looked grim-faced as the presenter, Robert Peston, read out Jeremy's post asking why she would not debate with him on television. The question, and her lame reply, made great content for Facebook and Twitter and was a massive hit. Jeremy's video about it on Facebook was viewed 3.76 million times and prompted more than 220,000 reactions, comments, and shares. His tweet racked up 2.69 million impressions and some 91,000 retweets, likes and replies.

An independent analysis[20] of social media by *Buzzfeed* found that 16 of the 20 most widely shared election stories in the week before our manifesto launch were either pro-Corbyn or anti-Tory. The story that travelled furthest and was seen most was a report on the *Independent*'s indy100site, headlined: "If 30 per cent more people under 25 vote, the Tories could lose the election."

Meanwhile, on the Electoral Commission website, people under 25 were signing up in their thousands. The manifesto leak had sparked a surge in voter registrations: from a daily run rate of 50 – 60,000, it had gone over the 100,000 mark. Of those registering, a third were 24 or younger and another third were 25 to 34.

By the fifth week of the campaign, there seemed to be green shoots everywhere. The question was, how fast would they grow?

---

[20] Buzzfeed News Social Barometer, 14.5.2017.

9 – Tories Play The Generation Game

"The great Tory reform of this century is to enable more and more people to own property."
Margaret Thatcher[1]

Whichever way you looked at it, the election had been called for tactical reasons. May claimed it was to strengthen her hand in the Brexit negotiations. Others saw it as a move to secure her leadership against internal enemies. Some Tories viewed it as a chance to keep Labour from power for a generation. One likely factor was that, without her own election mandate, she would continue to be a prisoner of the 2015 manifesto of her predecessor – as had been sharply demonstrated by the outcry that forced Phillip Hammond to back down after trying to increase National Insurance contributions for the self-employed in the March budget.[2] None of these motives went much beyond political expediency. Which is why, on Thursday, May 18, there was no reason to expect the Tory manifesto to contain a compelling big idea – and we would not be disappointed.

On the morning of its launch, two days after ours, it

---

[1] Margaret Thatcher, speech to the Conservative party conference, 10.10.1986.

[2] In the 2015 general election, the Tory manifesto promised there would be no VAT, NI or income tax rises for the next five years under a Conservative government. It was this pledge Philip Hammond had broken when he announced the increase in NI rates for the self-employed on 8.3.2017.

was encouraging to find the media talking about a Corbyn 'bounce.' In political parlance, it seems, there are bounces and there are surges, and sometimes it's very confusing. To my mind, a bounce is a pick-up in support after a specific event, whereas a surge is more sustained and substantial. A bounce, being a lesser thing, is not always easy to detect.

When going back over events for this book, I found the term 'Corbyn bounce' had been mentioned earlier than I can remember seeing it at the time. Credit must go to polling expert Matt Singh, who wrote a piece for the *Financial Times* website on Tuesday, May 16, the day of Labour's manifesto launch, saying the polls over the four weeks since the calling of the election showed Labour's share of the vote increasing at a faster pace than the Tories.[3] You could say four weeks makes it more of a slow surge than a bounce, but why argue with a positive? It roughly tallied with our assessment at the time that we had gained ground in two, dare I say it, waves: one in the first ten days of the campaign, the other in the period between the leak of the Labour manifesto (May 10) and its official launch (May 16).

By the morning of the launch of the Tory manifesto on May 18,[4] evidence of our progress was growing. Polls published that day by the *Times* (*YouGov*) and *Evening Standard* (*Ipsos Mori*) found Labour's support had increased by two and eight points respectively to 32 and 34

[3] Matt Singh, 'What is really happening in the run-up to June's election,' the Financial Times, 16.5.2017.

[4] The Tory manifesto was launched in Halifax on 18.5.2017.

per cent.[5] There was still a double-digit gap between us and the Tories, but social media was buzzing with talk of us bouncing. As the mainstream media gathered in Halifax for May's first foray into actually revealing some policies, even the commentariat was writing pieces mentioning it. What none of us expected, at that point, was how the Tory manifesto would help put even more spring into our bounce.

It's not true to say that the cynical Tory manifesto and May's poor performance gifted us the campaign – as the polls showed, we were already gaining ground by our own efforts – but there is no denying it contributed. The word 'cynical' is accurate because the manifesto was so blatant in its betrayal of older voters, suggesting the Tories believed their support was guaranteed whatever nasty medicine they dished out. (They had, after all, retained a big lead among the over 55s, despite shabbily betraying women born in the 1950s on the raising of the state pension age a few years earlier.[6])

At the launch of the manifesto, May borrowed much of our language, as she had previously. She spoke of "making Britain a country that works not for

---

[5] UK Polling Report. See also, for example, Sarah Ann Harris, 'Latest general election polls show Labour bounce as Jeremy Corbyn narrows gap with Tories,' the Huffington Post, 18.5.2017.

[6] The Tory government of John Major first introduced legislation to raise the state pension age for women to 65. In 2011, however, the Coalition government under David Cameron brought the increase forward without warning and also raised the pension age to 66, sparking the Women Against State Pension Inequality (WASPI) campaign.

the privileged few but for everyone," and of the Tories being a party that would put government "squarely at the service of working people." Using a rather feeble play on the words of John F Kennedy, she said the Tories would build "a country that asks not where you have come from but where you are going to."[7]

It was spun as a break with Thatcherism, but the only sense in which that was true was in her betrayal of people who had literally bought into the Thatcherite dream of being a property owner and were now being told it was contingent on them not falling ill in later life. The headline-catching policy in the manifesto, which came almost immediately to be called 'the dementia tax', was the inclusion of the value of someone's home, rather than just their savings, when calculating whether or not they would have to pay for their own social care.

Home ownership increased by a third in the Thatcher years, creating 4 million more owner-occupied households. About half of the increase was council houses and flats sold off at discounts of up to 50 per cent. Now, in this great act of treachery, the Tories were looking to get the money back to pay for social care.

At Southside, John McDonnell, Ian Lavery and several of us from the LOTO and shadow treasury teams had gathered in a committee room to watch May's speech and discuss how we should react to the manifesto. Deciding the main issues we would highlight was one of the easier decisions of the campaign. As well as forcing older people to pay for care if they need it with their

---

[7] US President Kennedy famously said in his inaugural address: 'Ask not what your country can do for you – ask what you can do for your country,' 20.1.1961.

homes, the Tories were going to make them go through a means test before getting Winter Fuel Payments and scrap the triple lock that guarantees pensions will rise by 2.5 per cent regardless of what happens to prices and earnings. They were leaving the Osborne tax giveaways to big business and the wealthy intact, including cutting corporation tax to 17 per cent by 2020. However, for everyone else, there could be higher tax bills: the 2015 manifesto promise not to increase income tax and National Insurance contributions was dropped.[8]

We lost no time in sending a statement out to the media saying that "behind the rhetoric, this is a manifesto that offers the majority of working people and pensioners insecurity with a huge question mark over their living standards." We did not need to do much more at that point, so huge was the outcry on social care.

Trouble was brewing for the Tories even before May was on her feet in Halifax. It is customary for the media to be fed some of the key points from a manifesto the day before its launch (the idea being to get coverage in two 24-hour news cycles). In this case, the tactic had prompted the *Radio 4*'s *Today* programme to interview Andrew Dilnot, who had chaired a Commission on Funding of Care and Support in 2011.[9] Having clearly been given advance warning of what was in the manifesto, he said:

---

[8] Of Cameron's 'triple lock' on taxes, May retained only the commitment not to increase VAT.

[9] Sir Andrew Dilnot, an economist and the warden of Nuffield College, Oxford, was appointed by Cameron's Coalition government to chair the commission. It recommended capping an individual's contribution to care costs at £35,000.

"People are faced with a position of no control; there's nothing that you can do to protect yourself against care costs. You can't insure it because the private sector won't insure it, and by refusing to implement a cap the Conservatives are now saying that they're not going to provide social insurance for it, so people will be left helpless knowing that what will happen, if they're unlucky enough to suffer the need for care costs, is they'll be entirely on their own until they're down to the last £100,000 of all of their wealth, including their house."

This, he pointed out, was "a classic case of market failure," yet May had promised in her speech to the Tory conference eight months earlier a new approach of the state providing what markets could not.

On *LBC Radio*, a woman caller told presenter Shelagh Fogarty:

"She's definitely lost (my vote) with this one. I couldn't believe what I was hearing this morning. It's a pure evil. It is definitely a death tax, another form of inheritance tax and I don't know what they're thinking....It's the nasty party back. This is a tax on people who have bothered to buy their own home and to invest a little bit of money into somewhere to live."[10]

Later, another caller into Iain Dale's programme, said:

"She [May] thought she was going to have such a landslide, that every one of us mugs that have voted Conservative all our lives would give her it.

---

[10] See: 'I was going to vote Tory until I saw the manifesto - callers tell Shelagh,' **www.lbc.org.uk**, 18.5.2017.

> My husband can't bring himself to vote for Labour,
> but I have already sealed my postal vote for the
> Labour party...I will burn my house down before I
> give Theresa May a penny of it."[11]

To add to May's woes, a Tory think tank, the Bow Group,
also came out strongly against the manifesto proposal,
calling it "a tax on death and on inheritance." Their
chairperson Ben Harris-Quinney, said:

> "It will mean that, in the end, the government will
> have taken the lion's share of a lifetime earnings in
> taxes. If enacted, it is likely to represent the
> biggest stealth tax in history, and when people
> understand that they will be leaving most of their
> estate to the government, rather than their
> families, the Conservative party will experience a
> dramatic loss of support."[12]

That afternoon, we worked on the different elements of
our response and finalised arrangements for our own
press conference the next morning. My focus was on the
key messages and graphics for the event. After kicking a
few ideas around, we settled on "Tory triple whammy for
pensioners" as a strapline, and I asked Krow
Communications to come up with something that would
work on social media and at the press conference. The
result was an image with the strapline above three giant
red boxing gloves saying on each in turn: "No triple lock",
"No winter fuel allowance," and "Pay for care with your
home." It was simple and did the job.

---

[11] See: 'Irate caller threatens to burn house down over Tory
manifesto,' **www.lbc.org.uk**, 18.5.2017.

[12] Bow Group press release, 'The biggest stealth tax in history,'
18.5.2017.

At the same time, we decided to dip into our digital budget to buy 'dementia tax' on Google AdWords. The way this works is that an advertiser can bid for a term so that their advert appears next to the Google search results when people look for that subject. We wanted anyone searching for information on the Tory proposal to see, at the top of the page, a link that would take them through to a Q&A the campaign had produced exposing how it would hit people. Google AdWords is usually seen by political campaigners as a way of getting information in front of 'opinion-formers,' such as journalists or policy wonks who are interested in a subject and can influence other people. In this case, I felt a large number of older voters alarmed about the dementia tax would also be searching for it. Google AdWords is not as targeted as Promote, but it is an effective campaign tool when a topic is hot and you need to influence the debate as quickly as possible. We would use it again later in the campaign for 'Brexit' and 'Shoot-to-kill.'

As we prepared for the next day and the weekend, one of the worries I had was the way the Tories were playing up a divisive 'inter-generational inequality' argument to justify the dementia tax. They had devoted a whole section of the manifesto – one of only five – to what they were calling "A Restored Contract Between The Generations." In the introduction, it said "the solidarity that binds generations" was "under strain" and that maintaining it would at times "require great generosity from one group to another – of younger working people to pay for the dignified old age of retired people, and of older people balancing what they receive with the needs of the younger generation." Giving older people "the dignity we owe them" and younger people "the opportunities they deserve" would, the manifesto said, mean facing "difficult decisions." Behind the euphemisms, this was a slippery exploitation of the word inequality to play one part of 'the many' off against another – a classic case of divide and rule, allowing the rich to continue to enjoy their tax breaks and hide most of their assets in tax havens.

The *Sunday Times* Rich List, published only two weeks earlier, showed that the real issue is the vast and accelerating disparity in wealth between a tiny minority and everyone else, whatever their age. The combined wealth of the 1,000 people on the 2017 list was £658 billion, a 14 per cent increase on the previous year. During the previous seven years of austerity, the wealth of those on the Rich List had almost doubled. Some older working people living in London may, during that period, have got lucky with the value of their own home, but that pales into insignificance compared to the wealth accumulated by the likes of Sir James Dyson (#14, £7.8 billion) or the Duke of Westminster (#9, £9.5 billion).[13]

Besides, as Anna Dixon of the Centre for Ageing Better had put it a few months earlier, the idea of inter-generational inequality "also ignores the way wealth is passed down between generations within families." Working class families are much better at solidarity between the generations than the Tories will ever be with the public finances. Some 75 per cent of people over the age of 65 own their own home, and most see it as an asset that will be passed on to their children,

---

[13] Rich List 2017, the Sunday Times, 7.5.2017.

grandchildren, nieces and nephews.[14]

Late that Thursday evening, I sent an e-mail to Seumas and Andrew Murray saying I thought a speech Jeremy was due to make in Birmingham that Saturday should be on the theme of "uniting generations" and "standing together to build a fairer Britain." It should spell out that the Tories have "made it impossible for young people to buy a home" and are now "making their parents use their home to pay for their care." We had already decided to make pensioners the theme of the weekend, followed on Monday by the announcement of our policy on tuition fees – the speech would link the two. Seumas and Andrew agreed and worked the idea into their draft for Jeremy.

The following morning's strategy meeting was one of the most upbeat of the campaign. The general feeling was that the mood was moving our way, but Seumas was concerned that we had not really landed a punch. In some ways, we didn't need to – disgruntled Tory voters were doing it for us – but there was a danger of our voice getting lost in the furore. We agreed that John McDonnell should make a specific call at the press conference for the Tories to immediately withdraw their plan to means test Winter Fuel Payments, and I was despatched to the venue to brief him. When I got to the venue near The Embankment, John was in a side room raring to go and took no persuading that we needed a strong line for the lunchtime bulletins. The press conference was well attended and largely achieved

---

[14] Anna Dixon, 'We need to stop our divisive obsession with intergenerational unfairness,' the Daily Telegraph, 6.11.2017. She is chief executive of the Centre for Ageing Better.

what we wanted: a platform for our response to the Tories and something visual for the mainstream media. But it did also confirm the correctness of our decision not to have too many press conferences because some of the journalists could not resist the opportunity to try to catch John out on things he had said decades earlier on Northern Ireland.

Leaving the venue, it took my eyes a while to adjust to the brightness of a sunny late spring day, and I realised just how little time I had spent outside in daylight since the election was called. I have a minor hereditary heart condition which causes chest pains when my weight goes above a certain level, and I had been having trouble because of the unhealthy diet and lack of exercise that went with the campaign. The previous day Karie had taken me in hand. When she discovered I had left my tablets in Cardiff, she insisted on dragging me to the nearest pharmacy where she impressively used her know-how as a former health visitor to blag a small supply that would get me to the weekend.[15] That Friday morning, I decided to walk the couple of miles to Southside and then go back to Cardiff earlier than usual on a mid-afternoon train. We still had nearly three weeks of campaigning to go, and I knew I needed to pace myself.

That Saturday, I watched the live feed of Jeremy's rally in Birmingham online. The text of the speech sent out in advance to the media was very good, but Jeremy decided to add to it – he wanted to have what he calls an

---

[15] Karie was a health visitor in Glasgow before becoming Unison's full-time head of health in Scotland and then moving to London to work for the union as head of health for the UK.

"off-piste" moment. Speaking at the International Convention Centre to an enthusiastic audience of supporters and their friends, he was bound to get a good reception. But the passage calling for inter-generational unity – both the original and Jeremy's additions – was interrupted six times by applause, sometimes mid-sentence. He was clearly echoing everyone's anger only two days after May had played the divisive 'inter-generational inequality' card.

After some introductory words, he came to the unity passage and delivered the opening part mostly as it was drafted:

"The Tory manifesto must be the most divisive for many elections. They are now pitching young against old. Their manifesto is typical of what a very well-known person once called a nasty party, as they attempt to set one generation against another. For pensioners they offer a triple whammy of misery: Ending the 'triple lock' which protects pensioner incomes, means-testing the Winter Fuel Allowance and slapping a 'compassion tax' on those who need social care by making them pay for it using their homes. Some claim that cutting support for the elderly is necessary to give more help to the young. But young people are being offered no hope by the Tories either – loaded with tuition fee debts, with next to no chance of a home of their own or a stable, secure job. We stand for unity across all ages and all regions in our country.

"It is simply wrong to claim that young people can only be given a fair deal at the expense of the old, or vice versa. We in this hall and in every street across the country know that the reality is we all depend on each other. That is why we are calling on the Tories to drop their anti-pensioner package immediately – older people should not be turned into a political football at this election at the behest of the Prime Minister. And we promise that a Labour government will make education free at all levels and build the homes young families need, offering the security of a home for life. It's something many people dream about, we want to make it a reality. Because our manifesto, this party, stands for the many against government by, of and for the few.

"We say that if we all stand together we can build a fairer Britain. There is no trade-off between young and old – and there should be no trade-off at all. Society should not be setting the future of our young against the security of our old."

And then Jeremy came to a passage he had added entirely:

"I find it deeply offensive that we should get into this kind of discussion and debate. Older people who've made such a fantastic contribution to our society, and in retirement continue to make that contribution in voluntary activities, in inspiring people, in supporting young people. And young people who seek the advice and solace of older people. *It's not a war between generations, it's a unity of generations to create a better society for all*."

The last sentence brought the house down, showing how

strongly people felt about the cynical divisiveness of the Tories. Jeremy going off-piste always worried the speechwriting team, but only because we feared it could create an awkward moment with the autocue or inadvertently introduce a phrase that could be misquoted. We wrote speeches knowing Jeremy's views and using the phrases he liked. But Jeremy had added a dose of passion. Out on the road, he was closer to the popular mood and becoming more assured as each day passed in responding to it. In this case, it was also personal: nothing angers him more than an attempt to pit people against each other.

Working through the afternoon at home, I followed Jeremy's journey north to the Wirral on social media. He was due to speak at a rally at West Kirby beach where thousands of people, including my youngest son, Josh, were gathering in a car park to hear him. Watching several video posts, I was taken aback by the size of the crowd on such a rainy and windy afternoon. But I was even more surprised a couple of hours later when I saw photographs on the LOTO WhatsApp group of staff in the stands at Prenton Park, the home ground of Tranmere Rovers. Jeremy was about to go on stage at the Wirral Live festival to speak to the 20,000 or so music fans. The operational note for the weekend had not mentioned the event. It was added at the last minute by Karie, who knew one of the organisers, despite initial objections from the police responsible for Jeremy's personal protection.

My anxieties, however, were about possible heckling rather than security: people were there for the music, not to hear what they might consider a gate-crashing politician. If going 'off-piste' in Birmingham was a risk, this was like Jeremy trying Olympic ski jumping. But it was a triumph: in a short speech Jeremy hit (apologies for the pun) all the right notes. You can't go wrong talking about working class communities building football clubs and making music on Merseyside. And, as he ended with a rousing "This election is about you and what we can achieve together," the crowd started singing 'Ohhhh, Je-re-my Cooorbyn, Ohhhh Je-re-my Coooorbyn' to the tune of *Seven Nation Army*. It was an unforgettable moment and – as someone born not far from Prenton Park[16] – one of the most emotional of the campaign. Within 24 hours, Jeremy's own posts about the event had reached more than 8 million people on Facebook and Twitter.

In the papers that Sunday, all the polls showed us increasing our vote share and closing the gap on the Tories. The best and closest from our point of view were those where the fieldwork had been done after the Tory manifesto was published, including *YouGov*'s poll for the *Sunday Times*, which had Labour only nine points behind the Tories on 35 per cent, the first poll of the campaign to show a single digit gap. *The Andrew Marr Show*, which was calling it the Tories' wobbly weekend, had interviews with both the work and pensions secretary, Damian Green, and John McDonnell on the respective manifestos. Green repeatedly refused to say at what level the means test would be set for Winter Fuel Payments, insisting it would be decided after the election. When Marr questioned him on the dementia tax, Green played the 'inter-generational fairness' card

---

[16] I was born in nearby Wallasey.

and argued it was unfair for people working now to pay taxes to fund care for pensioners. But Marr, with more than a hint at his own experience of how anyone can be struck by poor health at any time, put it to him that pensioners have paid taxes to insure themselves against bad luck:

> "It's very unfair that some people get dementia and some people don't. Under the original Dilnot system, we pooled the risk in society after a certain threshold and spread out the unfairness. If you are very unlucky and you get a terrible disease that means you are being looked after at home, maybe a stroke where you don't return to work or whatever it might be, then the rest of society will come in and help you. You don't have to pay again. Under the new proposals, you are basically on your own for most of it."[17]

Green was looking increasingly uncomfortable, and the debate about making pensioners pay with their homes, for care they thought they had paid for with a lifetime of taxes, would run and run on every media channel right through that day and into the next.

However, while the campaign clearly had the Tories on the ropes, someone nominally in our own corner could not restrain themselves from making mischief. The *Sunday Times* was running a report headlined "Don't mention Corbyn, aide tells Labour candidates" based on a leaked recording of a conference call briefing I had given the previous Wednesday. The report said that I had been asked by one of the 167 candidates on the call how canvassers should deal with voters who openly criticise

---

[17] The Andrew Marr Show, BBC, 21.5.2017.

Jeremy and quoted me as replying they should "focus...on the manifesto and the policies rather than individuals." For anyone who has been canvassing and knows how little time there is on the doorstep, my response would have seemed fairly standard. My own experience of canvassing is that you try to shift the conversation away from a point of disagreement, whatever it is, onto something that might be more fruitful. Besides, Jeremy himself would always put the emphasis on policy. It was another non-story, apparently supplied to Tim Shipman from a disappointingly disloyal candidate.[18]

Meanwhile, in the same newspaper, Seumas' predecessor as Labour's director of strategy and communications was giving further grist to the Tory mill by accusing Jeremy of "preparing for nothing more than his annual summer leadership contest." In a complete travesty of the truth, Tom Baldwin claimed:

"People were initially puzzled about why [Jeremy] was spending so much of this campaign addressing rallies of committed activists in seats unlikely to be on any target list until it was pointed out these were places where lots of the members who elected him to the leadership lived."[19]

How Baldwin knew where people who voted for Jeremy lived is intriguing given it was supposed to be a secret ballot. However, the seats Jeremy had visited were easy enough to check. Had he taken the trouble to do so, he

---

[18] Tim Shipman, 'Don't mention Corbyn, aide tells Labour candidates,' the Sunday Times, 21.5.2017.

[19] Tom Baldwin, 'Win seats, Jeremy, or do an Ed,' the Sunday Times, 21.5.2017.

would have found – as noted in Chapter 7 – that Jeremy was mainly visiting offensive seats. At this point, of the 48 seats he had been to, only 20 were Labour held. Of the 28 offensive seats, Labour went on to win 13 of them, and several more – such as Dunfermline & West Fife, Telford, Pudsey and Calder Valley – proved very close.

That Sunday afternoon, I returned to Southside to find the LOTO strategy group undistracted by sniping from the side-lines and eager to keep the momentum going. The priority, we agreed, was a major 'northern push' with shadow cabinet members mobilised to visit as many target seats as possible. And, in continuing the campaign to win more older voters, our central message would be that a means test for Winter Fuel Payments would be a prelude to an attack on other universal pensioner benefits such as free TV licences and prescription charges.

The deadline for voter registration was 24 hours away and all our teams were gearing up for a big final push, including an e-mailer to our supporter database and social media activity across all the feeds. The huge array of content we had ranged from numerous celebrity endorsements to a snappy 15 second video saying: "Good morning. Things to do today: register to vote, hit RT to remind your friends, put your feet up." To give the campaign a final boost, we released that evening the details of our pledge to abolish tuition fees with immediate effect, giving 18-year-olds sitting their A levels that summer "yet another reason to register to vote" before the deadline of midnight on May 22.

My first message on the morning of voter registration

deadline day was a welcome one from an old Labour friend in Sheffield, Debbie Woodhouse, another member of my informal focus group. She had not voted for Jeremy to be leader but was now pleasantly surprised by the way the campaign was going. "So many people I know are starting to think they may vote Labour, and I think this is because the message is getting out there about who he is and what he stands for," she said. She thought we were offering "a clear choice for the first time for decades for a new type of politics" and felt it was "a historic moment."

Within a few hours, Debbie's optimism was further vindicated by a shambolic U-turn from Theresa May on the dementia tax. In a speech that sounded panicky and Trump-like, she accused Jeremy of '"fake claims, fear and scaremongering" before surprising everyone by saying there would be "an absolute limit on the amount people have to pay for their care costs."[20]

Only a few days earlier her own health secretary, Jeremy Hunt, had argued a cap would be "unfair" because someone with a house worth "a million pounds, 2 million pounds" should not have their care costs limited and therefore "born by taxpayers, younger families who are perhaps struggling themselves to make ends meet."[21]

Hunt's professed concern about struggling young families was hypocritical and typically divisive, but his point on the cap does illustrate how any form of self-funding of care is hard to reconcile with being fiscally progressive (that is, raising money in proportion to

[20] Laura Hughes, 'Theresa May announces dementia tax U-turn,' the Daily Telegraph, 22.5.2017.

[21] Kate Proctor, 'Theresa May faces Tory unrest over unfair social care reforms,' the Evening Standard, 19.5.2017.

someone's wealth or income). Among home-owning pensioners, generally speaking, the more your home is worth, the more you benefit from a cap.

Labour's manifesto promised to build a National Care Service with an additional £3 billion of funding every year "to place a maximum limit on lifetime personal contributions to care costs, raise the asset threshold below which people are entitled to state support, and provide free end of life care." It goes on to say that in the long term we would "seek consensus on a cross-party basis about how (social care) should be funded, with options including wealth taxes, an employer care contribution or a new social care levy."[22] This was far better than the Tory position, but it still contained a concession to the concept of what is – however you look at it – means testing. The danger is that once you move from a social insurance to a partially self-funding model you are on a slippery slope: it becomes only a matter of where you draw the lines.

In my view, someone who has dementia or a severe stroke and needs ongoing care should be treated no differently from someone who has cancer, or any other condition that may involve costly treatment over a long period. Socialists, quite rightly, defend the principle of universality and argue that the question of inequality in assets and income should be addressed through a progressive tax system. The manifesto mentioned a wealth tax, but it also accepted the idea of some level of personal contribution. It was an understandable compromise in the time available to finalise our platform

---

[22] Labour party manifesto, 'For the many, not the few,' 2017, p71-2.

for the election, but the issue is not going to go away.

Those long-term policy questions, though touched on in our discussions that day, were not the most pressing concern. A crack had appeared in the now shaky Tory edifice, and we needed to shine a light on it. In discussing our immediate reaction to the U-turn, we agreed to focus on how unfair the Tory policy muddle was on the elderly. Not only had May abandoned her manifesto policy after only four days, she had also not said what the limit would be. We rushed a statement out from Andrew Gwynne saying she had thrown her own campaign into chaos and confusion:

> "By failing to put a figure for a cap on social care costs, she has only added to the uncertainty for millions of older people and their families. This is weak and unstable leadership. You can't trust the Tories – if this is how they handle their own manifesto, how will they cope with the Brexit negotiations?"

The Tories were desperate, meanwhile, to deflect attention from their dementia tax disarray. That morning, the Northern Ireland secretary, James Brokenshire, issued a press release "demanding Jeremy Corbyn and his top team come clean about their true attitudes towards IRA terrorism." The release said:

> "In recent days, Corbyn, his closest ally John McDonnell and shadow home secretary Diane Abbott have all been revealed as having extremely worrying views about the campaign of violence carried out by IRA terrorists. On Sunday, Jeremy Corbyn – who could be prime minister in 18 days – failed to condemn IRA bombing FIVE times."

The Tories attached to their release a transcript of an interview of Jeremy by Sophy Ridge on *Sky* the previous day. It was not true that Jeremy had failed to condemn the IRA – in fact, at one point he said "of course I condemn it" – but what Ridge was trying to do was get him to single out the IRA exclusively and not at the same time condemn the violence of loyalist paramilitaries, as he always did. The Tories may not have briefed Ridge, but it was certainly a convenient line of questioning that helped them move onto the attack.

Brokenshire's release challenged Jeremy to answer a series of very specific questions: Does he condemn the IRA's acts of murder unequivocally? Were the IRA terrorists? Did the deaths of members of the armed forces count as 'innocent lives'? And does he regard the armed forces and the IRA as 'equivalent' participants during the troubles? With media inquiries pouring in, James Schneider worked on Jeremy's response. The answers were direct (in order): yes; yes, the IRA clearly committed acts of terrorism; yes, all loss of life is tragic; no. These answers were, however, still put in the context of a statement giving Jeremy's more rounded view:

"I condemn all acts of violence in Northern Ireland from wherever they came. I spent the whole of the 1980s and 1990s representing a constituency with a large number of Irish people in it. We wanted peace, we wanted justice, we wanted a solution. The first ceasefire helped to bring that about and bring about those talks, which were representative of the different sections of opinion in Northern Ireland. And the Labour government in 1997 helped to bring about the Good Friday Agreement

(GFA), the basis of which was a recognition of the differing history, cultures and opinions in Northern Ireland. It has stood the test of time and it is still there.

"We have devolved administration in Northern Ireland, and I think we should recognise that that peace was achieved by a lot of bravery, both by people in the unionist community and in the nationalist community. They walked a very difficult extra mile under pressure from communities not to do so, both republicans and unionists walked that extra mile and brought us the GFA. And I think we should use this election to thank those who brought about the GFA, all of them. Those in government at the time and all those who did so much on the ground. Northern Ireland is a very different place. We're going to be working with the devolved government in Northern Ireland as well as the government in the Republic to ensure that Brexit doesn't bring about a barbed wire border. We don't want a hard border."

The final part of the statement reflected the growing confidence in the campaign that Jeremy could be the next prime minister, and would indeed be working with the Irish government and the devolved government in Northern Ireland on Brexit and other issues. Paradoxically, the Tory attack – by highlighting that Jeremy could be heading for Downing Street – may have helped our momentum. The Tories were beginning to look like a party running scared, and Jeremy was – with every speech and in brushing off the attacks – looking ever more confident and composed.

That Monday evening, news came through of a remarkable *YouGov* poll of Welsh voting intentions: Labour was up nine points to 44 per cent and the Tories were down seven points to 34 per cent. The end was far from nigh for Labour in Wales. Maybe I would be able to show my face in Cardiff, after all.

Jeremy Corbyn leaves his house the day after denying the Tories a majority.

London Borough of Barnet
Education Committee

HENDON COUNTY GRAMMAR SCHOOL,
GOLDERS RISE,
HENDON, N.W.4

01-202 9004

8th. July 1970.

HEADMASTER:
E. W. MAYNARD POTTS.
M.A., M.Sc., HON. F.R.I.B.A.

Dear Mr.Howell,

    I must congratulate you on your good fortune. Perhaps it would be more appropriate if I congratulated Berkeley on its wisdom in inviting you.

    I like your proposals for Stephen. He is very interested in the formation of public opinion through pressure groups. Even fleeting contact with an American university campus would give him first hand experience of techniques which have become so professional as to be self-defeating.

    We do much new work in the first three weeks of the autumn term. There will therefore be a great challenge to Stephen when he returns to face a mountain of work. There is even a risk that he will not be able to face it and will accept a lower standard of success than he has been achieving recently.

    Although I recognise this risk I am willing to accept it if Stephen is. In October the Jewish holy days are 1st, 2nd, 10th(Sat), 15th, 16th, 22nd, 23rd. They will slow the pace of new teaching in October and help Stephen to catch up lost ground.

Yours sincerely,

E.W. Maynard Potts

Headmaster.

My headteacher says I'm "very interested in the formation of public opinion through pressure groups." But there's a sting in the tail.

Peter Mandelson (bottom left) and me (top right) in a Hendon County sixth form photograph (1971).

Tony Benn delivers the George Caborn Memorial Lecture in 1985. I appear to be still writing my notes for the appeal. George was one of South Yorkshire's best-known union leaders. His son, Richard, was MP for Sheffield Central and later minister for sport.

Bernie Sanders speaks to a 13,000-strong crowd at the Los Angeles Coliseum on 4 June 2016, three days before the California Democratic primary.

The area set aside for media and campaign guests.

Actor and activist Susan Sarandon arrives to introduce Bernie Sanders.

Feel The Bern campaign T-shirts.

I'm official – showing off my parliamentary pass after collecting it.

Freshwater colleagues wish me luck in my indefinite leave of absence.

Canvassing for the local elections in Butetown ward, Cardiff with Derek Walker, Harry Edgeworth, Saeed Ebrahim and Lyn Eynon. Saeed won handsomely.

My photo of the scene on Westminster Bridge, just after a lone terrorist attacker had driven into pedestrians on 22 March 2017 (see Chapter 3).

Jeremy gives everyone a pep talk at the end of the five-hour 'lock down' following the Westminster attack.

Barry Gardiner and David Prescott watch the TV in the main LOTO office as Theresa May announces a snap election on 18 April, 2017.

My son, Gareth, and my granddaughter, Ilana, read a letter from Jeremy explaining why I would not be able to get to California for her fifth birthday.

LOTO team members gather for a quick snap with Jeremy just before moving to Southside for the campaign. Left to right, back row: Thomas Gardiner, James Meadway, Chris Flattery, Angie Williams, Ayse Veli, Rich Simcox; front row: Mark Simpson, Seumas Milne, Jeremy and Laura, Sian Jones, Sophie Nazemi and Liz Marshall.

Ken Loach briefs Jeremy ahead of filming an interview with Labour supporters for one of the party political broadcasts.

Jeremy and Laura relax ahead of filming with Ken Loach.

Chaotic scenes in Cardiff as Jeremy speaks to an unexpectedly large crowd on 28 April 2017, with Wales First Minister Carwyn Jones (bottom right).

My daughter, Cerys, canvasses in the local elections with my grandson, Gwilym, then just three months old.

Jeremy loves travelling by train, with his notebook always handy.

Jeremy chats to a supporter in Warrington on 29 April, one of hundreds of conversations he had during the campaign.

Tories wrap the Mansfield Chad on 3 May with an advert that plays the Brexit card but doesn't mention the party.

Theresa May looks miserable as Jeremy pops up with a question during her 'Facebook Live' on 15 May, 2017.

The Daily Mail and Daily Telegraph rubbish our leaked manifesto on 11 May, 2017 with almost identical headlines.

Ready to react to the Tory manifesto on 18 May 2017. Left to right: Rory MacQueen (Shadow Treasury team), John McDonnell, Ian Lavery, Suha Abdul (STT), James Mills (STT), Seumas Milne, Madeleine Williams (STT) and Karie Murphy.

The Daily Mirror leads with the Tory attack on Winter Fuel Payments the day after their manifesto launch.

Feeling very optimistic as Jeremy Hunt struggles to explain the Tory manifesto.

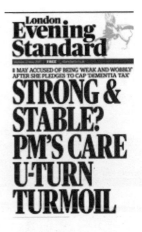

London Evening Standard

FREE standard.co.uk

MAY ACCUSED OF BEING 'WEAK AND WOBBLY' AFTER SHE PLEDGES TO CAP 'DEMENTIA TAX'

STRONG & STABLE? PM'S CARE U-TURN TURMOIL

Beccy Long-Bailey delivers our verdict on the Tory manifesto's 'Triple Whammy' at a press conference on 19 May 2017.

The Evening Standard reacts to May's U-turn on a dementia tax cap on 22 May 2017.

Register to vote today!
#YourVoteYourVoice

Above: Andrew Fisher ticks off constituencies visited in the glasshouse used by Jeremy and the LOTO strategy group.

Left: Our final social media reminder about voter registration on deadline day – 22 May 2017.

Jeremy speaks to an invited audience and the media as campaigning resumes following the Manchester attack.

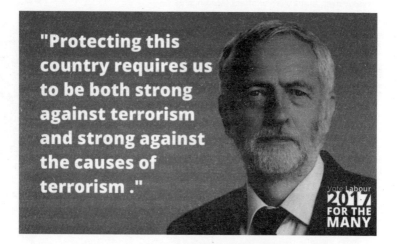

"Protecting this country requires us to be both strong against terrorism and strong against the causes of terrorism ."

An adaption of an old slogan sums up the two aspects of Jeremy's security stance.

BBC · Sign in · News · Sport · Weather · iPlayer · TV · Radio · CBBC · CBeebies · Food · iWonder · More · Search

NEWS

Find local news

Home · UK · World · Business · Election 2017 · Tech · Science · Health · Education · Entertainment

Jeremy Corbyn opposes 'shoot to kill' policy

The Labour leader Jeremy Corbyn has said in an interview with BBC Political Editor Laura Kuenssberg he is "not happy" with the shoot-to-kill policy in the event of a terror attack in the UK.

Asked if he was prime minister whether he would be happy to order police or military to shoot to kill if there was a terror attack on Britain's streets Mr Corbyn told the BBC he was "not happy with the shoot-to-kill policy in general" and "the idea you end up with a war on the streets is not a good thing... I think that is quite dangerous and I think can often can be counterproductive".

16 Nov | UK Politics

Share

MORE ON: Jeremy Corbyn

Security focus as campaign resumes

Corbyn criticises Tories in terror speech

What do party leaders do in their spare time?

Corbyn defence vow after Trident grilling

The BBC website page on shoot-to-kill as it was on 4 June 2017 - conflating shoot-to-kill 'in general' as a 'policy', which is illegal, with the legal use of lethal force to save lives during a terror attack (see Chapter 13).

The Tory 'dog whistle' AdVan tours the north-west. Why is Diane on there and not her Tory opposite number, Amber Rudd? (See Chapter 12).

LOTO strategy group members view the final cut of the campaign video. Left to right: Katy Clark, John McDonnell, Andrew Murray, Seb Corbyn, Leah Jennings (adviser to Jon Trickett), Seumas Milne, Jack Bond and Jon Trickett.

The Daily Mail and Sun do their bit for the Tories on the day before voting.

The LOTO communications team ready for the results on election night. Left to right: James Schneider, Ben Sellers, Rich Simcox, Angie Williams, Sophie Nazemi, me, Sian Jones, Joe Ryle, Jack Bond and Georgie Robertson.

Off-duty Labour staff celebrate at Southside as the gains roll in.

Seumas and Karie at home with Jeremy on election night.

Ian Lavery and Jeremy have a quiet moment at a reception for new Labour MPs on June 13.

L'myah Ross Walcott, Karie, Jennifer Larbie and Patsy Cummings enjoy election night.

Jeremy joins LOTO and campaign staff for a team photograph just after the election.

10 – Manchester – Tragedy and Terrorism

"And it's hard times again in these streets of our city.
But we won't take defeat and we don't want your pity
Because this is the place where we stand strong together
With a smile on our face, Mancunians forever."
Tony Walsh, Manchester poet[1]

At 5am, on the morning of Tuesday, May 23, I woke up to a text from Seb Corbyn and a missed call from the Labour press office. Seb had sent me a message at 11.24pm saying there were reports of an explosion in Manchester, but I had missed it, having already fallen asleep. Still slightly bleary, I checked the news online. The enormity of what had happened was immediately obvious from the headlines. Twitter was flooded with grim accounts of a bomb exploding and video clips of the panic at Manchester Arena as thousands of people – mainly teenagers – were leaving an Ariana Grande concert. Dozens had been injured, some were dead.

I phoned the Labour press officer who had been on duty overnight. Katy Dillon gave me a few more details and said the media were asking if we had suspended the campaign. I said I assumed we had – or would – but would check. Even more urgently, I called Jack Bond to stop any scheduled campaign tweets from Jeremy going

---

[1] Read at the vigil for the victims of the Manchester attack on 23.5.2017.

out. I then spoke to Karie who agreed campaigning had to be suspended. By 5.30am I was able to get back to Katy with a confirmed position that she could release in time for the 6am bulletins. My next port of call was Laura Parker, Jeremy's private secretary. She told me that Jeremy and the Prime Minister had spoken an hour or so earlier and had in fact already agreed to suspend campaigning "until further notice." Laura was keeping in touch with Alastair Whitehead, May's private secretary.

On the taxi journey into Southside, I tried to find out more about the attack and think through its implications. I knew Jeremy had spoken at a rally in Hull with John Prescott the previous evening, and that he was scheduled to go to Birmingham that morning to announce our housing manifesto with John Healey, the shadow housing minister. I presumed Jeremy had not come back to London overnight, which meant he had stayed in Hull or somewhere en route to Birmingham. Either way, he was somewhere in the north. The question was: should he come back to London or go to Manchester? It seemed unthinkable to me that he should literally turn his back on Manchester and head home when he was, broadly speaking, in the neighbourhood. That would be seen as heartless and, quite rightly, severely criticised. And yet, by going to Manchester, he risked being accused of showboating or trying to gain political advantage from a tragedy.

My mind went back to 1989 and the days immediately following the Hillsborough disaster[2] when I worked for

---

[2] On 15.4.1989, at Hillsborough stadium in Sheffield, 96 Liverpool supporters were unlawfully killed after police failed in their duty of care as fans arrived to watch an FA Cup semi-final between Liverpool and Nottingham Forest.

Sheffield City Council. The leader of the Council, Clive Betts,[3] asked me to go to Manchester airport with the Lord Mayor's driver to meet the then Labour leader Neil Kinnock and bring him back to Sheffield. Neil wanted to see what had happened for himself. It was to be a private visit, with no media involvement, and I would accompany him for the whole day, going first to Sheffield Wednesday's ground, then to the Royal Hallamshire Hospital, and finally to talk to traumatised staff at the mortuary. We spent the largest part of the day at the hospital where Neil spoke to Liverpool fans still recovering from injuries, and to their relatives and friends gathered in the corridors and waiting rooms. It was a harrowing situation that required the utmost sensitivity, and I thought Neil handled it with genuine empathy and solidarity.

You could not organise an under-the-radar visit like that now. The advent of 24-hour news, the internet and social media mean a Labour leader's movements are almost impossible to keep private − not least in the middle of a general election. We were worried in 1989 that Neil's visit would look like he was politicising Hillsborough. The risk of that with the Manchester attack, in the midst of a campaign, was infinitely greater. I was confident Jeremy would be acutely attuned to the feelings of those affected by the bombing, but I was also aware of the possibility of hostile sections of the media seizing on any comment or gesture that they could take out of context and portray negatively.

The 7am strategy call that morning took stock as best we could of the situation and agreed steps to

---

[3] Clive Betts is now MP for Sheffield South East.

communicate the suspension of campaigning to staff, candidates and agents. The question of Jeremy going to Manchester was raised but left for LOTO to discuss with Jeremy. In the longer 9am strategy meeting, Seumas pointed out that Jeremy and David Cameron had gone together to Birstall after the shooting of Jo Cox. But that was during a referendum when both leaders were campaigning for Remain. We knew May was going to go to Manchester that day, but it seemed inconceivable she would agree to go with Jeremy.

By mid-morning, we had been in touch several times with Jeremy and Sian Jones, the LOTO communications person who had accompanied him to Hull. They were still at a Premier Inn in Doncaster where they had stayed overnight. It was decided Jeremy should go to Manchester, subject to Andy Burnham's agreement. Jeremy wanted to speak to Andy himself.

While we waited for that discussion to take place, we agreed that Karie, Ian Lavery, Jack Bond and James Schneider should also go to Manchester to support Jeremy and protect him from a media scrum. In the account of this in another book about the election, it has been suggested that Ian – as the election co-ordinator – was considered a poor choice by a Labour figure in Manchester.[4] I had not heard that until I read the book, but I have to confess that I think it was my idea – it was certainly a decision I was party to. This was primarily because I thought Ian had the down-to-earth warmth and sensitivity needed for the visit. I also thought that it was important to have a shadow cabinet member from

[4] Tim Ross and Tom McTague, 'Betting The House,' Biteback Publishing, 2017, p290.

the north accompanying Jeremy to avoid it being perceived as Londoners descending on Manchester. I was not thinking of him at that moment as the election co-ordinator.

At 12.45pm, we had another conference call with Jeremy. By that time, he had set off for Manchester, having spoken to Andy. Jeremy said Andy was happy for him to attend a vigil that had been hastily arranged for 6pm that evening and then stay in the city for meetings the next day.

Jeremy arrived in Manchester just after 3pm. After a further conference call to run through his programme, he went to Manchester Town Hall with Karie and Ian for meetings with Sir Richard Leese, the leader of the City Council, and Andy Burnham, and to sign the book of condolences. He then recorded a pool clip for broadcast media and a piece to camera for Labour party use before going back to the Town Hall for the vigil with faith and community leaders, Liberal Democrat leader, Tim Farron, and home secretary, Amber Rudd.

It was Jeremy's decision to leave Manchester immediately after the vigil. Andy had mentioned staying for meetings the next day. There had been talk of visiting the hospital to see the injured and their families. But I think Jeremy felt he had shown his solidarity and done what was appropriate in the circumstances.

The next morning, he arrived at Southside in a solemn but determined mood. Karie had given the strategy group a schedule of his calls and meetings, one of which would be a meeting with the LOTO strategy group to take stock of the implications of the attack for the campaign.

On the train back to London the night before, he had

taken a call from Theresa May informing him that she would be announcing the raising of the security threat level from severe to critical, the highest level, for the first time in ten years. Her live television statement shortly afterwards was made dramatically from a presidential-style podium in Downing Street. She said the threat level was being raised because of "a possibility that we cannot ignore that there is a wider group of individuals linked to this attack." A plan called Operation Temperer was being activated so that military personnel could be deployed to guard key sites to free the police to patrol other areas. "While we mourn the victims of last night's appalling attack, we stand defiant," she said. "The spirit of Manchester – and the spirit of Britain – is far mightier than the sick plots of depraved terrorists. That is why the terrorists will never win, and we will prevail."[5]

Behind these Churchillian words, however, the Tories wanted general election campaigning to remain suspended until the following Monday. The Conservative chairman, Patrick McLoughlin, and his deputy, Stephen Gilbert, had separately said this to members of our team, and May herself had confirmed it in a call with Jeremy on Tuesday morning.

If one of the objectives of the terrorists was to derail our democracy, it seems they were willing to let them prevail on that score. But were we prepared to go it alone? And how should we resume campaigning, given the tragic circumstances and raw sensitivities?

Those were the big questions our strategy team faced as we gathered mid-morning to meet Jeremy and John McDonnell. The glasshouse was at greenhouse

---

[5] Theresa May, Downing Street statement, 23.5.2017.

temperatures that day. Outside, the emergency services seemed busy, their sirens adding to a sense of crisis. All the senior people in the Leader's team were present: Karie, Seumas, the two Andrews, Katy and me. Jeremy started by running through the security situation, his conversations with May and how the visit to Manchester had gone. He said the vigil had been attended by more than a thousand people and described it as having a "we're not going to be beaten" mood. He was in favour of resuming local campaigning the next day and national campaigning on Friday, and it was agreed he would put this directly to May on their call later that day. We would also seek the agreement of the other parties for this timetable and then make our final decision after we knew where everyone stood.

The manner of the campaign resumption would, we knew, have to be very measured. There would be no public rallies on Friday. Jeremy's only speech would be to an invited audience. He would not go on the road – we would find a central London venue. We did not, at that stage, discuss what he would say about the attack, but I doubt I was alone in taking it as read that he could not avoid the big questions it threw up. Only two weeks earlier, his speech at Chatham House had outlined why he thought the "war on terror" had made Britain less secure. He was going to be asked if that applied to Manchester, whatever he said in his first speech after the attack.

Jeremy took the call from May in the same room at 1.30pm. They discussed the suspension of campaigning, and Jeremy proposed a phased resumption from Thursday, arguing that we should not allow terrorists to close down democracy. May was taken aback. She wanted to delay a decision until Saturday. But Jeremy persisted and made it clear that, while we would prefer the timing to be agreed, we were considering resuming anyway.

The strategy group met after the call to firm up our plans swiftly. The feedback from the other opposition parties was that they wanted to resume campaigning as soon as possible. Our own position was already the subject of rumour and speculation on social media. We decided to give constituency parties – at their discretion – the option of campaigning the next day. Our party political broadcast on Brexit would also go ahead on Thursday evening. Jeremy would then speak on Friday morning at One Great George Street in Westminster. The main lines of his speech would be trailed, with no embargo, in time for the Thursday evening news bulletins.

Speech writing had been a team effort throughout the campaign. In this case, Seumas and Andrew Murray took the lead and had a working draft ready within 24 hours. When I saw it on Thursday afternoon, I had only a handful of comments that had more to do with tone and style than the substance of it. Overall I thought it was strong, sensitive to the situation and very much in line with Jeremy's long-standing approach.

The lines from the speech that we sent out to the media were in three parts. On Britain's values, Jeremy would say that "the solidarity, humanity and compassion that we have seen on the streets of Manchester this week" would be "the values that guide our government." He would argue that, while no government can prevent every terrorist attack if an individual is determined and callous enough to get through, it does have the responsibility of minimising that chance – to ensure the police have the resources they need, that our foreign policy reduces rather than increases the threat to this country and that, at home, we never surrender the freedoms we have won and that terrorists are so determined to take away.

On domestic policy, he would promise that Labour would reverse the cuts to our emergency services and go on to say:

"'Austerity has to stop at the A&E ward and at the police station door. We cannot be protected and cared for on the cheap. There will be more police on the streets under a Labour government. And if the security services need more resources to keep track of those who wish to murder and maim, then they should get them."

The third, and most controversial, part of the speech was on foreign policy. Reiterating his well-known views, he would say:

"Many experts, including professionals in our intelligence and security services, have pointed to the connections between wars our government has supported or fought in other countries and terrorism here at home. That assessment in no way reduces the guilt of those who attack our children. Those terrorists will forever be reviled and held to account for their actions. But an informed understanding of the causes of terrorism is an essential part of an effective response that will protect the security of our people that fights rather than fuels terrorism. We must be brave enough to admit the 'war on terror' is simply not working. We need a smarter way to reduce the threat from countries that nurture terrorists and generate terrorism."

Though the speech contained nothing I viewed as insensitive or inappropriate, I knew this was going to be a watershed moment for the campaign. As I left Southside that evening, I was aware of messages from the press office that an above-average media storm was brewing. One colleague feared we had "gifted the Tories a security attack on a plate" but I remained certain we had no choice, and confident it was the right thing to do.

A specific query from the *Today* programme asking which experts had linked foreign wars with terrorism was easy to handle. One of them, Richard Barrett, a former director of global counter-terrorism at MI6, argued that we need a "smarter" approach than "launching bigger bombs" only two days earlier – on the *Today* programme itself.[6] He said:

"We can go on and on saying, 'Oh, we must crack down on these people and launch bigger bombs' or whatever. That's not solving the problem that 15, 16 years after 9/11 we're facing a bigger threat than we did then. So, we have to do something a bit smarter than that, and I'm sure that is about engaging the community and letting the community, in a way, inform what we should be doing to prevent further attacks, because some of

---

[6] Richard Barrett, former director of MI6's global counter terrorism operations, speaking on Radio 4's Today programme, 23.5.2017.

the external stuff we're doing, some of the more obvious stuff we're doing, which is easier to do than the community level stuff, is not having the effect we want."

And there were others who had been even more explicit. In 2015, President Obama described ISIL as:

"A direct outgrowth of Al Qaeda in Iraq, that grew out of our invasion, which is an example of unintended consequences [and] why we should generally aim before we shoot".[7]

In 2016, the House of Commons Foreign Affairs Committee made a similar point in a report on Libya. In a conclusion that is particularly relevant given the Libyan background of the perpetrator of the Manchester atrocity, it said that Britain's intervention in 2011 had resulted in:

"Political and economic collapse, inter-militia and inter-tribal warfare, humanitarian and migrant crises, widespread human rights violations, the spread of Gaddafi regime weapons across the region and the growth of ISIL in North Africa."[8]

As I walked from Woodside Park tube station to where I was staying, Laura Kuenssberg called to talk about the speech. The Tories were already accusing us of "making excuses for terrorism." Weren't we, she asked, playing into their hands? Wouldn't making the speech only a few days after the attack leave Jeremy open to accusations of poor timing? My response was that the victims of terror

---

[7] Barack Obama, interview with VICE News, 16.3.2015.

[8] House of Commons Foreign Affairs Committee, 'Libya: Examination of intervention and the UK's future policy options' Third Report of Session 2016-17, HC119.

deserved honesty, not empty platitudes. I said we knew it was a political risk but Jeremy couldn't resume the campaign without talking about Manchester, and no one would respect him if he didn't say what he genuinely thought.

Laura reflected that view accurately in her live piece to camera on that evening's *Ten O'clock News*. She said that, while Jeremy would:

"Absolutely explicitly say it does not justify the actions of any individual terrorist, it does not justify the horror of what happened this week, he will be quite clear that, in his view, Britain's wars abroad have made things more not less dangerous."

She continued:

"His team are aware it's a controversial argument to make right now when the reality of what's happened is still so raw. It's not the first time that Jeremy Corbyn has made this case. He's held this belief for quite some time. Nonetheless, they are prepared for a barrage of criticism tomorrow when he gives this speech, but those people around Jeremy Corbyn, and Jeremy Corbyn himself, I think, believe that it would be dishonest, perhaps, and certainly not giving a full picture [not] to have a proper debate about why this happened and how it could be prevented in the future without looking at the whole situation. And, for them, that includes Britain's wars abroad."

That was a reasonable summary of our position. But other parts of the media and our political opponents were gearing up for a fierce attack. The *Sun* was calling

214

the speech "incendiary" and saying it "will spark outrage."[9] The defence secretary, Michael Fallon, was doing the rounds for the Tories, dubbing the speech as "ill-judged" and proof that Jeremy was "soft on terrorism."[10] And the former Lib Dem leader, Lord Ashdown, was accusing Jeremy of seeking to "politicise the events of the week."[11]

None of this was at all surprising. Jeremy had been living with attacks of this nature since being elected leader, and we knew that he would be subjected to them whether he tackled or tried to avoid the difficult issues. The Manchester speech was in line with our approach – whether on security, Brexit, or his own leadership style – of creating opportunities for people to hear his views in full in the hope that we could reframe the debate. Paradoxically, the campaign's success in doing this was adding to the pressure. With two polls that week showing the gap between us and the Tories narrowing to only five points, the possibility of winning was becoming very real – and none of us wanted to put it at risk.

I arrived at Southside on the morning of the speech resolved to read it through carefully again. When I did, I was reassured to find – as I had the first time – that Andrew and Seumas had done a very good job. The sensitive points were carefully crafted. We could back our arguments up. The balance and tone were right. After sending a couple of suggestions for small changes to Seumas, I turned my attention to writing a few notes

---

[9] The Sun, 26.5.2017.

[10] Michael Fallon speaking on Sky News, 26.5.2017.

[11] Belinda Robinson, 'Lord Ashdown savages Corbyn,' the Daily Express, 26.5.2017.

for Angela Smith,[12] who would be introducing Jeremy, before leaving for One Great George Street about ten minutes' walk away.

When I arrived, Jeremy was in an oak-panelled side room sitting with Laura at the far end of a large table making a few more last-minute changes before the speech went onto the auto-cue. Seumas, Diane Abbott, Shami Chakrabarti, and Emily Thornberry were huddled with them. Angela was standing to one side and I made a bee-line for her to see if she was happy with her introductory notes. She seemed calmer than me, but then this was the first time I'd allowed myself out of the engine room to hear Jeremy speak. I felt more nervous than if I was delivering it myself.

As the events team called time, I walked through to the hall where the meeting was being held with Diane, Laura and Shami. We entered through the double doors that Jeremy would use a few minutes later and were met by a wall of photographers and a crescendo of clicking cameras. I ducked to the back and found a spot to stand just behind one of the TV cameras. When Jeremy walked in, the photographers pressed forward again, hiding him from view. It took Angela several minutes to calm them down so we could have a minute's silence for the Manchester victims.

Jeremy delivered the speech well. This was not a day for oratory. His calm sincerity was exactly what was needed. We wanted the millions watching on TV and online to think about the words he was saying, not be stirred by rhetoric. After he had finished, he left the

[12] Baroness Smith is shadow leader of the House of Lords. She was MP for Basildon from 1997 to 2010.

rostrum and the room immediately, as planned. We had decided there would be no questions, the media had the speech, and we wanted them to have to quote from that rather than divert the story onto their own agenda.

That did not, of course, stop some of them editorialising. On the *BBC* lunchtime news, Norman Smith described the speech as "hugely contentious" and said it had already been widely criticized, not only by Conservatives, "but also some in the Labour party who are aghast he should make this sort of speech so soon after an atrocity." Smith sneered at Jeremy for thinking he had a responsibility for starting a discussion about how we try to avoid atrocities like Manchester, and claimed that he would not take questions "because of the backlash he will face over this speech."[13] Smith's report had more of his own editorialising than it did clips from the actual speech, and we complained about it to the *BBC*.

By contrast, Krishnan Guru-Murthy on *Channel 4 News* was willing to challenge the Tories on their position on the issue. In an interview that evening with Fallon, he asked the defence minister to respond to a quote:

"Isn't it possible that things like the Iraq war did not create the problem of murderous Islamic fundamentalists, though the war has unquestionably sharpened the resentments felt by such people in this country and given them a new pretext?"

Fallon condemned the comment, thinking it had been made by Jeremy, but Guru-Murthy then revealed that Boris Johnson had said those words in response to the 7/7 London bombings in 2005 that killed 52 people.

[13] Norman Smith, BBC, 26.5.2017.

Johnson also went on to say "the Iraq war did not introduce the poison into our bloodstream but, yes, the war did help to potentiate that poison."[14]

Fallon's gaffe left both Tory ministers looking as foolish as each other, for Johnson had only the previous day joined the chorus condemning Jeremy. He said – in contrast to his words 12 years earlier – it was "absolutely monstrous" for anyone to "subtract from the fundamental responsibility of those individuals, that individual in particular, who committed this atrocity."[15]

The public deserve better from politicians, whatever their party, than this kind of slippery shifting of position. There is nothing wrong, of course, with politicians changing their mind, but they should do so openly and explain their reasons. Apart from that being right in principle, it is also harder these days for anyone to get away with inconsistency and hypocrisy when the public have easy access to so much information.

As the Fallon interview was being shared far and wide on social media, *YouGov* put a poll in the field that found a majority (53 per cent) agreed that wars the UK has supported or fought are responsible, at least in part, for terror attacks against our country. This was more than twice the proportion who think they are not responsible for terror attacks (24 per cent). They found voters from across all parties more likely to side with Jeremy's stance

---

[14] Krishnan Guru-Murthy quoted Boris Johnson to Michael Fallon on Channel 4 news, 26.5.2017.

[15] Boris Johnson was speaking at a press conference with US secretary of state Rex Tillerson, as reported by the BBC in 'General election 2017: Corbyn pledges change at home and abroad on terror,' 26.5.2017.

than not.[16]

A week later, an *ORB* survey for the *Independent* found three-quarters of people agreed Britain's military involvement in Iraq, Afghanistan, and Libya had increased the risk of terrorist acts. Even among Tory voters, 68 per cent thought foreign wars had added to the risk of terrorism at home. The figure for Labour supporters was 80 per cent.[17]

Jeremy was honest with voters about his views on terrorism and security, solely because he would not have wanted it any other way. But it was reassuring and rewarding to find that honesty was also the best policy from an electoral point of view. We went into the penultimate weekend of the campaign feeling we had done the right thing.

---

[16] Matthew Smith, 'Jeremy Corbyn is on the right side of public opinion on foreign policy,' YouGov, 30.5.2017.

[17] Andrew Grice, 'Majority of British voters agree with Corbyn's claim UK foreign policy increases risk of terrorism,' the Independent, 6.6.2017.

11 – The Show Goes Epic

"The idea is to generate a climate of 'epic-ness' and political centrality – to be what everyone else is talking about, expressing their opinions on, imitating and criticising. "
Jorge Moruno, Podemos

Cup Final day may not be the big deal it used to be in football terms, but it gave some welcome respite from the Manchester tragedy and an opportunity for people to come together in a positive way. After Celtic had beaten Aberdeen 2-1 at Hampden Park in Glasgow, Arsenal won by the same score against Chelsea, with Jeremy in the crowd supporting his local team. "Great to be at Wembley to watch Arsenal defy the odds and win the #FACupFinal for a record breaking 13th time," he tweeted afterwards.

That morning Jeremy had been out on Hackney Marshes with a group of young footballers to launch Labour's policy of ensuring that 5 per cent of Premier League revenue from TV rights is invested in the grassroots game. Showing a few nice touches himself for the media, he said:

"Too often, youth football teams can't find pitches to play on, and when they do they're expensive and the facilities aren't fit for purpose. All-weather pitches are like gold-dust and coaching badges can cost unaffordable amounts. Labour will ensure the footballing talent of young girls and boys is harnessed, and football is a game for the many, not the few."

Jack Bond, meanwhile, kept the football theme going throughout the day on Jeremy's Twitter feed with quotes from some of the sport's icons such as Brian Clough ("I think Socialism comes from the heart") and Bill Shankly ("The socialism I believe in is everyone working for the same goal and everybody have a share in the rewards").[1] Both were retweeted more than five thousand times.

The Labour campaign returned to the question of security on the Sunday by announcing a plan to recruit 10,000 more police officers, 3,000 more firefighters, 3,000 more prison officers, 1,000 more security and intelligence agency staff, and 500 more border guards. Diane Abbott, as shadow home secretary, was on *The Andrew Marr Show* to discuss our policies, though you would not have known it from the aggressive questioning about things she is reputed to have said in the distant past.

Early in the interview, Andrew Marr had erroneously implied she had specifically voted against proscribing Al Qaeda "just before 9/11," but Diane explained – I thought clearly enough for any open-minded person

----

[1] Brian Clough, an outstanding manager for Derby County and Nottingham Forest, supported the miners' strike and was a founding sponsor of the Anti-Nazi League. When he died in 2004, aged 69, more than 14,000 people attended his funeral. Bill Shankly, who established Liverpool as one of the leading clubs in Europe, was known for his strong socialist convictions and down-to-earth honesty. After his death in 1981, aged 68, the club honoured him with a statue and the Shankly Gates at Anfield.

listening – that the vote had actually been against a widely-cast proscribed list that included organisations she considered dissidents rather than terrorists. The home secretary of the day, Jack Straw, had not given MPs an opportunity to vote separately on Al Qaeda, or any other organisation. Her answer did not spark a major controversy that day, but it would later be cunningly cut into the nastiest Tory attack of the campaign.

Behind the scenes, the weekend was a hotbed of discussion about the shape of the final days, with even a leading figure in Podemos in Spain chipping in with a few suggestions. Jorge Moruno, a strategist for the movement's leader, Pablo Iglesias, urged us to create a climate of "epic-ness" in which our plans become "a new project for the whole country" and our core supporters are excited by the idea that "we can do this."

In their panic, the Tories were sounding the alarm bell so loudly about Jeremy that they were inadvertently making him politically central and helping to create Moruno's sense of epic-ness. In an Op-Ed in that weekend's *Sun on Sunday*, Theresa May said:

"The choice facing the British people at the general election is becoming ever clearer — and the stakes could not be higher. If my party loses just six seats, we would lose our majority and Britain would have a hung Parliament. With the Liberal Democrats and the Scottish nationalists ready to form a coalition of chaos to prop him up, Jeremy Corbyn could be walking through the door of 10 Downing Street in 12 days' time as prime minister."[2]

Gone was the talk of a landslide to strengthen her hand

---

[2] The Sun on Sunday, 28.5.2017.

with Brussels. Now May was reduced to a desperate plea to "stop Corbyn."

As ambitious as we had been from the outset, the reality of the gap narrowing meant every decision had to be weighed more carefully. The agonising question at this crucial point was how to be even bolder in our approach without making any mistakes that would set us back. That was the underlying dilemma as the LOTO strategy group met that Sunday evening to discuss the shape of the final stage of the campaign. What was the upside and what were the risks if Jeremy took part in the *BBC* leaders' debate on Wednesday evening, regardless of whether May turned up or not? Was Trafalgar Square – for which we had police permission – the best place to hold our final big rally 36 hours before polling? Had we done enough to make our position on Brexit clear? How should we allocate the unexpectedly large flow of cash coming in online? How could we fit in the policy announcements postponed after the Manchester attack, not least our core 'wealth creation' strategy?

With Jeremy back on the campaign trail, speaking at a rally in Glasgow with Ian Lavery, nine of us gathered at Southside to make some decisions – politicians John McDonnell, Jon Trickett and Andrew Gwynne, Unite's Andrew Murray and LOTO's senior staff: Karie, Katy, Seumas, Andrew Fisher and me. Everyone had a spring in their step. The week ahead was full of opportunities to get our message across through the big broadcast events of the election – *Sky* and *Channel 4*'s *May v Corbyn: The Battle for Number 10* on Monday, Jeremy's appearances on *Woman's Hour* and *The One Show* on Tuesday, the *BBC* debate on Wednesday, and a *BBC Question Time* special with the two leaders on Friday. It did not look like May would budge on her refusal to debate head-to-head with Jeremy, which meant they would appear in separate segments of the *Sky-Channel 4* and *BBC* programmes.

The Wednesday leaders' debate remained a dilemma. Pressure from some of our supporters for Jeremy to take part was growing. A member of my personal focus group, Ivor Gaber, had argued for Jeremy to take part in *ITV*'s opposition leaders' debate two weeks earlier, saying it was a "golden opportunity to reach many of our waverers" and "a gamble worth taking."[3] Our reticence then was mainly based on wanting to keep the focus on the Labour-Tory debate and May's refusal to go head-to-head with Jeremy. But the *BBC* debate was different because the Tories would be represented by a senior cabinet minister, Amber Rudd, and May's absence would be even more conspicuous.

Most of us were beginning to think Jeremy should do it, but we could afford to delay a final decision until after the Monday *Sky-Channel 4* programme. That left our alternative nominee, Emily Thornberry, in the unenviable position of having to be prepared without knowing if she would be needed, but it made sense to judge the mood as late as possible and, meanwhile, continue to reap the news value of the speculation about whether Jeremy would appear or not.

The week's television commitments filled much of the grid, but we also had to slot in some important policy announcements – funding for childcare on Tuesday, public ownership of rail on Thursday, wealth creation on Friday, and back to pensioners and care for the weekend.

---

[3] Ivor Gaber, Professor of Journalism, University of Sussex.

And then there was Brexit, and what else we could do to get across our message that the Tories were not to be trusted to defend working people in the negotiations with Brussels. Jon Trickett had reported that voters were moving back to us from UKIP in strongly pro-Leave Labour areas. People were afraid, he said, of what was going to happen to them if there were to be another five years of Tory government. The triple whammy of attacks on pensioners had shown the Tories in their true colours and alarmed many older people.

Though May was still playing the Brexit card in a big way, undecided potential Labour voters did not trust the Tories. In recent private polling, they overwhelmingly agreed that Theresa May's Tory party protects the wealthy and would not look after working people. And, on Brexit, we had scored markedly better than the Tories when they were asked who could be trusted to put jobs first in the negotiations. Intriguingly, the age profile of the 375,000 Facebook views of our Brexit PPB – broadcast on television at the end of the previous week – was markedly older than for any of the other campaign videos. It was clear that Brexit was key to reducing our deficit among older working-class voters, not by pandering to prejudices on free movement, but by exposing the Tory agenda of a post-Brexit de-regulated, cheap labour Britain. We decided that Jeremy should make a speech specifically on Brexit in pro-Leave Basildon, squeezing it into the week's densely-packed grid on the Thursday.

Looking beyond that to getting out the vote in the final week, we revisited the original campaign plan to have a big final rally in London to enthuse supporters.

The events team had investigated various venues and secured Trafalgar Square for Tuesday, June 6. At first this was considered quite a coup, but the more we talked about it, the more reservations grew about it looking like a stereotypical protest rally open to any fringe sect to turn up and gift the Tory media an opportunity to contrive images of Jeremy addressing 'extremists'. Seumas was hankering instead for us to emulate the French left candidate Jean-Luc Melenchon, who had spoken at a rally in Dijon just before the presidential elections a few weeks earlier and appeared simultaneously as a hologram at six other events around the country. The risk of this going horribly wrong was all too obvious, but everyone was up for being 'epic' if we could find the means to do it. We decided to ditch the Trafalgar Square option and hold the main rally in Birmingham with a satellite video link to five other venues if the hologram idea proved too problematic.

All our planning at this crucial stage in the campaign was made much easier by the donations pouring in online and the generous support we had received from the unions, especially Unite. It is never the case that money is no object in the labour movement, and we were always mindful that every donation was hard-earned cash from people with not a lot to spare. But we were – at this crucial point in the campaign – seeing a virtuous circle of growing support enabling us to be more ambitious about events while also ramping up spending on digital and newspaper advertising.

Jeremy arrived back from Glasgow that Monday and went straight to a hotel in West London to prepare for the *Sky-Channel 4* debate with Seumas and Andrew

Fisher. The format of the debate was that each leader in turn answered questions from a studio audience before being quizzed by Jeremy Paxman, who was playing the lawyer trying to break a witness in a movie.

Paxman's theme for his opening questions to Jeremy was views he had previously expressed that were *not* in the manifesto. After an initial exchange on the Trident nuclear weapons programme, Paxman quoted Jeremy saying in 2013 that he favoured banks being in public ownership:

Paxman: You said that in 2013, and it doesn't get into the manifesto, does it?

Jeremy: What we seem to be struggling with here is an understanding of a process that brings about a manifesto...

Paxman (waving manifesto): What we're struggling with is how much this represents what you believe...

Jeremy: I am not a dictator who writes things to tell people what to do. This is a product of a process in our party. That's why I was elected leader, to give a voice to the members and those that are affiliated to our party.

Paxman's hectoring continued across more subjects that were not in the manifesto, but Jeremy looked comfortable as he batted them away. And, when Paxman said "there is nothing in this manifesto about getting rid of the monarchy," he threw him an exasperated look and said pointedly, "there's nothing in there, *because we're not going to do it*." It earned him an outbreak of laughter at Paxman's expense – and the loudest applause of the evening.

Nevertheless, the prosecutor stuck doggedly to his search for a trip wire that would catch Jeremy's ankles. Questions followed on Brexit, immigration, the Falklands and drone strikes. When Paxman finally reached Afghanistan and asked why Jeremy had criticised the killing of Osama Bin Laden, Jeremy was still unruffled and earned another round of applause for firmly defending the rule of law. "Because I think he should have been arrested, and I think he should have been put on trial, and he could have been," he said to applause.

It was one of his best media interviews of the campaign, and much stronger than the robotic and evasive performance of May. In answering questions from the studio audience, she would not say what the cap on social care costs would be and was flummoxed when a midwife said of extra NHS funding that she would "believe it when I see it." Even May's claim that Labour's manifesto figures didn't add up was greeted with laughter by many in the audience.

At Southside, about twenty or so people were crammed in one meeting room running a social media support operation, encompassing not only our own Twitter and Facebook feeds, but also those of other campaign supporters. As the commentariat pontificated about who had 'won' the debate, social media gave its own answer in an outpouring of Theresa May GIFs mocking her performance. The comedian, David Schneider, posted one of a woman falling off a treadmill, with the words "Theresa May's election campaign so far." Another portrayed the reaction at Tory HQ through a clip from the spoof disaster movie, *Airplane*, with the actor Leslie Nielsen in front of a burning building waving people away, saying: "Please disperse. Nothing to see here." My favourite is a clip of a solitary audience member standing up to applaud May with a post saying: "That standing ovation in full." The irony was brutal, but it had been invited by the Tories' decision to build their campaign around May while relentlessly vilifying Jeremy. Chris Graham in the *Daily Telegraph* concluded: "Overall, if the GIFs are anything to go by, it was seen as a car crash performance."[4]

As ever, how people perceive something can be more important than how it actually was. May's performance was not as disastrous as the GIFs portrayed it, but she had set herself up for a fall by using 'strong and stable' *ad nauseum*, and then refusing to take part in a direct debate with Jeremy. The atmosphere at the joint strategy meeting the next morning was euphoric. Patrick could hardly contain his enthusiasm. He wanted us to tell the media that evening that Jeremy would take part in the *BBC* leaders' debate the next day so that the story would run for 24 hours, putting May under huge pressure. It was a great idea – except that it was, ultimately, Jeremy's decision, and he was already out and about visiting a nursery to launch our policy of 30 hours of free childcare a week for two to four-year-olds. His next stop would be the BBC Broadcasting House for *Woman's Hour*, and then he would be going to *Mumsnet* for a live online Q&A. Our first chance to speak to him would be after that, while he was travelling to the launch of our 'Race and Faith' manifesto in Watford. In our enthusiasm to be 'epic', we

---

[4] Chris Graham, '#Theresamaygifs: Prime Minister mocked on social media for debate performance,' the Telegraph website, 30.5.2017.

had crammed his day with so much there was precious little time for any discussion with him, not to mention for him to digest all the briefings he had been given.

Something had to give – and it did, on *Woman's Hour*, with millions of people listening. When the presenter Emma Barnett asked him how much the childcare policy would cost, Jeremy was stumped and started to look the figure up on his iPad. Barnett did not hesitate to tell listeners what Jeremy was doing and pressed her point by saying:

"You've announced a major policy and you don't know how much it will cost. Is this not exactly the issue with people and the Labour party, which came up under Gordon Brown, that we cannot trust you with our money?"

Jeremy was initially flustered but quickly recovered his composure and, polite as ever, said: "Can we come back to that in a moment?" What the listeners did not know was that Emma Barnett had the figure in front of her in the briefing we supplied, as we did with all the interviews, before Jeremy arrived.

A test of a good media performer is not whether or not they make occasional mistakes on air, which everybody does, but how quickly they recover. On that basis, as interview car crashes go, this probably ranked as a bump rather than a write-off. But it did have a knock-on effect on our plans for the *BBC* debate because our conference call with him while he was on his way to Watford was monopolised by how to handle the fall-out from *Woman's Hour*. As expected, the cost of the childcare policy was raised in media questions at the 'Race and Faith' event, and this time Jeremy handled it well. But then he had to come back to London for *The One Show*, and it was still not a good time to distract him with the dilemma of the *BBC* debate.

By that stage, I was on a train to Cardiff - for the funeral of former Welsh Labour leader Rhodri Morgan[5] - and ignoring messages from journalists who wanted to wheedle out of me what Jeremy was likely to do. The media thought we were deliberately keeping them guessing, but the truth was that Seumas did not get a chance to speak to him about it until after *The One Show*, and then he wanted to discuss it with John McDonnell and other key colleagues, some of whom had reservations. On the morning of the debate, Karie and Seumas met Jeremy to make a final decision. They thought he should take part. He said: "We're still behind. The only way to close the gap is to do it."

Rhodri's funeral was being held at the Senedd building about ten minutes' walk from my home and, as you do when you are so near a venue, I cut it fine to get there. When I arrived, the Neuadd — the Senedd's reception area — where the service was to be held was already packed and hundreds of people were overflowing onto the steps outside and across the Cardiff Bay quayside beyond. I should have expected this. It was not for nothing that, in Wales, Rhodri was called the father of the nation. Everyone used his first name, whether speaking about him or to him. More importantly, as my daughter Cerys pointed out in a Facebook post, he in turn

---

[5] Rhodri Morgan was leader of the Welsh Labour party and First Minister for Wales from 2000 to 2009. He had also been a Westminster MP from 1987 to 2001. He died on May 17, 2017, aged 77.

invariably remembered other people's names.[6]

Much like Jeremy, Rhodri was unaffected by his political status and always ready to talk on an equal footing with anyone. I had first met him in the early 1990s when he was sitting unobtrusively in the stand at Cwmbran Stadium watching some athletics – a sport we were both involved in – wearing shorts and a T-shirt, plucking sandwiches from a plastic bag. He was a Westminster MP then. Later, after he became First Minister, we worked together on Wales' successful bid to stage the 2010 Ryder Cup and in promoting Wales in the build-up to the event. It was typical of Rhodri that, by retiring in 2009, he left his successor, Carwyn Jones, to enjoy hosting the biggest sporting event ever to be held in Wales while he moved gracefully into an elder statesman role as a regular *Western Mail* columnist and Chancellor of Swansea University.

The funeral went on far longer than planned, but it was somehow apt that there were so many speeches and an abundance of anecdotes and humour. Rhodri would undoubtedly have enjoyed it. But what really said everything about him for me was the choice of music and the collective show of appreciation as he took his final leave. Wales, internationalism, and working class solidarity were each represented in *Hen Wlad Fy Nhadau*, *Nkosi Sikelele*, and the *Ballad of Joe Hill*.[7] Then, as the

---

[6] Cerys attended Caerleon Comprehensive School. One year, Rhodri came to present the school prizes. Whenever he saw either of us afterwards, he always remembered her name.

[7] In order: Wales' national anthem, the anthem of the African National Congress, and a song that pays tribute to the American union activist, Joe Hill (1879 – 1915).

coffin was carried from the Senedd building and down the steps, someone did what the rest of us were thinking of doing – with one clap they set off sustained applause that did not stop until he was in the hearse and had disappeared around the corner of the building. It was the most moving funeral farewell I've ever witnessed.

At the refreshments afterwards, conversation inevitably moved from Rhodri to the general election. I chatted to Cardiff Central Assembly Member, Jenny Rathbone, and the Cardiff North candidate, Anna McMorrin, about how the campaign was going in Wales. Both were very upbeat, but I was shocked to find that Anna, who had given up her own job, was running the campaign without any other full-time help. This beggared belief. I could understand people doubting the realism of LOTO's campaign to win strategy in April – but not at the end of May. Cardiff North was our 17th most winnable seat, and Jeremy had visited it at the start of the campaign. With only a week until polling day, it should have been brimming with support. I promised to raise the issue at the first opportunity.

By the time I had left the Senedd for the railway station, Jeremy had announced, at a rally in Reading, that he would be taking part in the *BBC* debate. Among others, I texted Laura Kuenssberg to apologise for not responding to her messages asking what was happening. She had set off for Bristol, where Jeremy was originally due to be speaking that evening, and then had to turn around to go to Cambridge for the debate. An unnamed source had claimed that Jeremy's late change of plan was prompted by wanting to "move on fast" from his memory lapse on the cost of the childcare policy. I pointed out that the fall-out from the *Woman's Hour* interview had only delayed a decision, not changed it, but it was clear Jeremy's participation was being presented in some quarters as a salvage operation rather than in the positive way we wanted. On the streets of Cambridge, however, that did not dampen the reception Jeremy was given as he was driven to the venue. Seumas, who was in the car and is not prone to exaggeration, says he was "startled and moved" by the response from people of all ages who, once they saw the police outriders and spotted Jeremy, started clapping. From Cardiff to Cambridge, it seems people like honesty and authenticity.

When I arrived back at Southside that evening, there was a buzz of anticipation about the debate. The social media support team had gathered in a meeting room on the second floor as before. Most of the other staff were on the eighth floor with an abundant supply of pizza. Once the debate started, it was soon obvious we had made the right decision. Jeremy looked comfortable and the audience responded so well to him that Nigel Farage, predictably, complained it was full of "paid up Corbynistas." Having all seven parties represented made it a scrappy affair, and Tim Shipman of the *Sunday Times* was about right in tweeting:

> "Corbyn's done well enough but hard to stand out from the cacophonous crowd. May loses but not as much as she would have if she had turned up."

It was a pointed swipe at May for her poor performance in the campaign from a commentator who would normally be supportive. Jeremy being there was positive on all counts. For the Tories, there was only damage limitation. Her stand-in, Amber Rudd, was credited by the

Sun columnist, James Forsyth, with "holding her ground pretty well." However, in repeatedly telling Jeremy that there was no "magic money tree" for public services, Rudd gifted us an easy social media counter attack on tax havens and tax cuts for the rich that would run and run.

As the debate was finishing, news came through of a *YouGov* poll putting the Tories on 42 per cent and Labour on 39 per cent. The gap of three points was down from seven only five days earlier, and that was from interviews carried out before the debate. Was there a limit now to how ambitious we could be? Late that evening, I exchanged e-mails with Ben Nolan, who was orchestrating the online fund-raising. He had drafted an appeal from Jeremy, ready to go out at 8am the next morning saying "we need £120,000 before polling day to guarantee our teams have everything they need." Fund-raising psychology leans to setting targets that can be beaten, but the reality was the Tories were still outspending us by a massive margin on digital and newspaper advertising, and we needed as much cash as we could get our hands on. I replied: "£120,000 doesn't seem much. We could do with a hell of a lot more!" We agreed to up the target to £500,000.

The mood in Southside was palpably upbeat that Thursday morning. My first port of call was Iain McNicol's office to discuss Cardiff North. There was no disagreement – he acted immediately to arrange more support for Anna. When the general secretaries of affiliated unions arrived for their usual monthly meeting, they also seemed bullish. After I gave an outline of the campaign so far and our plans for a final push, Patrick reeled off statistics for all the activity so far and said how proud we all were of the campaign we had run. "It was one of the most fascinating campaigns in British history," he said. The meeting was a far cry from the gloomy gathering on local election day only four weeks earlier. We were all slightly 'unhinged' now in our enthusiasm, and that was only to be welcomed.

On a LOTO senior management call that morning, Jeremy continued in similar vein. After reeling off a list of Tory marginals he wanted to visit, he said:

"This chance isn't going to come again. It's our big, big moment. We've got to throw everything at it in the last week."

We agreed that, as well as the six simultaneous rallies on the Tuesday evening before polling, the campaign bus would take Jeremy from Glasgow to London on the final Wednesday, making stops in Lancashire, north Wales, and the Midlands before delivering him to his eve-of-poll rally in Islington. Such was the mood that, for the first time collectively, we also discussed forming a government. If there was a hung parliament and we were the largest party, or the Tories were but could not muster any allies, we would stake a claim to do it on a 'confidence and supply'[8] basis.

As Jeremy travelled to Basildon that afternoon to make a speech about Brexit, there was every reason to feel his words would now be monitored closely in Brussels as those of a possible future prime minister. The

---

[8] Confidence and supply is not the same as a coalition. It's an agreement to support a minority government on motions of confidence and other key votes, but it does not involve having places in the cabinet. The Tory-DUP deal is 'confidence and supply.'

central point he was going to make was that crashing out of the EU would be "the worst outcome for Britain" because "there is no such thing as 'no deal'." He said:

"Britain is leaving the EU. If we leave without a positive agreement, because we have needlessly alienated everyone, we still have to trade with the EU, we will still have terms for that trade, and very bad ones. So, no deal *is* in fact a bad deal. It is the worst of all deals because it would leave us with World Trade Organisation tariffs and restrictions, instead of the access to European markets we need. That would mean adding tariffs on the goods we export – an extra 10 per cent on cars – manufacturers would leave for the European mainland taking skilled jobs with them. In sector after sector, 'no deal' would prove a disaster."

Back at Southside, the focus was on more mundane matters. A further £250,000 from Unite meant we had a budget to ensure more offensive seats would benefit from newspaper advertising and a final direct mail letter to voters from Jeremy. Meanwhile, money had been pouring in all day in small online donations at a rate of more than £1,000 a minute. By mid-afternoon, it was clear we would easily raise £500,000 and, even then, the flow of financial support was not likely to abate any time soon.

We allocated all the new money to digital advertising, taking the budget well over the million mark. This financial firepower allowed us to make some key spending decisions for the final phase of the campaign in a digital strategy meeting later that afternoon. To reach more young voters, we decided to advertise on Snapchat, becoming the first UK political party to do so. Across all social media, we would prioritise three subjects and target them by age: tuition fees to 18 to 25-year-olds, pension and dementia tax related posts to people over 50, and NHS content to those in between. We also decided to buy 'Brexit' on Google AdWords for three days to ensure anyone writing or posting about it was certain to see our material.

A video of London-based American actor Rob Delaney calling for people to vote Labour was among several pieces of new content we had to play with. In it he explains he can't vote but has lived in Britain for three years and pays taxes here. With his usual dry humour, he then says:

> "I had a baby here, through my wife's body – she had it, I watched. That baby was born in the NHS, which is the greatest thing I have ever experienced in my life. So please support Labour, tell your friends and family. Maybe they have bodies that require the NHS, or children with minds that need, for example, a school. So, vote Labour and together we can build a Britain for the many not the few."

It was a nice piece, but something we didn't know then would later make his video especially poignant: his baby son, Henry, was undergoing treatment for a brain tumour and would die eight months later. In a statement on Facebook announcing Henry's death, Rob said:

> "The NHS nurses and doctors and the home carers and charity workers who helped our family survive Henry's illness will be my heroes until the day I die. I am desperately sad right now, but I can say with authority that there is good in this world."

He urged everyone not to take the NHS for granted and "to take concrete and sustained action to support [it] however you can."[9]

---

[9] Statement posted on February 9, 2018.

12 – The Tories Play The Race Card

"If they take you in the morning, they will be coming for us that night."
James Baldwin, letter to Angela Davis[1]

What do you do when nasty doesn't work? The Tories' relentless personal attacks on Jeremy, John McDonnell, and Diane Abbott had not stopped Labour's support surging. The gap between the two parties in some of the polls was now within the statistical margin of error. The ones showing bigger Tory leads were still weighted heavily against young people voting. But the Tories must have been tracking applications to register to vote as closely as we had and will have known they were in trouble. The election could go either way. It was a far cry from all the talk of a Tory landslide. And we were about to find out how desperate they were.

The first clue was a curious one: an AdVan was driving around the north west of England displaying a Tory poster that did not make much sense. One half of the poster was blue with a picture of Theresa May and the strapline "The best Brexit deal." The other half was red with "Brexit shambles" above a picture of Jeremy and

---

[1] Letter sent by author James Baldwin to activist and academic Angela Davis in 1970 as she faced murder charges for which she was later found not guilty. An iconic figure in African-American politics, Davis was an honorary co-chair of the Women's March on Washington on January 21, 2017.

Diane. It was odd: why have the shadow home secretary on the poster and not her opposite number, the actual home secretary, Amber Rudd, on the other side with May? Why bring either of them into an advert about Brexit? The obvious answer was that the Tories were playing the race and immigration card in a heavily Brexit-voting area. It was not explicit, but it was hard to see any other explanation for Diane being on there.

It was Thursday, June 1. Until 3.58pm, it had been – despite the troubling AdVan – one of the best days of the campaign. Jeremy had done well in the *ITV* debate. The meeting with the unions that morning was upbeat. Donations were flooding in online. *YouGov* had published a seat projection saying the Tories would not get an overall majority. I sent it to my son, Gareth, in California, saying: "Just enough for Labour to form a government."

Then an e-mail landed in my inbox. It was Karie sending me a link to a Tory Facebook advert. I clicked through to find the title graphic of a 67-second video with, in white reversed out on black, the words: "If Corbyn wins, Diane Abbott will be in charge of national security." Underneath the video was the branding for the Tory page on Facebook and more text: "If the Conservatives lose just 6 seats there will be the chaos of a hung parliament with Jeremy Corbyn as prime minister and Diane Abbott home secretary. SHARE this video so everyone knows that's a risk not worth taking."

The advert started with solemn violins dramatising the voice of *BBC* presenter Andrew Marr, who was out-of-vision saying, "Shortly before 9/11…." Then Marr came into view with the words, "you voted against proscribing Al Qaeda as an organisation."

The sequence continued:

Diane: The legislation brought forward was a whole list of...

Marr: Which I have here.

Diane: Organisations.

Marr: Al Qaeda, Egyptian Islamic Jihad, the Armed Islamic Group, Harakat Mujahideen, the Liberation Tigers of Tamil, the Palestinian Islamic Jihad.. Which of these should not be proscribed?

With those words, another white-on-black graphic came up with the words: "She would be in charge of tackling terrorism." That all took 30 seconds, about the longest most people will view a video on Facebook before moving on to other posts. The editors had done their work well: the claim that Diane had "voted against banning Al Qaeda just before 9/11" was established in the first 10 seconds. Millions would have seen it.

Having watched the original interview on *The Andrew Marr Show* the previous Sunday, I was aware that the vote had not simply been for or against banning Al Qaeda. It was far more complicated than that, both politically and procedurally.

The video is a masterpiece of dishonest editing. At one point, while Marr is talking, there is a cut-away to Diane wriggling uncomfortably. To many people that would look like shiftiness and guilt. To someone in the trade, it was a sign of an edit being hidden by the producer. I was pretty certain that people were not being shown whole extracts from the interview, but tiny fragments joined together, out of sequence, to sustain a false impression.

I immediately flagged it to Labour's legal team and

asked them to get a transcript of the full 14-minute Marr interview for comparison. When it came the next day, it ran to nine pages and more than 2,500 words. The Tories had used only 52 of Diane's words juxtaposed against 114 – mainly accusatory – words from Marr.

On the programme, the question about Al Qaeda followed a more general exchange between Marr and Diane about debates in the House of Commons on anti-terrorism legislation in which Diane said:

> "What you have to remember is that on many of those occasions, I and Jeremy Corbyn were going through the lobby with Tory MPs."

This, she pointed out, included Theresa May, who had voted against the 2005 Prevention of Terrorism Bill,[2] the introduction of ID cards, and the use of control orders without sufficient legal intervention. Diane continued:

> "My point is... nobody votes against these things without a lot of thought, and the view of myself and Jeremy and most of the members of the Conservative Party, including David Davis, at the time, was this was counter-productive counter-terrorism legislation. And some of the positions we voted for were upheld in the courts."

Not surprisingly, none of this was used in the Tory video. The fragments they chose were all from the part of the interview that followed, the transcript of which is

---

[2] Theresa May and Diane Abbott both voted against the Prevention of Terrorism Bill 2005 on its third reading. Among the other Labour MPs voting against the legislation were Tam Dalyell, Alice Mahon, Barbara Follett, Jeremy Corbyn and John McDonnell. It was subsequently amended in the Lords and some of its provisions were over-turned in the courts.

reproduced in Appendix 5. By comparing this with the video, you will see that the Tories have removed, firstly, Diane's explanation that some of the organisations were seen as dissident rather than terrorist groups and, secondly, Marr's reference to the Kurdistan Workers party, who many people would have known were involved in fighting ISIS.

The interview was aggressive – and I would later discover that it was itself misleading in several ways – but, nevertheless, it was possible to discern from it that Diane had voted against a list that she thought was too broad in the organisations it was proscribing. Contrary to the impression given by Marr's opening question, and then exaggerated in the Tory video, the vote had been for or against a long list of groups and *no* specific vote had been taken on Al Qaeda.

But much more work would have to be done to sustain a legal challenge to the Tories. Everything in the transcript would have to be checked against the facts. In the case of the Al Qaeda allegation, this would mean identifying exactly when those debates had taken place and finding and reading the *Hansard* reports of them. And that was a lot to tackle on the final Friday before polling with Jeremy about to take part in the *BBC*'s live *Question Time* debate.

I had spent much of that final Friday of the campaign working on a new release about the 'dementia tax', which highlighted how people needing care who owned average and lower-priced homes would be hit much harder, relatively, than those with expensive properties.[3]

---

[3] At a cap on care costs of £100,000, a person with a house worth £217,500 (at the time, the UK average) would pay up to

Seumas had gone to York with Jeremy to prepare for the *Question Time* programme. At Southside, the communications team was gearing up to provide the usual live social media and press office support for Jeremy.

I discussed the Tory attack video with Gerald Shamash, Labour's retained solicitor, and John Stolliday in Labour's compliance unit. Both had gone through the whole transcript in detail, and we agreed there was enough of a case to answer for it to be worth troubling Diane for her comments and seeking the advice of a specialist media lawyer.

In an e-mail later that evening, after the *BBC* debate, Diane confirmed that her objection to the proscribed list had been linked to the fact that it included the Kurdistan Workers party (PKK). She said the large Kurdish community in her constituency saw the PKK as being a dissident organisation campaigning for the rights of Kurdish people within Turkey rather than being terrorists.

I read Diane's explanation in the early hours of Saturday morning while on a train back to Cardiff. My knowledge of Kurdish politics was sketchy, but I knew enough to understand that she had been responding to a legitimate point of view among her constituents. The PKK's armed conflict with the Turkish authorities since the 1980s not only had strong support among Kurds in Britain, but was also viewed by many, internationally, as justified in a struggle for independence and akin to anti-colonial resistance in Africa. Turkey itself had faced repeated criticism from the European Court of Human

---

42% of its value, whereas the most someone living in a £1m home could lose is 10%.

Rights for its brutal treatment of the Kurds and suppression of Kurdish political parties. Over the years, Turkey had come under pressure to negotiate with the PKK.

But to what extent was any of this relevant to the security of the people of Britain? With the benefit of more time, I have now read the *Hansard* transcript of the debate in the House of Commons that Andrew Marr used to ambush Diane. It took place on March 13, 2001 when the then home secretary, Jack Straw, proposed a motion proscribing 21 organisations, including the nine named by Marr in the interview with Diane. Proscription was part of a new Terrorism Act adopted by Parliament only two weeks earlier. It made it a criminal offence to belong to, or invite support for, one of the organisations listed, or to "display articles in public" in a way that arouses "reasonable suspicion" that an individual is a supporter of a proscribed organisation. The penalty for proscription offences was up to ten years in prison.[4]

This meant a Hackney resident of Kurdish origin who wore a badge supporting independence from Turkey would be at risk of arrest and imprisonment, even though no evidence was being presented by Jack Straw to show the PKK posed a terrorist threat in Britain itself.

Diane was far from alone in having concerns about the proscribed list. In the debate in 2001, the first challenge to it came from the Liberal Democrat foreign affairs spokesperson, Menzies Campbell, who asked:

"Does the Secretary of State understand the discomfort that some of us feel at the notion that 21 organisations should appear in the motion that

---

[4] See: Terrorism Act 2000, Proscribed Organisations.

we are debating, and that there has not been an opportunity to deal with each on an individual and separate basis?"[5]

From the Labour backbenches, Jim Marshall, the MP for Leicester South, agreed with Campbell that it was "unfortunate that we cannot debate each organisation on the list." He said:

"There is grave disquiet in the Sikh community about the inclusion of the International Sikh Youth Federation. That organisation is active in my constituency and I have been involved with it."

Fellow Labour MPs Fiona Mactaggart (Slough), Dennis Turner (Wolverhampton South East), and Alan Simpson (Nottingham South) raised the same issue.

For Plaid Cymru, Simon Thomas, the MP for Ceredigion, pointed out that "at least one of the 21 organisations on the list has been on a ceasefire for 18 months" and wanted to know if Straw would "de-proscribe organisations if ceasefires hold."

Straw batted the questions away before gaining some respite when Ann Widdecombe, the then shadow home secretary, spoke at length in support of the proscribed list for the Tories. But some on her own benches were still not persuaded. Lichfield MP, Michael Fabricant, expressed doubts about the Iranian opposition movement, Mujaheddin e Khalq, being on the list when it was fighting to establish a democratic regime. His Tory colleague, Douglas Houg, MP for Sleaford and North Hykeham, agreed, saying:

"The real problem is that we do not have a clue

---

[5] All the quotes from the debate are taken from Hansard, 13.3.2001.

about the strength of evidence on which the right hon. Gentleman (Straw) relies. We have to accept his word. Does the hon. Gentleman agree that that is too fragile a basis on which to proscribe an organisation?"

Labour MPs Robin Corbett (Birmingham, Erdington) and Steve McCabe (Birmingham, Hall Green) were also concerned about the inclusion of the Mujaheddin. McCabe described it as "astonishing" that the Iranian opposition group should be placed on the list when the Home Office "accepts membership of that organisation or association with it (as) proper grounds for asylum in Britain."

William Thompson, the Ulster Unionist MP for West Tyrone, accepted that many of the 21 organisations were "involved in violence in other parts of the world," but said:

"The judgment that we have to make is whether they have been involved in violence in the United Kingdom. An order proscribing every organisation involved in violence around the world would be very wide and difficult to police."

In the most wide-ranging speech of the debate, the MP for Islington North asked Straw whether or not the list had been influenced by pressure from the governments of Turkey, India, Sri Lanka and Iran to clamp down on the political activity of their opponents. Jeremy said Muslim, Sikh, Tamil and Kurdish communities in Britain were being given the message that we are banning their organisations because they are calling for fundamental change in their home countries. "We will be in danger of criminalising – or driving into the hands of criminals – a lot of people who have no wish to take part in criminal activities," he added.

Diane's contribution to the debate was a brief interjection during Jeremy's speech. She said (and I quote in full):

"While no one denies the atrocities perpetrated by some groups on the list, what we are attempting to scrutinise tonight is the process, the thinking and the procedure behind this type of proscription. The history of Britain's withdrawal from empire is littered with groups that were described as terrorists but survived to take tea with the Queen."

Replying for the Tory frontbench, Buckingham MP John Bercow told Straw he should address the concerns raised about individual organisations. He said:

"It is obviously a weakness of the arrangement that the Government have adopted that there is no opportunity to cherry pick and consider the merits of each organisation. We are invited *en bloc* to give our approval or *en bloc* to withhold it."

At no point in the debate did anyone mention Al Qaeda, never mind speak against it being on the list. At that time, Al Qaeda's operations were largely limited to Afghanistan and Pakistan. It would be six months before the group made its murderous presence felt in New York. If the list was meant to be preventative, it patently failed to make any difference. You don't need a proscribed list to investigate terrorism. If the intelligence and police services suspected anyone of plotting to fly planes into the twin towers, they could have acted. They would not have said 'we can't do anything because they are not proscribed.' But, if there was to be a proscribed list, no one was arguing for Al Qaeda to be left

250

off it.

When the vote on the motion to adopt the list was taken on March 15, 2001, the Labour and Tory front benches united to deliver a majority of 396 to 17 with 246 MPs abstaining or absent. The 17 against comprised all four Plaid Cymru MPs, one Tory MP (Peter Lloyd) and 12 Labour MPs (among them Tony Benn, Dennis Skinner, Alan Simpson, Jeremy and Diane). A large proportion of the abstentions were Liberal Democrat and Scottish National Party MPs, including their respective leaders at the time, Charles Kennedy and Alex Salmond. The two Tories and five of the Labour MPs who spoke in the debate also abstained.

What is clear to me from this is that *The Andrew Marr Show* breached *BBC* editorial guidelines in ambushing Diane in the way it did. *BBC* programmes must, of course, ask searching questions of those who hold public office, as the guidelines say. But that it is in the context of striving to avoid "knowingly and materially misleading our audiences"[6] and of ensuring output is based on "fairness, openness, honesty and straight dealing."[7] The guidelines say "contributors and audiences will be treated with respect."[8]

The Andrew Marr Show must have known – assuming they had done their own research and not simply used a Tory briefing – that reservations about the proscribed list spanned the political spectrum. They must also have known that categorising Al Qaeda as a terrorist organisation was not questioned by anyone. Yet Marr's opening question gave viewers the impression that Diane had voted specifically against proscribing Al Qaeda. And, by adding

---

[6] BBC Editorial Guidelines, Editorial Values, Clause 1.2.1 Trust.

[7] Ibid, Clause 1.2.7 Fairness.

[8] Ibid, Clause 1.2.7 Fairness.

"just before 9/11," he seemed to be inferring culpability with that atrocity.

Had the Marr team dug a little deeper, they would also have discovered that influential voices in Washington are now saying that Turkey's hostility to the PKK has hampered the fight against ISIS. The Bipartisan Policy Center, which includes former Senator Bob Dole and other prominent Republicans among its board members, produced a report in July 2016 which accused Turkey of prioritising the fight against the PKK over ISIS and of making it "more difficult for the United States to achieve its strategic objective of degrading and destroying the terrorist group."[9]

Of course, priorities in Washington change. But that is precisely why Jeremy, Diane and others have argued that security threats to the British people should be judged independently, on their own merits, rather than be subservient to shifting US global interests or dictated by pressure from other countries generally.

That Saturday morning, I was pretty sure – without having had time to do my own research – that the *BBC* had misled its audience and gifted the Tories the material they needed to make Diane look soft on terrorism, or worse. But, as the media lawyer advising us pointed out, the law can be a clumsy tool. The Tories would play for time if we mounted a libel action, and the police would be reluctant to apply electoral rules that ban the making of false statements.[10] With the polls less than a week away, and the attacks on us multiplying, was this an issue we should choose to fight on? Millions were pinning their hopes on us winning the

---

[9] Bipartisan Policy Centre, 'Turkey vs. ISIS and PKK: A Matter Of Distinction,' July, 2016, p1.

[10] Section 106, Representation of the People's Act.

election – or at least denying the Tories a majority – and we owed it to them to do whatever best served that cause.

Often these questions are settled by the circumstances. When Seumas phoned me to discuss the *Question Time* debate, his main worry was how the Trident issue was playing out in the media. The consensus of the commentariat was that May had done better than previously, but had struggled on social care and nurses' pay. Their verdict on Jeremy was that he had looked at ease and come across well until pressed on nuclear weapons.

That was probably about right. Jeremy had begun to look uncomfortable towards the end of a grilling from David Dimbleby and several audience members on whether or not he would ever "press the red button." His argument that negotiating to prevent threats emerging was far better than the appalling idea of anyone ever using a nuclear weapon was never going to satisfy some of them, and they seemed to have Jeremy on the ropes until a young woman in the audience earned the biggest cheer of the evening by saying:

"I don't know why everyone in this room seems so keen on killing millions of people with a nuclear bomb."

It was impossible to judge what effect the 'red button' question would have on people's voting intentions, but it was clear we needed to move on to other issues. I phoned Andrew Murray who suggested we challenge May on her claim during the programme that "there is no magic money tree." He thought we should make tax havens and the Tory tax cuts for the wealthy the theme of a speech Jeremy was due to make in Carlisle on Sunday evening. A conference call with Jeremy that morning gave the idea the go ahead, while also agreeing that Seumas should summarise the key lines of argument on nuclear weapons ready for the issue surfacing again.

Jeremy sounded uncharacteristically worn-out after a gruelling week of debates, interviews, and speeches. His stamina had been awe-inspiring but he was markedly less upbeat on the call than usual, and I wondered if the pressure of a long campaign was beginning to tell. Not that he was alone. There were a few tears in the campaign team in the final two weeks. It was mainly exhaustion from the long hours. But there was also the pressure of success: an underlying anxiety that a false move could undo the progress we had made. No one wanted to let Jeremy, the party or themselves down.

That afternoon there was little respite. It was the final Saturday before polling, and the political journalists were restless, hungry for some red meat to get their teeth into. Among them Ben Riley-Smith, the *Telegraph*'s assistant political editor, wanted to know why Jeremy had called for Hamas, the Palestinian Islamic movement, to be taken off the proscribed list in a television interview in 2009. Ben had provided a transcript of the interview in which Jeremy pointed out that Hamas was the elected government in Gaza and that former US president Jimmy Carter had met Hamas representatives. It was a non-story, but that would not stop the *Telegraph* making something of it. We issued a short comment from the Leader's spokesperson, saying that Jeremy was echoing a political consensus that was emerging across Europe and the US at that time, and believed it wasn't possible to achieve peace in the Middle East without recognising the elected government in Gaza.

The piece appeared online that evening under the headline: "Revealed: Jeremy Corbyn called for Hamas to be removed from banned terror list." The report was a familiar cocktail of innuendo, with the word 'terror' and 'terrorist' used several times, and reference made to the fact that supporting a proscribed group is a criminal offence. For good measure, it quoted Andrew Bridgen, the Tory candidate for re-election in North West Leicestershire, saying Jeremy had "some very strange friends and is no friend to the UK."[11]

It was fairly standard *Telegraph* stuff, but the issue itself serves to illustrate the point that Jeremy, Diane and others were making in the 2001 debate that criminalising people for the stance they take on a conflict in another country is fraught with problems. Where do you draw the line? Should Jimmy Carter have been arrested for advocating the inclusion of Hamas in the peace process? What do you do with people imprisoned for supporting a proscribed organisation when the political sands shift and Western governments take them off the list? Tony Blair, who was prime minister when Hamas was proscribed, admitted recently that he had been wrong. "In retrospect," he said "I think we should have, right at the very beginning, tried to pull [Hamas] into a dialogue and shifted their positions."[12]

---

[11] Ben Riley-Smith, the Sunday Telegraph, 'Revealed: Jeremy Corbyn called for Hamas to be removed from banned terror list,' 4.6.2017.

[12] In an interview with Don Macintyre for his book 'Gaza: Preparing for dawn,' Blair said: 'In retrospect I think we should have, right at the very beginning, tried to pull [Hamas] into a dialogue and shifted their positions. I think that's where I would be in retrospect. But obviously it was very difficult, the Israelis were very opposed to it. But you know we could have probably worked out a way whereby we did – which in fact we

Not for the first time, Jeremy was vindicated. But Blair's U-turn came five months after the election, and too late to help the campaign.

That evening, I phoned Diane to pass on the comments of the lawyer and see what she thought we should do. She was subdued, but focused and objective. Whatever anger she felt personally, her political mind was analysing what the attacks on her meant for the campaign. She said it felt like she was "at the epicentre of all the racism the election was throwing up." She had expected some "dog whistle racism" because of the immigration issue, but this was more direct:

> "The question the Tories are really putting is: do you want a black woman to hold a significant position of power?"[13]

I could not disagree. It was hard to see any other explanation for her image being on the AdVan, or for singling her out for their final attack video. It was sickening. But I was not sure what we could do at that point to take a stand against it. The campaign was going so well in almost every other way. Was our best response to the attack on Diane to focus all our energy and resources on a final push around our positive agenda? Or could we find a way of exposing the dishonesty of the Tory video that would help us defeat them? We agreed to mull it over and talk again.

---

ended up doing anyway, informally.' Reported in the Observer, 14.10.2017.

[13] Research by Azmina Dhrodia for Amnesty International found that Diane received 45 per cent of all abusive tweets sent to female MPs in the six weeks before Election Day, published 6.9.2017.

A poll released later that evening put that dilemma into even sharper focus. Conducted by *Survation* for the *Mail on Sunday*, it found there was just one point in it: 39 per cent were intending to vote Labour compared to 40 per cent favouring the Tories. The *Mail* was also carrying an Op-Ed from May oozing desperation. If Labour won, she wrote, "our economy would collapse and Britain would be the laughing stock of the world." Jeremy was "waffling and weak" on just about everything, including "keeping us safe." In a line that was cringingly unoriginal and an inept hostage to fortune, she said "we have seen this movie before and we know how it ends: in calamity for our country."[14]

So, who would do a better job of keeping us safe from calamity? At 10.04pm, that question would be posed in the most tragic of ways, yet again, when three terrorists drove a van into pedestrians on London Bridge and went on a stabbing rampage in the nearby restaurants and pubs.

---

[14] Theresa May, the Mail on Sunday, 4.6.2017.

13 – Tragedy Sparks Hope

"So why don't we go,
Somewhere only we know?"
Rice-Oxley, Chaplin and Hughes, sung by Lily Allen[1]

There was chaos on all the roads approaching London Bridge. Karie Murphy was on her way out when she saw the trouble ahead. The Champions League final had been played in Cardiff that evening and, at first, she thought it was rowdy football fans who had been watching in the local pubs. It was soon obvious that it was something much more serious.

Once back in her flat, she made some calls. It would be an hour or so before the full bloody reality of it would be clear. By then, Jeremy was on standby to make a statement and she had started liaising with the other parties. But she could not get through to anyone at Downing Street or the Conservative campaign headquarters. No one was picking up.

At 12.50am, the Unite branch secretary at Guy's Hospital phoned her. "I thought you would want to know," he said. "Kirsty is dead." Karie could hardly speak: Kirsty Boden was the nurse who looked after her on the recovery ward when she donated a kidney two years

---

[1] Lily Allen gave permission for her cover of 'Somewhere Only We Know' to be used by Labour for its 2017 general election campaign video. The song was written by Tim Rice-Oxley, Tom Chaplin and Richard Hughes.

earlier. The 28-year-old Australian was out with friends at a pub near London Bridge when the attack happened. She was killed after running towards danger to see if she could help the people who had been hit by the van. As she knelt over someone, she was stabbed herself.

As the night went on, the details of the attack became clearer. Seven people were confirmed dead and many more were injured. The three perpetrators had been shot dead by police. But, even by the time of the 7am call, there had still been no communication with Downing Street. The Tories had unilaterally announced a suspension of campaigning and were not answering Karie's calls. There was, however, agreement with the Liberal Democrats and Greens on a 12-hour suspension of the national campaigning, with local activity allowed to continue.

By 8.44am, we had put out a statement from Jeremy expressing his shock and horror at the attacks. It continued:

"My thoughts are with the families and friends of those who have died and the many who have been injured. Today, we will all grieve for their loss. I would like to thank the police and emergency services for their bravery and professionalism in acting to save lives and deal with these appalling acts of terrorism, as well as NHS staff and members of the public who sought to protect others.

"The Labour party will be suspending national campaigning until this evening, after consultations with other parties, as a mark of respect for those who have died and suffered injury. Those who wish to harm our people, divide our communities and attack our democracy will not succeed. We will stand together to defend our common values of solidarity, humanity and justice, and will not allow terrorists to derail our democratic process."

It was a non-partisan statement consistent with our approach to the Manchester attack. May, however, was preparing to sing from a very different hymn sheet. With all the polls in the Sunday papers showing a further narrowing of their lead – and the *Survation* one suggesting it was down to only one point – the Tory campaign was about to abandon what little dignity it had left. Instead of being prime ministerial, May chose to use a mid-morning statement in Downing Street – her first public appearance after the attack – to announce a politically--charged set of proposals for regulation of the Internet, "stamping out extremism" in the public sector, giving the police "all the powers they need" and increasing "the length of custodial sentences for terrorist-related offences – even apparently less serious offences."

Mother Theresa had shed her caring skin and revealed the authoritarian inner-self. Signing off a billboard campaign saying, "In the UK illegally? Go home or face arrest" – as she did as home secretary – was only a foretaste of how far she could go. These proposals, though lacking in any detail, were a recipe for a form of McCarthyism. So loosely is the word 'extremist' bandied about, the implication was that anyone with an alternative view on regime-change wars or how to fight ISIS could lose their jobs or even go to prison.

But there were other flaws: firstly, May had actually

been responsible for cutting police numbers, making her toughness sound hollow and hypocritical; and secondly, it had already been revealed that the perpetrator of the Manchester attack was known to the intelligence services – there were therefore questions to ask about operational failures before discussing purges in the public sector and new police powers.

An hour or so later, on *Radio 4*'s *World This Weekend*, Emily Thornberry wisely resisted being pushed by Mark Mardell into commenting on the substance of May's proposals. After Emily said she did not want to be "dragged into plans at this stage" so soon after the attack, Mardell pressed her on whether or not there was too much tolerance of 'extremism' in Britain.

Emily: Of course, I agree that there is too much extremism in Britain and it needs to be tackled. Exactly how that is, is something that is certainly open to debate and discussion. None of the things which I understand she is proposing in her four-point plan are immediate steps and so I regret the timing of it.

Mardell: You think she was being too political? Why do you regret the timing?

Emily: Because there is an agreement between the parties that there would not be party political campaigning until this evening or tomorrow.

Mardell: And do you regard what she said as party political campaigning?

Emily: I think it is drawing us into a debate. I think there is time enough to discuss these issues. As I say I don't think anything that she is proposing is anything that needs to be or will be dealt with tomorrow. I don't think there is anything which is immediate steps that she is putting forward. And obviously if it was then that would be a different matter. But, you know, to come out on to the steps of Downing Street immediately in the aftermath of a terrible outrage like this was not something that would be expected.

Mardell: Do you think she has broken the agreement that you've spoken of?

Emily: I just simply regret the approach that she has taken.

Emily had handled difficult media interviews well throughout the election, but this was probably her best moment – a masterclass in not getting drawn. We had already decided that Jeremy would devote a large part of a speech scheduled for that evening in Carlisle to tackling the meat of the security issue again. In batting Mardell's questions away, Emily was holding our line that national campaigning had been suspended until then, out of respect for the London Bridge victims and their families.

The Carlisle speech, which had been due to be on the economy, was being re-worked by the two Andrews and Seumas as Emily was speaking. My own day was about to go in a different, though not unrelated, direction. Just after 3pm that afternoon, John McDonnell texted me to say the *BBC* website was still using a clip from an old Laura Kuenssberg interview with Jeremy, conducted a few days after terrorist attacks at the Stade de France and the Bataclan theatre in Paris had left 130 people dead.[2] It was, he pointed out, the clip that had been used in a *News at Six* report nearly two years earlier that the *BBC* Trust ruled inaccurate and a breach of impartiality because it gave the false impression that Jeremy was opposed to the use of lethal force in such circumstances.[3]

I could tell from his texts that John was incandescent. When I looked at the webpage, I could see why. Not only had they used a clip from the old interview, the accompanying text said Jeremy was "not happy" with a shoot-to-kill policy *"in the event of"* a terror attack on Britain's streets. The copy was completely at odds with the *BBC* Trust ruling and the position that Jeremy had often reiterated that he supported the use of whatever force was necessary to save lives. To make matters worse, that page was the top trending item on the *BBC* website and being shared widely across social media by supporters of the Tories. By 4.16pm, the *Sun's* website was running a story about the conveniently rediscovered clip under the headline: "Jez gun row – Video of Corbyn saying he opposes shoot-to-kill policy rises to the top of *BBC* website in wake of London attack."

I phoned Katy Searle at the *BBC* immediately to lodge our objections and say we were taking legal advice. In a written reply an hour or so later, she said the complaint upheld by the Trust was "not against the online story, but against the broadcast piece" and that "online material is

---

[2] The perpetrators of the Paris attacks on 13.11.2015 were shot or blew themselves up.

[3] BBC Trust, Editorial Standards Findings, Appeals to the Trust and other editorial issues considered by the Editorial Standards Committee; September, November 2016 and January 2017, issued January 2017; News at Six, BBC One, 6.11.2015.

rarely taken down as it forms part of the archive." She said she had taken advice herself and was "happy that we have broken no election rules."

This did nothing to quench the red-hot blaze of anger inside the Labour party. After discussions with John, Iain McNicol and Shami Chakrabarti, it was agreed that we should set up a conference call that evening to get a barrister's opinion on our options. In the meantime, Jeremy was on his feet in Carlisle giving a speech that, in the febrile atmosphere of the day and with polling stations opening in less than 90 hours, would be scrutinised word by word.

After expressing "love and solidarity" to the families and friends of those who have died and been injured, and paying tribute to the emergence services and everyone who acted selflessly to save lives, Jeremy said:

"The violence and brutality of last night's attack, the targeting of innocent people going about their ordinary business is a depravity familiar from similar attacks in Manchester, across Europe, the Middle East and beyond. That is why we are ready to consider whatever proposals may be brought forward by the police and security services more effectively to deal with the terrorist threat.

"If Labour is elected I will commission a report from the security services on Friday on the changing nature of the terrorist threat. Our priority must be public safety and I will take whatever action is necessary and effective to protect the security of our people and our country. That includes full authority for the police to use whatever force is necessary to protect and save life as they did last night and as they did in Westminster in March.

"You cannot protect the public on the cheap – the police and security services must get the resources they need, not 20,000 police cuts. Theresa May was warned by the Police Federation but she accused them of 'crying wolf'. As Labour has set out in our manifesto, we will recruit another 10,000 new police officers, including more armed police who need to be properly rewarded as well as a thousand more security services' staff to support our communities and help keep us safe."

Jeremy went on to talk about why the election must go ahead and the choices the British people face on June 8. Then he returned to his main theme with a direct reference to May's comment that morning that "difficult conversations" had to take place on extremism.

"And, yes, we do need to have some difficult conversations starting with Saudi Arabia and other Gulf states that have funded and fuelled extremist ideology. It is no good Theresa May suppressing a report into the foreign funding of extremist groups. We have to get serious about cutting off the funding to these terror networks, including ISIS here and in the Middle East. No government can prevent every attack, sometimes the most depraved and determined will get through, but the responsibility of government is to do everything we can to minimise the risk."

The speech was crystal clear: Jeremy said he would give "full authority for the police to use whatever force is necessary to protect and save life." At the same time, he put May on the spot over police cuts and links with Saudi Arabia, using her 'difficult conversations' theme to turn the question round.

Looking back on the campaign, I realise this was Jeremy's 'Philadelphia moment'. The Chatham House speech had laid the foundations on security and the post Manchester speech built on them, but Carlisle was the moment when everything hung in the balance. It is important to be prepared for those situations, but you can't predict when they are going to happen. You simply have to know that 'Philadelphia moments' exist, and rise to the challenge when they come along. The essence of it is that, when faced with a crisis that poses questions that could make or break a campaign, you not only choose to deal with the issues head on but you do it, as Obama did in 2008, on your own terms and with integrity.

Spectator columnist Stephen Daisley described Jeremy's Carlisle speech as "the best of the campaign so far,"[4] and much of the media was leading with the line that "you can't protect the public on the cheap."[5] The *Sun,* on the other hand, had to square Jeremy's words with its previous misrepresentations by calling it "a dramatic Corbyn U-turn on shoot-to-kill". The *Sun* claimed that, in saying the police should use "whatever force is necessary" to protect lives, Jeremy was going back on his 2015 comment that he was "not happy with a

---

[4] Stephen Daisley, 'Jeremy Corbyn has just given the best speech of the election campaign so far,' the Spectator website, 4.6.2017.

[5] Laura Kuenssberg, 'London attack: Corbyn criticises Tories in terror speech,' BBC, 4.6.2017.

shoot-to-kill policy in general."[6]

Note the words 'in general'. What the *BBC* Trust's ruling hinged on was whether Jeremy had been responding to a question about shoot-to-kill generally or in the context of an immediate threat to life specifically. In the *News at Six* report, Laura Kuenssberg's scripted voice-over said she had asked Jeremy whether or not he would be happy for British officers to pull the trigger in the event of a Paris style attack. However, when the Trust examined the full interview, they found the question actually put was more widely framed:

"Would you be happy to order people – police or military – to shoot-to-kill on Britain's streets?"

The Trust therefore ruled that, while there was no deliberate attempt to mislead, "the *BBC* was wrong to present an answer Mr Corbyn had given to a question about 'shoot-to-kill' as though it were his answer to a question he had not in fact been asked."[7]

The distinction between shoot-to-kill 'in general' and the police using lethal force when lives are at risk is not a semantic one. It is critical because the latter is legal and the former is not. That Sunday evening, it was good to have the benefit of Shami Chakrabarti's advice. Ahead of the conference call at 10.30pm, she circulated an internal note making the legal position on shoot-to-kill clear.

---

[6] Harry Cole and Alain Tolhurst, 'Jeremy Corbyn U-turns on his long-held concerns over police shoot-to-kill policy in response to London Bridge attack,' the Sun, 4.6.2017.

[7] BBC Trust, Editorial Standards Findings; Appeals to the Trust and other editorial issues considered by the Editorial Standards Committee; September, November 2016 and January 2017, issued January 2017; News at Six, BBC One, 6.11.2015, p18.

Opening with my favourite legal phrase, she said:

"For the absolute avoidance of doubt, Jeremy Corbyn, the Labour Party, UK criminal and human rights law all support the use of necessary lethal force in the circumstances of a terrorist attack in order to protect innocent lives. This is different from what may be described as 'shoot-to-kill policies'... whereby suspected members of terrorist groups are deliberately killed when they might have been investigated and /or arrested. Here the use of lethal force is contrary to law."

Many journalists – either through ignorance or bias – were conflating two entirely different questions. Any coverage saying Jeremy had changed his view was therefore based on a false premise. Finding a remedy, however, for the *BBC*'s continuing misrepresentation of Jeremy's views was more complicated. The 10.30pm call discussed the potential for a libel action, a formal complaint to the *BBC* and a referral of the issue to the police under Section 106 of the Representation of the People's Act.

The latter was by a long way the most drastic of the options. The Act makes it a criminal offence to publish "any false statement of fact in relation to the candidate's personal character or conduct" unless the person has "reasonable grounds for believing, and did believe, that statement to be true." In saying that Jeremy would not be happy with the police shooting to kill "if there was a terror attack on Britain's streets," the *BBC*'s website was, to my mind, saying something about Jeremy's character, with implications for his fitness for office, that it knew absolutely to be untrue because of the Trust's clear ruling. However, we were all conscious of the far-reaching consequences of using Section 106, both in its impact on the already toxic election battle and in its potential for restricting free speech longer term. It was not a course of action we could recommend without further advice and discussion. A formal written complaint to the *BBC* was, however, a different matter, and we decided to go ahead with that without delay.

Over the next hour or so, a letter was prepared, which Gerald Shamash sent to James Harding, the *BBC*'s head of news, at 12.27am on Monday, June 5. After summarising the facts, it said we were "very concerned about the damage this inaccurate content will do to Mr Corbyn's reputation and the impact it may have on the outcome of the general election." It asked the *BBC* to remove the content immediately and publish a correction.

The shoot-to-kill issue was so sensitive and urgent that I had to abandon my plan to return to London that Sunday evening. It was not something I could break away from or deal with on a train. To complicate matters, I also had to rearrange holiday plans made earlier in the year. My wife and I were booked on a flight to Los Angeles that Wednesday to spend a few weeks with our son and his family in California. I had decided to delay my departure the moment the election was called – in fact, Jeremy sent a nice letter to my eldest granddaughter, Ilana, apologising in advance for me missing her fifth birthday on the Sunday after polling day – but I could not change the flight until I was clearer about our chances of winning. Having reached the point where I could not prevaricate any longer, and given how close some of the polls were, I decided I should be around long enough to help out if Jeremy was called on to form a government – I delayed going to the US until Wednesday, June 14.

On the Monday morning, the shoot-to-kill controversy was gathering pace. Still in Cardiff, I phoned Karie to discuss the situation. We agreed to take further advice from Martin Howe, a solicitor who had acted for Jeremy previously. The overnight letter had formally registered our complaint, but we wanted Martin to put together a more comprehensive argument based on the *BBC* Trust ruling and the *BBC*'s editorial guidelines.

That morning, the campaign also arranged – at very short notice – a press conference at midday to push our message that the Tories had put austerity ahead of safety by cutting police numbers. Karie and the team had lined up the unions representing workers in the emergency services to speak and arranged for Keir Starmer to chair.

The Tories, meanwhile, were still trying to damage Jeremy on shoot-to-kill. At 12.14pm, they did Laura Kuenssberg a grave disservice by posting a clip from her 2015 interview on the official Conservative party Twitter feed with a tweet saying:

"The shoot-to-kill policy saves lives – Jeremy Corbyn opposes it. Retweet to let everyone know."

And thousands did, helping to keep the topic trending on both Twitter and the *BBC* website.

The *BBC* had not, at that stage, responded to our complaint. While they were considering it, one of their political correspondents was interviewing Jeremy for a routine 'pool clip' that would be shared with the other broadcasters. Afterwards, Sian Jones, LOTO's head of media, who was with Jeremy at the time, alerted me to questions she thought sounded like they might have been inspired by the *BBC*'s lawyers. When I saw the transcript, I could see her point:

Alex Forsyth, BBC: You said in November 2015 that you were not happy with a shoot-to-kill policy. Last night you said you back the police using all reasonable force. Were you wrong in 2015?

Jeremy: What I said in 2015 was taken totally out of context, and there was a complaint made and the complaint was upheld by the *BBC*.

Forsyth: I've got your words. These are your words. 'I'm not happy with a shoot-to-kill policy in general. I think it's quite dangerous and it can often be counter-productive.' That was your view in 2015. What's your view now?

Jeremy: My view has not changed. In a defensive position, where security of the individuals is at stake, then what happened in Westminster, what happened over the weekend is about saving people's lives.

Forsyth: So, you back shoot-to-kill now?

Jeremy: What I back is a police force that is adequately prepared and able to deal with a terrorist attack, such as we had on Saturday where they had to take the necessary action.

Forsyth: So, you were wrong in 2015? I just want to be clear again.

Jeremy: Let's be very, very clear because the complaint made to your organisation, the *BBC*, was upheld by your own trust at that time.

Forsyth: You said I'm not happy with shoot-to-kill. I think it's quite dangerous. Have you changed your mind?

Jeremy: I've not changed my mind. What I said was I wanted our police to be able to act in a defensive capacity. I don't want, nobody wants the police going out shooting people. They don't want to do it. Nobody wants to do it. In the situation they faced at the weekend, or faced at Westminster, they took the necessary action. And I made it very clear that we want more police on the streets, including police that can take the necessary action to protect and save life.

Notice how Alex Forsyth used the term 'shoot-to-kill' without any qualification three times in her questions, but added 'in general' only on the one occasion she quoted what Jeremy had actually said in 2015. It was extraordinary – after two years of controversy about this – that *BBC* journalists were still confusing an unlawful *general* shoot-to-kill policy with the lawful use of "all reasonable force to save lives."

Whether this cross examination was influenced by lawyers eager to catch Jeremy out, or was simply a case of a journalist not understanding the issue is hard to say. It may be that everyone involved in this at the *BBC* was overcome by an urge to vindicate Laura Kuenssberg's original report. In doing so, however, they were re-cycling the same error as if the technicality of the *BBC* Trust's ruling being specific to the *News at Six* item meant it did not provide a precedent for reporting of Jeremy's views going forward. Anyone who reads the ruling will see that it made the general point that the *BBC* has to take particular care to achieve a high standard of accuracy when reporting "matters of considerable importance." The Trust said:

"The United Kingdom's response in the event of a Paris-style attack here was a crucial question at a time of extreme national concern. The audience would have an expectation that a scripted item on one of the *BBC*'s prime time television news programmes on such a day would reflect with the greatest accuracy what the Leader of the Opposition had said on the matter."[8]

The Trust was very clear that the question of authorising the police to shoot-to-kill when terrorists are "in the act of killing or threatening to kill civilians" had not in fact been put to Jeremy at all. Yet the entire *BBC* website copy, and Alex Forsyth's questions, were based on the premise it had been. Whether intentional or not, this failure to accept the implications of Trust's ruling had the effect of aiding the Tories and misleading the public on "a crucial question at a time of extreme national concern."

That evening, having arrived at a hotel near Southside, where I would stay for the rest of the campaign, I discovered Donald Trump had entered the fray with an attack on Sadiq Khan in a tweet saying:

"Pathetic excuse by London Mayor who had to think fast on his 'no reason to be alarmed' statement. MSM[9] is working hard to sell it."

In reply, Jack Bond had put out a tweet on Jeremy's behalf, which quoted Trump's post, saying:

"Sadiq Khan has spoken for London and our

---

[8] BBC Trust, Editorial Standards Findings, Appeals to the Trust and other editorial issues considered by the Editorial Standards Committee; September, November 2016 and January 2017, issued January 2017; News at Six, BBC One, 6.11.2015, p18.

[9] Shorthand for 'mainstream media.'

country in standing up to hate. That is how we stop terrorists winning, not by promoting division."

As a measure of the relative reach of the two parties on social media, Jeremy's post supporting Sadiq was retweeted more than 23,000 times, generating 4.3 million 'impressions', compared to roughly 4,500 retweets for the Tory shoot-to-kill post earlier in the day.

In the final days of the campaign, with attacks on us intensifying, online channels for reaching voters directly had become more important than ever. Our video post on the same day saying "you cannot protect communities on the cheap or by disregarding the opinions of the police" was viewed more than 3 million times on Facebook and Twitter. We had also bought 'shoot-to-kill' on Google AdWords so that people using that search term would be offered a link to Jeremy's Carlisle speech.

At 9.10am on the Tuesday of the final week of the campaign, Martin Howe sent James Harding, director of news and current affairs at the *BBC*, a letter outlining our objections to the website content. When the reply came at 4.27pm that afternoon, it simply reiterated the previous argument that the Trust's ruling applied only to the *News at Six* reports and insisted there was nothing wrong with the other material.

In the intervening period, Seumas and I had discussed whether or not to release our letter to the media. These are finely judged tactical questions, and there are always arguments both ways. Seumas was worried about the legal challenge becoming the story and fueling more bad coverage on shoot-to-kill. I had initially leaned towards releasing the letter feeling that, as we had already taken such a big hit on the issue, there could only be an upside to showing how strongly we rejected the way Jeremy's views had been portrayed. By Tuesday afternoon, however, the shoot-to-kill story was no longer featuring among the five 'most watched' items on the BBC news website, and none of us wanted to risk reviving it. Besides, the campaign was about to enter its final 36 hours with the staging of six simultaneous rallies across Britain, followed the next day by Jeremy's final sweep through the country from Glasgow to his own constituency of Islington North with four stops en route.

At that stage, the overwhelming priority was to enthuse our supporters to 'get out the vote' with a positive message of hope, and we had a few things in our back pocket. Ken Loach had saved the best until last with the fifth – and his third – party political broadcast of the campaign on the NHS. It told the story of what under-funding means for patients through the voices of health workers struggling with it day to day. Towards the end, consultant paediatrician Tony O'Sullivan broke down after talking about a child with severe mental health problems needing a hospital bed and the nearest one being 100 miles away. When I viewed it with Ken and his team in the editing suite a few days beforehand, no one could speak for a moment afterwards. I am sure most of the 8 million viewers who watched it on television felt the same.

And then there was our campaign video. This was Seumas' pet project. He wanted something like the Bernie Sanders campaign video, which had Simon and Garfunkel's *America* accompanying a montage of clips of people and rallies. After persuading him that *Jerusalem* was not quite right for our equivalent, we had given it to a team to come up with some suggestions and plan whatever new filming was needed. My input was marginal. On one occasion Laura Murray, who was co-ordinating the project, found her father, Andrew, and me and asked us to listen to some options for the music. Later she posted on WhatsApp:

> "Dad and Steve weren't super helpful... But they thought the Lily song would have more broad appeal."

The view of the old fogies was shared by most people involved – so, *Somewhere Only We Know* was chosen. The final video, which we launched online at 2pm the day before polling, captured the mood and hopes of the campaign perfectly. It was viewed 2.4 million times on Facebook and Twitter.

The Tuesday evening rallies were also a huge success. Jeremy spoke in Birmingham with a celebrity and musical line-up that included Steve Coogan, Ben Elton, Maxine Peake, Wolf Alice, Clean Bandit and Reverend and the Makers. The other rallies in Barry, Brighton, Glasgow, Croydon and Warrington had their own speakers and performers, but Jeremy's speech was transmitted live by satellite to all the venues. Those simultaneous rallies were the crowning achievement of our brilliant events team. Altogether more than 15,000 supporters turned up at the six venues. On Facebook, the Birmingham rally was seen by another 2 million people after being shared more than 40,000 times. In a matter of hours, 85,000 people had 'liked' or 'loved' it. Chloe Green, the social media manager at Southside, described it as Labour's "most successful piece of content of all time," and heaped praise on the LOTO-Southside events teams, saying:

"I got a glimpse of just how much work goes into
an event and I am infinitely impressed and in awe.
It looked sensational."

Behind the scenes, however, a new drama was unfolding. In a heart to heart with Karie, Diane Abbott had revealed – as the rallies were taking place – that she had Type 2 diabetes, which she was struggling to control. The intensity of the campaign had made it hard to manage her diet and medication. Now she was facing unimaginable pressure: the Tory vilification of her that started before the London Bridge attack was escalating by the hour. Karie felt it would be best for her and the campaign if she took a break.

Early Wednesday morning, Karie called to brief me to be ready to inform the media, once she and Seumas had discussed the situation with Jeremy. My feeling – not having spoken to Diane – was that the Tories were using her as a punchbag, and, if it was putting her health at risk, she should step aside. It would leave them throwing their fists at thin air.

After getting the nod from Seumas, I gave the story to Kevin Maguire at the *Mirror* and Laura Kuenssberg at the *BBC*, confident that both would handle an issue of that nature sensitively. (Laura may seem a counter-intuitive choice given the wrangle with the *BBC* over shoot-to-kill, but I saw that as an institutional issue and did not hold her personally responsible for the way her 2015 material was now being misused). Fifteen minutes later, at 8.57am, the Labour press office issued a one sentence statement saying Jeremy had asked Lyn Brown to stand in for Diane as shadow home secretary for the period of her ill health.

Lyn is the MP for West Ham and was in Diane's team as shadow minister for policing. She would be the first to admit that her profile is so low she would not register in a name recognition poll. When I phoned her that morning she was very reticent about the whole situation. She said she was "very fond" of Diane and described herself as "a working class girl who wasn't even supposed to be an MP, never mind shadow home secretary." This was a horrible situation for everyone, and it makes me angry even now to think about what Diane must have gone through in that election. But I think it was in the best interests of the campaign that she stepped aside at that point. Lyn was a real trooper for stepping in, and Diane deserves enormous respect for handling the situation with such dignity and discipline.

The polls on the final day were all over the place. *Survation* had Labour and the Tories only one point apart for the second time in four days. *YouGov*, whose poll the previous week had narrowed the gap to three-points and provoked ridicule from May's pollster, Jim Messina,[10] was now suggesting the Tories had opened up a seven-point lead. Late in the afternoon, Patrick Heneghan scurried into Jeremy's room where Andrew Murray and I were working to say a *BMG* poll for the *Glasgow Herald* was forecasting a 46 to 33 per cent win for the Tories. Andrew and I looked at each other and shrugged. We had not taken much notice of *BMG* throughout the campaign, why start now?[11]

That evening, as Jeremy was arriving in Islington for

---

[10] Jim Messina tweeted (31.5.2017): 'Spent the day laughing at yet another poll from YouGov.'
[11] UK Polling Report.

his final rally, the digital team had everything set up for polling day. For the first time in the UK, Labour had built a polling station finder and lined up a social media advertising campaign targeted at groups who might need a bit of a push to turn out. Over the next 24 hours, it would be visited by 1.24 million people, 61 per cent of the traffic coming from Snapchat.

When I left, Southside was nearly deserted. Many of the staff were out in constituencies around the country. Others had gone to hear Jeremy speak in Islington. As I walked back to my hotel, I thought we had done everything we could – and definitely enough to give the Tories a fright – but I did not appreciate then quite how different Britain would seem in 24 hours' time. As Jeremy would say on election night: politics has changed, and won't be put back into the box it was in.

14 – Game Changer

"I was wrong [about Jeremy Corbyn]. I am very surprised, an earthquake has happened in British politics and I did not foresee it."
Peter Mandelson, *World At One*, BBC Radio 4[1]

Midday. Friday, June 9. Theresa May was at Buckingham Palace seeking the Queen's permission to form a government. Jeremy was at home in Islington ready to take over as prime minister if she failed. With the seven Sinn Fein MPs not taking up their seats, the magic number of MPs needed to form a government was 322. The Tories, with 317 seats, would need the support of the 10 Democratic Unionists (DUP). The 262 seats Labour had won meant there was an arithmetic possibility of Jeremy leading a minority government on a 'confidence and supply' basis with the tacit support of the smaller parties.

The pressure was on May. She had failed spectacularly in her snap election gamble. In early interviews John McDonnell had made it clear Labour was ready to form a government and used May's own 'coalition of chaos' catchphrase to describe a possible Tory-DUP deal. The Twitterati were speculating about a Tory coup, and the bookies were narrowing the odds for bets on Boris Johnson or David Davis taking over. When May returned from the Palace, she jumped the gun, breaching protocol,

---

[1] Interview on the World At One, 9.6.2017.

by saying she *had* formed a government. However, it would take a further 13 days and the inducement of £1 billion of taxpayers' money for the DUP's pet projects before that would actually be true.

Southside was almost deserted when I got back there after a few hours' sleep. I had spoken to Seumas and would stay in the office that afternoon to ensure we had media interviews covered and to sign-off Op-Eds and other content. Everyone was exhausted. Even the ever-reliable Barry Gardiner needed some arm twisting to do another stint in the Westminster studios. Shami Chakrabarti shared the load as she was already lined up for a special *BBC Question Time* that evening.

Never one to miss an opportunity to influence events, Peter Mandelson texted Seumas and me to say we should listen to his interview on the *Radio 4*'s *World At One*. He had adjusted swiftly to the new situation and, with characteristic ease, found an angle to turn it to his advantage. After acknowledging he had been wrong about Jeremy and praising his "sure-footed campaign," he said he remained "unconvinced" by his ability to win a majority down the line, and argued that he needed to "build on what he's achieved" if he wants Labour to win. What he meant by this became clearer in other interviews that day by Peter's close allies: Lord Blunkett, one of Jeremy's fiercest critics, called on him to "heal the rift" with the PLP by allowing it to elect the shadow cabinet; and Chuka Umunna, who had previously ruled himself out of a shadow ministerial role under Jeremy, said he was now prepared to take one.

When the LOTO strategy group met the next day, the overwhelming feeling was that the existing shadow cabinet had proved to be a winning team and that the only pressing issue was the need to fill vacancies created by MPs standing down. It would be Jeremy's decision, but the success of the campaign meant there was no reason for him to bow to pressure from any quarter.

With all the voting figures collated, the scale of the campaign's success could be quantified. Labour had increased its share of the vote from 30.4 per cent in 2015 to 40 per cent – the biggest advance from one election to another since 1945. In securing 12.9 million votes, Labour had won more support than in any election since 1997. It was also the first election since 1997 in which Labour had secured a net increase in seats. In Scotland, we had won seven seats, reversing the long-term decline that had left us with only one in 2015.

In my home city, Anna McMorrin had won Cardiff North for Labour for the first time since 2005, one of three gains in Wales as Labour won 49 per cent of the vote, its biggest share since 1997. When I met Anna at Westminster on the Tuesday after the election, she was still absorbing her surprise success and wearing a smile that I suspect had been a permanent fixture since election night. Anna has worked as campaigns director for Friends of the Earth Cymru and as a special adviser to Welsh government ministers. She had not voted for Jeremy in the two leadership contests, but, as a new MP, was unencumbered by the events of the previous summer and eager to play a role in mounting a challenge to the Tories as they clung to power. She would, a few weeks later, become parliamentary private secretary to Barry Gardiner, the shadow international trade secretary.

When the new PLP met for the first time that evening,

the atmosphere could not have been more different to the one I had found when I first started the job. Jeremy was given a hero's welcome, with supporters and critics alike uniting in a standing ovation to show appreciation for the campaign he had led. In his speech, he said:

"This is a government on notice from the voters. Parliament will now be front and centre stage. We can defeat this government and prevent it forcing through austerity for which it has no mandate if we are fast on our feet and remain united. We will use every opportunity to block cuts to vital public services and attacks on pensioners' incomes. We *can* see off their unpopular plans to cut the winter fuel allowance for millions of pensioners, introduce a dementia tax on social care and ditch the triple lock, and force them to row back on the bedroom tax, the public sector pay cap, if we work together as a united team. Theresa May has no mandate and no legitimacy for policies that do not have the support of the majority of the British people."

It would soon become clear that the campaign had already won some of those battles by denying the Tories a majority. The Queen's Speech[2] two weeks later was notable more for what was not in it, than what was. There was no mention of means testing winter fuel payments, ditching the triple lock or introducing a dementia tax. Gone too were plans to scrap free school meals for younger primary school pupils and to create more grammar schools. There was no mention either of the manifesto promise of a vote on overturning the foxhunting ban.

---

[2] Queen's Speech, Hansard, 21.6.2017.

Labour may not have won the election, but nor had the Tories, and that in itself had forced them to abandon some of their nastier policies. There would be plenty of battles ahead, but the new parliamentary arithmetic meant the Tories could be held to account every step of the way – not least if their approach to Brexit threatened jobs or employment and consumer rights.

In calling a snap election, the Tories had tried to use Brexit for party political advantage. Their calculation was that by making Europe the central issue they could annihilate Labour in Brexit-leaning areas. In the Copeland by-election, the increase in the Tory share of the vote corresponded almost exactly to the fall in the UKIP share.[3] This fed their belief that voters who Labour had progressively lost to UKIP over the previous decade would switch *en masse* to the Tories in a general election. To achieve this, they had to do two things: firstly, they had to present the election as being about Brexit and who could be trusted to deliver it, and secondly, they had to play down a Tory brand that was, for many people, still toxic in Labour's heartland. Their campaign strategy of talking about 'Theresa's team,' attacking Jeremy's competency and hardly ever mentioning the Tory party was cynical but entirely rational *if* their premise was correct that they could make negotiating Brexit – not domestic policy – the primary factor in how people voted. The core flaw in this was not so much poor delivery, though May's inability to build a rapport with voters was undoubtedly a factor, but a

---

[3] In the Copeland by-election, the Tory share of the vote increased by 8.5 percentage points to 44.2% and UKIP's share fell by nine points to 6.5% of the vote.

failure to interpret the EU referendum result and the mood of the electorate correctly.

They assumed Brexit was the pre-eminent fault-line in British politics and underestimated opposition to austerity. While the former divides the country in a way that could have been helpful to the Tories in taking Labour seats, anger about austerity had the potential to unite people for change regardless of their views on Europe. However, the two issues had become entwined in the lead-up to the referendum with the Leave campaign not only falsely claiming austerity could be ended by reinvesting the money spent on EU contributions in the UK economy and the NHS,[4] but also manipulating discontent over low wages and poor services to stir up anti-immigrant feeling. The challenge for us had been to disentangle these issues and move the focus from Brexit to austerity.

Analysis since the election of the factors influencing how people voted suggest that Brexit was the single most important issue for only one in three voters – and many of them were Remain voters looking to reverse or 'soften' Brexit.[5] A study of the media coverage of the election by Loughborough University found Brexit featured prominently in the first and fourth week of the campaign but fell away in the other weeks.[6]

During the campaign we saw evidence that the Tory

---

[4] See for example: 'EU exit would banish UK austerity, says John Redwood,' BBC website, 22.3.2016.
[5] The British Election Study, 'The Brexit election? The 2017 general election in ten charts.'
[6] '2017 General Election Media Analysis - Key Findings,' Loughborough University.

strategy was not working as early as the second week of May when Southside's digital expert Tom Lavelle drew our attention to Google election search data that he said was "truly fascinating." He was right. Among other things, it showed that Brexit – in that week – was fourth behind tax, housing, and the NHS in the issues people were searching for information about. This was confirmed soon afterwards by our private polling, which found that Brexit was markedly behind the NHS as the issue that most concerned potential Labour voters.[7]

The Tories were, as ever, out of touch. Brexit was undoubtedly a burning issue for many voters on both sides of the argument, but the Tories failed to appreciate how angry people were about the injustice of cuts in services and living standards for them while a favoured few were doing very nicely – benefiting from tax giveaways and amassing vast wealth.

The art of elections – or any contest, for that matter – is to play to your own strengths while exploiting the weaknesses and failings of your opponents. Some of Jeremy's Labour critics were, however, quick to seize on the latter to argue that the Tory campaign was so bad that we should have won outright. Peter Hyman, who headed strategic communications for Blair during the build up to the Iraq war, told the *Observer* on the Sunday after the election that "it was an election that, with the

---

[7] When we asked 1,839 potential Labour voters to choose up to three issues that concerned them most, 58% said the NHS and 40% said Brexit. The fieldwork was undertaken from May 16 to 18.

right people and programme, was easily winnable."[8]

A few weeks later, Bridget Phillipson, Labour MP for Houghton & Sunderland South, developed this argument in a lengthy piece in the *New Statesman*. Her main contentions were that Labour had followed a "core vote plus protest vote strategy," failed "to make much progress (in winning) previous supporters of the Conservative party" and become "a party of graduates and young people, a party of the socially liberal." She wrote:

"The miracle of this election isn't that we did so well. It's that, up against what appears to be an election special of *The Thick Of It*, we nonetheless contrived to lose – and then reimagined that as success."[9]

My initial reaction to this was bemusement. The 'core vote' point was a re-run of an old argument that I thought we had long moved on from. When Ed Miliband was leader there had been a debate between 'core vote' advocates who wanted Labour to edge back to its traditional values, and those who thought Labour could win only by staying in the Blairite centre and attracting 'floating voters.' The 2015 election showed convincingly that this debate was going in ever diminishing circles. Voters were weary of the merry dance of virtually indistinguishable Westminster actors. Many either chose to stay at home or discarded traditional loyalties to give

---

[8] Michael Savage, 'Former Blair aide says party lost an easily winnable fight,' the Observer, 11.6.2017

[9] Bridget Phillipson, 'The 2017 election was far from a triumph – Labour must do a lot more to win,' the New Statesman, 12.9.2017.

their votes to parties that were, in one way or another, challenging the centrist consensus. For the first time in nearly a century, the three major parties could not between them win the support of more than half the electors. And that was the registered electors – millions more were on the sidelines, too alienated even to sign up to vote.

The most dramatic manifestation of disillusionment with Westminster centrism was Labour's meltdown in Scotland, where we lost all bar one of our seats. In England and Wales, meanwhile, our position was being eroded in different ways by UKIP, the Greens, and Plaid Cymru. This allowed the Tories to win a parliamentary majority with nearly a quarter of a million fewer votes than had prompted Neil Kinnock to resign in 1992.[10]

How could you talk about 'floating voters' in the conventional centrist sense when people were scattering in all political directions? How could you base a strategy on a core vote when it had disappeared from under your feet in one of your heartlands? If further evidence was needed of a sea change in politics, it was provided by the EU referendum in 2016 when 17.4 million voters rejected the advice of all the major political parties to vote Leave.

Having been involved in virtually all the strategy discussions leading up to and during the election, I can honestly say I never once heard anyone talk about a 'core vote plus protest vote' strategy or anything that implied it. The LOTO position was unequivocally that we were campaigning to win a majority of seats with policies that

---

[10] In 1992, 11.56m votes gave Labour only a 34.4% vote share, whereas the 11.33m votes won by the Tories in 2015 gave them a 36.9% vote share and a parliamentary majority.

would transform society in the interests of the great majority of people. Jeremy was challenging not only seven years of Tory austerity but also the neo-liberal orthodoxy that had been entrenched since the Reagan-Thatcher era. As far as we were concerned, it would be from the outset a Labour campaign like no other.

In adopting this approach, we achieved unprecedented success in shifting opinion, a process that started well before the Tories published their manifesto and began to flounder. The polls may have produced widely varying estimates of the support for Labour and the Tories at any given point, but they were consistent with each other in showing that the Labour surge was greatest at two points: during the ten days immediately after the election was called, and in the seven days after our manifesto was leaked. The crisis in the Tory campaign was as much *caused by* the pressure the popularity of our policies put them under as it was by their own undoubted miscalculation that voters would back them on Brexit whatever nasty surprises their manifesto contained.

The polls suggest that in the final two weeks of the campaign, the desperate smear tactics deployed by the Tories had a degree of success in slowing our advance. Could we have done more to combat them? We expected attacks on Jeremy, John and Diane, and were quick to rebut them when they came, but the bankrupt Tory tactics were predictable, and it is arguable we could have had more material ready to pre-empt or counter them. A progressive party that seriously threatens the power and privileges of a rich elite has to assume it will face ruthless resistance and can never be too well prepared for it.

There were, of course, other things we could have done better. The decisions we correctly took midway through the campaign to sharpen our messaging on Brexit, especially in communicating to northern working class voters, could have been implemented more swiftly. With hindsight, we could and should have put more resources into Scotland. As mentioned in Chapter 8, though we were diligent in showing how individual policies would be funded by matching tax measures, we did not – for a variety of reasons – do enough to explain how all the manifesto commitments were underpinned by a coherent investment-led wealth creation strategy.

Overall, however, it is remarkable how massively the campaign moved opinion in eight short weeks. The British Election Study, which tracks the opinions of 30,000 respondents before, during, and after an election, concluded that the campaigns mattered more than in "any British election in recent memory" and that Labour had been successful in winning over a majority of the switchers (people who changed from one party to another during the eight weeks) *and* a majority of those undecided at the outset. It said:

> "Our pre-election survey, carried out in April and May, found that the Conservatives enjoyed a healthy lead over Labour – of 41 per cent to 27 per cent but by the last three days of the campaign the daily panel put the two main parties neck-and-neck. Overall, 19 per cent of voters switched parties between the April/May survey and the election. This is similar to the amount of "churn" we saw in 2015, when 17 per cent of voters switched parties, and slightly less than

at the 2010 and 2005 elections. The significant difference in 2017 was that the flow was overwhelmingly in one direction. In 2015, Labour and the Conservatives both won about a quarter of these late switching voters – effectively cancelling each other out. In 2017, however, Labour won 54 per cent of switchers [and] more than half those who hadn't made up their mind before the campaign."[11]

Far from not making much progress in winning over Conservative voters, as argued by Bridget Phillipson, the campaign actually did very well on that score.

There is always scope for more analysis of all the factors and trends at work to help hone future campaigning, but that should not detract from the achievement of dramatically reversing a decline in the Labour vote that started under Tony Blair. The 2017 campaign attracted 2.2 million more votes than Labour won in 2001 and 3.5 million more than in 2015.

Labour's share of the vote increased in every region and nation. At the low end, Scotland saw only a 2.8 percentage point increase. Wales was at the top of the scale with a 12.1 point improvement. Across the regions of England, the increase in our vote share was remarkably consistent, ranging from 8.5 points in the North to 11.4 in the South West.

Bridget cites the loss of Mansfield and North-East Derbyshire as evidence of support for Labour "slowly fading" in traditional working-class seats, yet Labour's share of the vote actually *increased* in these

---

[11] The British Election Study, 'The Brexit election? The 2017 general election in ten charts.'

constituencies.[12] The fact that it did so by less than the nine-point national average (five and three points respectively) is hardly sufficient evidence for Bridget's sweeping assertion that Labour is becoming a party of metropolitan socially-liberal graduates – especially not when we gained seats such as Bury North, Crewe & Nantwich, Warrington South, Peterborough, Ipswich, and Colne Valley with big increases in our vote share. Moreover, according to *Ipsos MORI*, while we did win more support than the Tories from people with a degree, we also increased our vote share among the DEs – semi-skilled, unskilled and unemployed manual workers – and retained a large lead over the Tories in that social group.[13]

A point that stands out from the *Ipsos MORI* figures is that *young* DE voters (aged 18 to 34) favoured Labour over the Tories by a staggering 70 to 18 per cent. The challenge for Labour in building on the 2017 campaign is that while that poll suggests young DE voters backed Labour more heavily than *any* other group – of any combination of age and social class – they also had the lowest turnout figure (at just 35 per cent, much lower than both older DE voters or young ABC1 voters). Clearly, while Labour's message resonated with a great many

---

[12] For further analysis of Mansfield, North East Derbyshire and the three other seats we lost (Stoke South, Walsall North and Middlesbrough South & East Cleveland), see Andrew Murray, 'How do we build on Labour's election results? Not by misunderstanding our position with working class voters,' Labour List, 14.7.2017.

[13] Ipsos MORI, 'How Britain voted in the 2017 election,' 20.6.2017.

young working-class voters, we need to convince far more of them that elections can make a difference.

The argument that Labour is turning its back on white working-class voters comes with some questionable policy baggage. Graham Jones, MP for Hyndburn in Lancashire, was quoted in the *Guardian* saying:

"How thick does this party have to be? We have not learnt the lessons from the rise of the BNP [in the 1990s]. Our core voters cannot be taken for granted...We have to talk about their concerns – counter-terrorism, nationalism, defence and community, the nuclear deterrent and patriotism."[15]

This assertion presents a caricature of white working-class voters that is not supported by any evidence. Of course, there will be some who did not vote Labour because they had been swayed by media attacks on Jeremy on defence and security. But the polling following the Manchester attacks showed that 80 per cent of Labour voters agreed with him that foreign wars had added to the risk of terrorism at home.

The evidence is mixed on how much these issues influenced the way people finally voted. In the private polling we conducted during the election, only 4 per cent of a big sample of potential Labour voters chose 'defence' when they were given an opportunity to select three issues that concerned them most. The issue was way behind the NHS (58 per cent) and Brexit (40 per

---

[15] Rajeev Syal, 'Senior Labour figures clash over concerns of working-class voters,' the Guardian, 4.7.2017.

cent) in the rankings.[16] This polling was admittedly in the field before the Manchester and London Bridge attacks, but it seems unlikely those events and Jeremy's reaction to them changed people's views on the central issues in the election, given that our polling figures continued to improve. To the extent that defence might have been of more concern, it appears to have had a net positive effect on our support.

The idea that defence and counter-terrorism is losing us core voters also has to be squared with the fact that Labour lost 5 million votes between 1997 and 2010 when the party's stance was much more 'hawkish.' As Andrew Murray argued in an analysis for *Labour List*:

"To put it starkly – if working-class people stopped voting Labour in 2005 or 2010 for defence-related reasons, it would have been because New Labour fought too many wars, not too few. Of course, it would be likely that the loss of working-class support in those years was as much or more to do with actual and perceived government failures on economic and social issues, including the disappearance of so many manufacturing jobs and widening inequality."[17]

So, what then did produce a result that took my old friend Peter Mandelson and so many others by surprise? What were the key ingredients of the campaign that fuelled the Corbyn surge and denied the Tories a

---

[16] Polling by BMG of a sample of 1,839 'potential Labour voters,' which was in the field May 16-18.

[17] Andrew Murray, 'How do we build on Labour's election results? Not by misunderstanding our position with working class voters,' Labour List, 14.7.2017.

parliamentary majority?

In a *Guardian* interview shortly after the election, Emily Thornberry, the shadow foreign secretary, gave the credit to our policies. "I love Jeremy, but the star of the show was the manifesto," she said.[18] And she's absolutely right, in one sense, of course. To adapt Bill Clinton's words: 'It's the politics, stupid.' Or, as I might say, 'it's the political narrative, stupid.' People were weary of austerity and angry at the unfairness of it being applied against the many but not the few. The rhetoric that free markets and globalisation deliver prosperity was increasingly at odds with the reality of most people's lives. The foreword to the manifesto told the story of how people were being held back, and how it could be different. The rest of the manifesto backed it up with policies that gave substance to a different kind of society. Many of them were individually very popular. But, more importantly, the over-arching story offered hope and struck a chord.

But a great manifesto cannot communicate itself. You have to tell people about it and get them engaged. So how did we do that so successfully in such a short space of time? In my view, there was no single magic ingredient. Rather, there were five major factors that we managed to combine rapidly into a highly effective campaign, despite starting with a much smaller budget than the Tories.

The first was that Jeremy is a great message carrier. This wasn't obvious to the Tories because of his low personal ratings prior to the election. They attacked him as if he was a liability to Labour, but we were confident

---

[18] Interview with the Guardian, 30.6.2017.

that his ease with people and willingness to discuss the issues would cut through, once he was given the obligatory fairer hearing on broadcast media. Our polling of potential Labour voters (cited earlier) found that television ranks higher than any other medium as a source of information on current affairs (72 per cent) and in the trust they place in it (46 per cent). It also showed that, while they use social media and newspapers as sources, the trust levels are low: 6 and 12 per cent respectively. Television coverage was therefore critical. And, paradoxically, the two years of attacks on Jeremy probably helped us. They appear to have made people more curious to see what he was like and, once they had, they were pleasantly surprised. Even though Labour's own pollsters were hugely pessimistic about Labour's chances, their data showed that a lot of people liked the fact that he was a politician who was prepared to go against the grain.[19] The British Election Study concluded that a favourable shift in people's perception of Jeremy was the biggest single factor in the campaign's success. It said:

> "The main reason that Labour gained so much in the campaign at the expense of the other parties is the strong performance of Jeremy Corbyn, especially relative to Theresa May. At the start of the campaign, Corbyn lagged far behind May in leader 'like scores', with an average score of 3.5, slightly worse than Ed Miliband's at a similar point in 2015. By the end of the campaign Corbyn had

---

[19] In an early campaign poll, BMG found that 36% of Labour 'considerers' agreed or strongly agreed that 'Corbyn is a leader with the strength to go against the grain,' 26.4.2017.

caught up with May on a score of 4.4."[20]
While television – both the debates and all the other appearances – gave Jeremy a platform for reaching the electorate as a whole, the rallies were also important in winning support and engendering enthusiasm. Jeremy had an astonishing work rate: he travelled about 7,000 miles during the campaign and spoke at 100 rallies and campaign stops. Most of these were not 'gatherings of the faithful,' but events that attracted a large proportion of the people living in the areas where they were held. For the tens of thousands who went to them, they were – to use the words of Bernie Sanders quoted earlier – "unforgettable and extraordinarily powerful."

The second factor was that we had an overwhelming advantage in boots on the ground. With 500,000 plus members, Labour had more than three times as many people to call on as the Tories. From the day the election was announced, when Jeremy visited the Tory-held marginal Croydon Central, we saw huge numbers turning out to campaign with him and other shadow cabinet members. And, as the campaign grew, so did the flow of cash to finance it: online fund-raising alone raised more than £4 million in donations averaging £19. With a similar sum coming from union affiliates, we began to match the money the Tories had from wealthy donors. As Jeremy put it in his speech to the Labour party conference, three months after the election "hundreds of thousands organising online and on the ground [outplayed] the

---

[20] The British Election Study, 'The Brexit election? The 2017 general election in ten charts.'

Tories' big money machine."[21]

The third factor was the hugely successful voter registration campaign we launched on April 29 using the #RegisterToVote hashtag. The campaign was built around video messages from sport, music and TV stars such as Ronnie O'Sullivan, Lily Allen, Neville Southall, Danny De Vito, Lowkey, Jme, Stormzy, and Rag n Bone Man. Overall, nearly 3 million people applied to vote through the Electoral Commission's website. While this was only 17 per cent higher than in the six weeks leading up to the 2015 election, the crucial difference was the mix: more than 2 million – 69 per cent of the total – were under 34. There was a 36 per cent increase in voter registration among those 34 and under. Narrowing it to the under 25s, the increase was 51 per cent. Some have called into question the idea that there was a 'youthquake,' but the voter registration figures confirm that the campaign excited and interested young people on a scale not seen for generations.

The flow of the registrations over the campaign is also interesting in that it mirrors the upward movement in Labour's polling. There was a big surge in registrations in the first week (an 81 per cent increase on 2015). They then settled at about 40,000 registrations a day until we launched our campaign on April 29. At that point, registrations started to climb steadily, reaching 60,000 plus a day just after the local elections. As with the polls, a big step-change came just after the manifesto was leaked: in one day – Saturday, May 13 – 113,983 people registered. After that, the daily figure stayed above the

---

[21] Jeremy Corbyn, speech to the Labour party conference, 27.9.2017.

100,000 mark on all bar two days of the final ten days, peaking at 622,389 on deadline day: Monday, May 22.

The fourth – and probably most talked about – ingredient of the campaign's success was our use of social media. Jeremy's personal social media presence was huge at the outset. By the end of the campaign, his Twitter following had grown 32 per cent to 1.2 million and the likes for his Facebook page had increased 31 per cent to 1.21 million. His Twitter feed racked up a staggering 1.5 million retweets in eight weeks. Video posts on both channels were viewed 73 million times. Alongside this, Labour's Facebook page saw likes reaching nearly a million (up 44 per cent), and the party's Twitter following rose to nearly half a million (up 24 per cent). With donations flooding in, we were able to complement this extraordinary organic presence with smart tactical use of paid-for digital advertising to reach demographic groups under-represented in our organic following, and to reinforce calls to action. This included the online 'get out the vote' campaign that saw 1.24 million people visit our Polling Station Finder.

As discussed in Chapter 6, the creativity of the content is especially important on social media because people will not share dull posts, even if they agree with them. In this respect, the campaign scored exceptionally highly. The levels of engagement achieved – such as the 73 million video views on Jeremy's feeds – show just how talented our teams were. And this was supplemented by some equally effective content generated by our supporters, especially Momentum.

The paid element of the digital advertising campaign added vital extra reach, generally using the same content. For example, in the 24 hours after our Brexit party-political broadcast was posted on Facebook, it was seen organically by 318,097 and reached a further 429,530 people through paid advertising. By paying, we were able to target half a million voters who our data categorised as 'Labour leavers' – known supporters who were moving away from us because of Brexit.

The fifth and final factor was our strategic decision to tackle tough issues pro-actively. This goes against conventional wisdom, but we thought perceived weaknesses on Europe, Jeremy's leadership, and national security could actually be strengths – *if* we could reframe them. Besides, a progressive leader facing a hostile media is never going to be allowed to side-step attacks. We had planned to take this direct approach at the outset, such as with the Chatham House speech, and the decision was vindicated when the two terrorist atrocities put security and leadership centre stage.

In all of this, we were undoubtedly aided by the wooden performances of Theresa May and a disastrous Tory manifesto. Under pressure, the Tories had no plan B. As our support grew, they simply escalated their smear campaign and spent millions on scurrilous attack ads. But this only deepened the perception – especially among young people – that they had nothing positive to offer. Suddenly, in the final two weeks, a Corbyn-led government was seen as a real possibility.

By denying the Tories a majority, the campaign has stopped the Tories from imposing a raft of new austerity measures on the British people. The political situation has been transformed. The Tories are on the defensive, and Labour has every chance of winning an election when it comes. May's reaction to our success has been to adopt some more of our language and hint at concessions she might make on policy. However, this does not help the millions who are held back by a rigged system and need action now to tackle the problems they face. Nor does it impress some of her staunchest supporters. Tim Wallace, the *Daily Telegraph*'s senior economics correspondent, lamented after the election that the government "seems determined to forget free market ideas and adopt watered down Corbynism instead." He continued:

> "Corbyn has truly shifted the UK's economic debate to the left... If the Tories can only offer Corbynism-lite, voters will conclude they may as well choose the real deal."[22]

Clearly, the Tories are wrong-footed and divided on how to respond to such a successful challenge to the neo-liberalism that has monopolised political debate in Britain for decades.

For Labour, there can be no going back. Whether it's the collapse of Carillion, or the neglect of elderly people needing care, the free market system has failed millions miserably. Labour's manifesto not only offered hope, it also outlined practical solutions. As Wallace acknowledged, the debate has truly shifted.

Reflecting on the campaign at Labour's conference in September 2017, Jeremy summed up the new mood:

> "It is often said that elections can only be won from the centre ground. And, in a way, that's not wrong – so long as it's clear that the political

---

[22] Tim Wallace, 'Pandering to Corbynism will just give labour the keys to Number 10,' the Daily Telegraph, 8.11.2017.

centre of gravity isn't fixed or unmovable, nor is it where the establishment pundits like to think it is. It shifts as people's expectations and experiences change and political space is opened up.

"Today's centre ground is certainly not where it was twenty or thirty years ago. A new consensus is emerging from the great economic crash and the years of austerity, when people started to find political voice for their hopes for something different and better. 2017 may be the year when politics finally caught up with the crash of 2008 – because we offered people a clear choice. We need to build a still broader consensus around the priorities we set in the election, making the case for both compassion and collective aspiration. This is the real centre of gravity of British politics. We are now the political mainstream."[23]

In making that political shift, the election was certainly a game changer. Now the battle continues to win the game – for the many, not the few.

---

[23] Jeremy Corbyn, speech to the Labour party conference, 27.9.2017.

Appendix 1

Who's who[1]

Shadow Cabinet members who were heavily involved in national campaigning[2]

Jeremy Corbyn	Leader of the Labour party
Tom Watson	Deputy Leader of the Labour party
John McDonnell	Shadow Chancellor of the Exchequer
Diane Abbott	Shadow Home Secretary
Emily Thornberry	Shadow Foreign Secretary
Jon Trickett	Shadow Minister for the Cabinet Office
Ian Lavery	Joint Election Campaign Coordinator
Andrew Gwynne	Joint Election Campaign Coordinator
Barry Gardiner	Shadow International Trade Secretary
Shami Chakrabarti	Shadow Attorney General
Keir Starmer	Shadow Brexit Secretary
Angela Rayner	Shadow Education Secretary
Jon Ashworth	Shadow Health Secretary
Rebecca Long-Bailey	Shadow Business Secretary
Richard Burgon	Shadow Justice Secretary

---

[1] In all cases, the roles given are those the person was in during the campaign.

[2] These are the shadow ministers with whom I worked most closely in the campaign. It is not a full shadow cabinet list.

Leader of the Opposition's (LOTO) staff[3]

Karie Murphy	Executive Director of the Leader's Office
Andrew Fisher	Executive Director of Policy
Seumas Milne	Executive Director of Strategy & Communications
Steve Howell	Deputy Executive Director of Strategy & Communications
Katy Clark	Political Secretary
Amy Jackson	PLP Liaison Manager
Laura Parker	Private Secretary
Ayse Veli	Diary Manager
Janet Chapman	Political Co-ordinator
Jennifer Larbie	Head of International Policy
Niall Sookoo	Director of Campaigns
James Schneider	Head of Strategic Communications
Sian Jones	Head of Media
Jack Bond	Digital Officer (supported by Ben Sellers during the campaign)
Sophie Nazemi	Press Officer
David Prescott	Policy Communications Manager
Angie Williams	Press & Events Officer
Kat Fletcher	Head of Events & Visits

---

[3] This is a list of LOTO staff mentioned in the book, which is inevitably biased towards my communications role. Apologies to those former LOTO colleagues not listed. You were all great to work with!

Marshajane Thompson   Events Manager

The LOTO communications team was reinforced for the campaign by Georgie Robertson, Joe Ryle, Lizzie Mistry, Rich Simcox and Steve Hoselitz (see Chapter 6)

Labour party staff

Iain McNicol	General Secretary
Emilie Oldknow	Executive Director, Governance, Membership and Services
Patrick Heneghan	Executive Director, Elections, Organisation and Campaigns
Simon Jackson	Director of Policy and Research
Ben Nolan	Director of Member Mobilisation & Engagement
Tom Geldard	Director of Campaigns & Corporate Communications
Ben Soffa	Head of Digital Organising
Clair Pryor	Head of Corporate Communication
Tom Lavelle	Head of Digital Campaigns
Chloe Green	Social Media & Web Content Manager
Neil Fleming	Head of Labour Press Office
Stephanie Driver	Head of Regional Media
Carol Linforth	Director of Events

<u>Others</u>

Len McCluskey   General Secretary, Unite
Andrew Murray   Chief of Staff, Unite
Ken Loach   Director, Sixteen Films
Rebecca O'Brien   Producer, Sixteen Films
Olwyn Silvester   Producer, Bedlam
Jem Bendell   Professor of Sustainability Leadership, University of Cumbria
Marc Lopatin   Communications Consultant.

Appendix 2

Key Dates

Tuesday 18 April

Theresa May announces a snap general election on June 8.

Jeremy welcomes the election and sets off for Birmingham for a planned visit to a Carers Hub to launch Labour's policy of a £10 increase in the £63.10 per week carers' allowance.

Wednesday 19 April

Labour's National Executive Committee meets.

Jeremy campaigns in Croydon Central.

Thursday 20 April

Jeremy addresses a packed rally at Church House, Westminster.

Friday 21 April

Jeremy visits Swindon, Bristol and Cardiff, where he is joined by First Minister for Wales Carwyn Jones.

Saturday 22 April	Jeremy visits Manchester Central, Warrington South, and Crewe & Nantwich.
Sunday 23 April	Jeremy appears on *The Andrew Marr Show*.
Monday 24 April	Campaign strategy is agreed by LOTO and joint strategy group.[1]
	Jeremy speaks at the Scottish TUC in Aviemore and at a rally in Dunfermline with Scottish Labour leader Kezia Dugdale.
Tuesday 25 April	Shadow cabinet meets for last time before the election.
Wednesday 26 April	Final Prime Minister's Questions.
	Jeremy campaigns with NHS nurses in London.

---

[1] LOTO had its own strategy group, and there was also a joint strategy group comprising the campaign co-ordinators, Ian Lavery and Andrew Gwynne, other key politicians, and senior party and LOTO staff.

Thursday 27 April	Joint strategy meeting debates 'campaign to win.' Jeremy visits a housing project in Harlow.
Friday 28 April	LOTO staff move to Labour head office at Southside, Victoria Street, for the rest of the campaign.
Saturday 29 April	Jeremy speaks on his approach to 'leadership' in London. Twitter launch of Labour's voter registration campaign.
Sunday 30 April	Labour announces a 20 point workers' rights package. An *ORB* poll for the *Sunday Telegraph* puts the Tories on 42 per cent and Labour on 31 per cent. Labour averages 30 per cent in four polls, an improvement of more than four points since the campaign started. Jeremy campaigns in Telford.

Monday 1 May	Labour calls time on bad landlords with new rights for renters.
	Jeremy campaigns in Battersea.
Tuesday 2 May	Labour announces a plan to recruit 10,000 more police (and most of the media turn it into a memory test for Diane Abbott).
	Jeremy is interviewed by Labour supporters for Ken Loach directed party political broadcast.
Wednesday 3 May	Tories attack Labour for "tax bombshell" – we reply with a list of "10 Tory mistakes amongst many."
Thursday 4 May	Campaign representatives meet the general secretaries of Labour-affiliated trade unions to discuss financial support.
	Local elections – polling day.
Friday 5 May	Labour loses council seats and

most pundits see the results as evidence May will get the landslide she wants, but Professor John Curtice says: "Don't be fooled... the Tories still face an uphill battle in their bid to crush Labour."

Jeremy visits Liverpool and Manchester where Steve Rotheram and Andy Burnham respectively have won metro mayoral elections convincingly.

Saturday 6 May	Jeremy speaks at a rally in Leicester and visits Derby North.
Sunday 7 May	Labour pledges not to increase VAT or National Insurance contributions and to restrict income tax rises to the top 5 per cent.

Shadow chancellor John McDonnell gives keynote speech setting out Labour's economic policy in detail.

The *Sunday Times* quotes anonymous sources falsely claiming "Corbyn's team have abandoned hope of winning."

Monday 8 May	Britain's largest trade union, Unite, donates £2.25 million to support the campaign.
	Jeremy visits Worcester and Warwick & Leamington Spa.
Tuesday 9 May	Flanked by the whole shadow cabinet, Jeremy sets out Labour's agenda at the official campaign launch in Manchester.
	The campaign bus takes Jeremy to four constituencies in the north west before heading across the Pennines to Morley & Outwood.
	6.5 million television viewers watch actor and Labour activist Maxine Peake present the campaign's first party political broadcast, produced by Olwyn Silvester, Bedlam Productions.
	Posts on Twitter and Facebook, highlighting how a third of the 100 richest people in Britain are Tory donors reach more than 5 million people.

Wednesday 10 May	Angela Raynor and Becky Long-Bailey join Jeremy in Leeds to launch Labour's plan for a National Education Service.
	Jeremy visits five constituencies in Yorkshire.
	Labour's manifesto is leaked to the *Daily Mirror* and *Daily Telegraph* before it has been formally endorsed by the party's Clause V meeting.
Thursday 11 May	The Clause V meeting, representing all parts of the party, adopts the manifesto.
Friday 12 May	Jeremy gives a keynote speech on peace, human rights, and security at Chatham House.
Saturday 13 May	Jeremy visits three constituencies in Norfolk.
Sunday 14 May	Labour announces plans to combat tax evasion.
	Grime artist Jme supports Labour

in a video with Jeremy.

Monday 15 May	Jeremy speaks at Royal College of Nursing conference in Liverpool, then visits Calder Valley and Leeds North West.
	Jeremy puts question to Theresa May during her 'Facebook Live' with *ITV*'s Robert Peston. His own Facebook and Twitter posts publicising the intervention are seen by more than 5 million users.
Tuesday 16 May	Labour launches its manifesto in Bradford.
	Jeremy visits three Yorkshire constituencies.
	Matt Singh, writing for the *Financial Times*, identifies a 'Corbyn bounce' in the polls.
Wednesday 17 May	Ken Loach's profile of Jeremy is watched by 7.2 million television viewers, and millions more on social media.

Thursday 18 May	The *Times* and *Evening Standard* publish polls showing a surge in Labour support.
	Theresa May launches Tory manifesto in Halifax and faces instant anger about the dementia tax – people's homes being used to pay for care.
Friday 19 May	Labour holds press conference on the "Triple Whammy" of a dementia tax, means testing of Winter Fuel Payments and scrapping of the Triple Lock pension guarantee.
	Jeremy campaigns in Bedford, Peterborough and Stevenage.
Saturday 20 May	Jeremy speaks on intergenerational unity at a rally in Birmingham.
	Thousands turn out for Jeremy's rally at West Kirby beach in West Wirral.
	When Jeremy speaks to an audience of 20,000 at the Wirral Music Festival the singing of 'Ohhhh Je-re-my Coooorbyn'

breaks out to the tune of *Seven Nation Army*.

Sunday 21 May	Jeremy campaigns in Liverpool.

Four Sunday newspaper opinions polls put Labour on 34 per cent or more, two have the gap with the Tories down to single digits. (All were understating Labour's position, but the trend is clear).

Monday 22 May	Jeremy campaigns in Hull, Scarborough and Goole.

May announces a U-turn on capping the dementia tax – having said there would not be a limit, now she says there would be one, but she does not say at what level.

The deadline for voter registration sees a surge in applications via the Electoral Commission website – 622,389 register in one day, nearly three quarters of them under 35.

A terrorist detonates a bomb at the Manchester Arena, as thousands are leaving at the end of an Ariana Grande concert. It kills 23 people and injures hundreds more.

Tuesday 23 May	All parties suspend campaigning.
	Jeremy attends vigil on steps of Manchester town hall.
Wednesday 24 May	Campaigning remains suspended.
	Theresa May wants campaigning to stay suspended until Monday, but Labour and the other parties favour resumption on Thursday or Friday.
Thursday 25 May	Labour campaigning resumes at a local level.
	Labour's party political broadcast on Brexit goes ahead.
Friday 26 May	Jeremy speaks to an invited audience and journalists about the Manchester attack. He makes clear terrorists should be "reviled and held to account for

321

their actions" but also argues that wars Britain has fought abroad have fuelled terrorism and not increased security at home.

The Tories accuse Jeremy of being "soft on terrorism" and the *BBC*'s deputy political editor, Norman Smith, describes the speech as "hugely contentious." But polls later find 75 per cent of public agree with Jeremy.

Saturday 27 May

On Cup Final weekend in England and Scotland, Labour launches its football policy.

Jeremy attends FA Cup final at Wembley to see his home side, Arsenal, beat Chelsea 2-1 to win the trophy for a record 13th time.

Sunday 28 May

Labour outlines its security policy, including recruiting more police, firefighters, prison officers and border agency staff.

Jeremy campaigns in Glasgow.

Monday 29 May	Jeremy gives as good as he gets in an interview with Jeremy Paxman during *Sky-Channel 4* election programme.
Tuesday 30 May	Labour launches its policy of extending childcare support.
	Jeremy has an awkward moment on *Woman's Hour* when he does not have the cost of the childcare policy to hand (though the presenter has it in a briefing and fails to tell her listeners).
	Jeremy launches Labour's 'Race and Faith' manifesto in Watford.
	Jeremy appears on *The One Show*.
	John McDonnell presents a party political broadcast on the economy, directed by Ken Loach.
Wednesday 31 May	Jeremy decides to take part in the *BBC* leaders debate and announces his decision at a lunchtime rally in Reading East.
	People on the streets of Cambridge applaud Jeremy as he

is driven to the *BBC* debate.

Jeremy is so well received by BBC audience that Nigel Farage claims it is packed with "paid-up Corbynistas."

Thursday 1 June

Campaign has upbeat meeting with union general secretaries.

Appeal to supporters following the *BBC* debate raises £470,000 online in under 8 hours – £1,000 a minute.

Jeremy speaks on Brexit in Basildon.

A Tory AdVan tours north west with a photograph of Diane Abbott alongside Jeremy under the heading "Brexit shambles." The other half is Theresa May below "The best Brexit deal." Oddly, there is no image of Amber Rudd, who Diane shadows as home secretary.

Tory video attacking Diane appears online.

Friday 2 June

Campaign seeks legal advice on

Diane attack video.

Jeremy takes part in the *BBC*'s *Question Time* debate in York.

Saturday 3 June

Jeremy campaigns in three Tory held seats in the East Midlands.

The *Mail on Sunday* releases *Survation* poll putting Tories on 40 per cent and Labour on 39.

Tories step up their attack with a Theresa May Op-Ed in the *Mail* saying Jeremy was "waffling and weak" on "keeping us safe."

At 10.04pm, three terrorists drive a van into pedestrians on London Bridge and go on a stabbing rampage. Seven people die, including the three attackers.

Sunday 4 June

All parties suspend campaigning until the evening.

Theresa May breaks convention to make a politically-charged speech on 'extremism' in Downing Street.

Two-year old text about 'shoot-to-kill' starts trending on the *BBC* website. It gives a false impression of the position Jeremy has always held on the use of lethal force to protect lives during a terrorist incident, confusing this with his opposition to 'shoot-to-kill in general,' which is illegal.

The *BBC* refuses to remove the content.

Jeremy makes his position clear in a speech in Carlisle, which one commentator describes as the best of the campaign.

Monday 5 June

Labour submits complaint to the *BBC* on the 'shoot-to-kill' content.

The Tories promote the *BBC* website page on social media.

Jeremy visits four constituencies in the north east, ending with a huge rally in Gateshead.

The final Ken Loach party political broadcast on the NHS is watched on television by 8 million viewers and millions more on social media.

| Tuesday 6 June | Jeremy campaigns in Telford. |

Jeremy speaks at a rally in Birmingham, which is transmitted live by satellite to simultaneous events in Barry, Brighton, Croydon, Glasgow and Warrington. More than 15,000 turn up at the six venues and 2 million watch via Facebook.

| Wednesday 7 June | Diane Abbott stands down temporarily as shadow home secretary on health grounds. |

Labour launches its campaign video, using Lily Allen singing *Somewhere Only We Know* as a soundtrack.

Jeremy travels from Glasgow to London via north Wales in a final tour ending with a packed eve-of-poll rally in Islington.

| Thursday 8 June | Voters across Britain turn out in numbers not seen for 20 years. |

Labour's polling station finder is used by 1.24 million people.

At 10pm, exit poll suggests Tories will take 314 seats and fail to win a majority. It predicts Labour will win 266 seats, 34 more than in 2015.

Friday 9 June

Once all the votes are counted, Britain has a hung Parliament with the Tories on 317, Labour on 262 and the other parties taking 71 seats.

Labour has achieved its best vote since 1997 and the largest increase in its vote share since 1945. The party has won 12.88 million votes, 3.5 million more than in 2015.

The Queen invites Theresa May to form a government, but it takes two weeks and £1 billion in spending promises for her to strike a deal with the Democratic Unionist party.

Appendix 3

The 2017 General Election: facts, figures and comparisons[1]

The headlines:

- The number of people casting a vote – more than 32 million – was the highest for 25 years.
- The turnout – measured as a percentage of registered voters – was 68.8 per cent, the highest for 20 years.
- In the 6 weeks leading up to the deadline for voter registration, 2.94 million people registered to vote, an increase of 17 per cent on 2015.
- Of those who registered to vote, 1.05 million were aged 18 to 24, an increase of 51 per cent on 2015.
- Labour won 12.88 million votes – its best result since 1997 and an increase of 3.53 million on 2015.
- Labour won 262 seats (up from 232 in 2015) – its largest contingent in the House of Commons since the 2005-10 parliament.
- Labour gained 36 seats and lost 6[2], giving a net gain of 30.
- Labour achieved a net gain in seats at a general election for the first time since 1997.

---

[1] House of Commons Library, Research Briefing, 'General Election 2017: full results and analysis,' 22.9.2017.

[2] The comparison is with 2015 and therefore Copeland, which was lost in a by-election and not regained, counts in the 6 lost seats.

- The Tories (with 317 of the 650 seats) lost their overall majority and could only form a government by doing a deal with the Democratic Unionist party.
- Labour won more than 40 per cent of the vote for the first time since 2001
- Labour's share of the vote was 9.6 percentage points higher than in 2015 – the largest increase in its vote share from one election to another since 1945.
- Labour's share of the vote increased in every region and nation.
- The increase in Labour's share of the vote in England was relatively even across all regions, ranging from 8.6 percentage points in the North East to 11.5 points in the South West.
- Labour's share of the vote in Scotland and Wales increased by 2.8 and 12.1 percentage points respectively.
- Britain elected more than 200 female MPs for the first time. Of the 208 women elected, more than half are Labour.
- Parliament is more diverse than ever – 52 MPs are from black and minority ethnic backgrounds.[3]

---

[3] Ibid, p7

Votes and seats summary: 2017 and 2015

	2017			2015[5]		
	Seats	**Vote**	**Share %**	**Seats**	**Vote**	**Share %**
Conservatives	317	13,636,684	42.4%	330	11,299,609	36.8%
Labour	262	12,877,460	40.0%	232	9,347,273	30.4%
Liberal Democrats	12	2,371,861	7.4%	8	2,415,916	7.9%
Scottish National Party	35	977,568	3.0%	56	1,454,436	4.7%
Democratic Unionists	10	292,316	0.9%	8	184,260	0.6%
Sinn Fein	7	238,915	0.7%	4	176,232	0.6%
Plaid Cymru	4	164,466	0.5%	3	181,704	0.6%
Greens Party	1	525,665	1.6%	1	1,111,603	3.6%
UKIP	0	594,068	1.8%	1	3,881,099	12.6%
Ulster Unionists	0	83,280	0.3%	2	114,935	0.4%
SDLP	0	95,419	0.3%	3	99,809	0.3%
Speaker/Independent	2	50,447	0.2%	2	52,396	0.2%
Other parties	0	295,975	0.9%	0	388,343	1.3%
Totals	**650**	**32,204,124**	**100%**	**650**	**30,697,525**	**100%**

---

[5] House of Commons Library, Research Briefing, 'General Election 2017: full results and analysis,' 22.9.2017.

Labour: seats, gains, votes and share of the vote in 2017, compared to 2015

	Seats			Votes		
	Won	Total	Gains/ Losses[6]	000s	Share %	Increase[7]
UK	262	650	+30	12,878	40.0%	+9.6
England	227	533	+21	11,389	41.9%	+10.3
Wales	28	40	+3	771	48.9%	+12.1
Scotland	7	59	+6	717	27.1%	+2.8
Regions of England						
North East	26	29	- 0	710	55.4%	+8.6
North West	54	75	+3	1,973	54.9%	+10.2
Yorks & Humber	37	54	+4	1,277	49.0%	+9.9
East Midlands	15	46	+1	955	40.5%	+8.9
West Midlands	24	59	-1	1,175	42.5%	+9.6
Eastern	7	58	+3	1,012	32.7%	+10.7
London	49	73	+4	2,087	54.5%	+10.8
South East	8	84	+4	1,326	28.6%	+10.3
South West	7	55	+3	875	29.1%	+11.5

---

[6] Net figures.
[7] Percentage points.

Labour election trends: UK 1997 – 2017[8]

	1997	2001	2005	2010	2015	2017
Votes (000s)	13,518	10,725	9,552	8,607	9,347	12,878
% of UK vote	43.2%	40.7%	35.2%	29.0%	30.4%	40.0%
Seats won	418	412	355	258	232	262

Voter registration – applications to Electoral Commission website in five weeks to deadline[9]

	2017	2015	% change in 2017
18 – 24	1,051, 308	696,366	+51%
25 – 34	972,680	788,457	+23%
35 – 44	432,220	439,727	–2%
45 – 54	244,604	299,952	–18%
55 – 64	134,865	163,105	–17%
65 – 74	70,797	83,094	–15%
75 and over	31,759	44,818	–29%
Total	2,938,268	2,515,519	+17%

---

[8] Ibid, p12.

[9] The point to note is that voter registration was not only 17% higher, but it was also even more heavily weighted towards younger voters than usual.

The Swing Paradox

Many experts analyse British elections mainly in terms of the 'swing' from Tories to Labour, or vice versa. This dates from the days of two party politics, when the decisive issue was their relative support. As a methodology for understanding shifts in opinion, it became less useful with the emergence of third parties and the significant movements in their support.

In this election, there was a 4.4 per cent swing to Labour from the Tories because, while the share of the vote of both parties went up, Labour's went up by more. However, this clouds the impact of movement *away* from third parties – notably UKIP and the SNP – which had a huge bearing on the outcome and produced a concentration of support behind the two major parties (82.3 per cent) not seen since 1970. This may mean that swing analysis comes into its own again. In this election, however, it does still tell only part of the story.

For example, in Scotland, the 2017 election saw a swing from Labour to the Tories of 5.5 per cent. This sounds disastrous for Labour, but it obscures the fact that both parties increased their share of the vote at the expense of the SNP, whose share of the Scottish vote fell to 36.9 per cent from 50 per cent in 2015. But the SNP vote share is still well above the 19.9 per cent it achieved in 2010. The main issue for Labour in Scotland is therefore not so much the battle with the Tories as winning back seats lost to the SNP in 2015. Of the 60 seats Labour needs to win at the next election to form a majority government, 16 are in Scotland – and all of them are SNP held.

Similarly, in England, the swing comparison from one region to another is distorted by the collapse in support for UKIP, which saw its share of the UK vote plummet to 1.8 per cent compared to 12.6 per cent in 2015. Because UKIP's vote is unevenly spread, this helped the Tories more in some regions than others. For example, Labour's share of the vote increased by similar amounts in Yorkshire & Humberside and London – 9.9 and 10.8 percentage points respectively – and yet the swing to Labour from the Tories was markedly different – 1.0 and 6.3 points respectively. A six-fold difference in the swing on the strength of only a small difference in the increase in Labour's vote share is explained largely by the fact that UKIP had twice as much support to lose in Yorkshire & Humberside than in London[10] – giving the Tories an opportunity to use Brexit to increase their vote share in the former by just over half the regional fall in UKIP's share.[11]

Swing analysis can be helpful in raising questions, but you have to dig much deeper to find the answers to them. In the case of Scotland and much of England north   of Watford, the tendency to talk mainly in terms of Labour-

---

[10] UKIP's share of the vote in Yorkshire & Humberside and London in 2015 was 16% and 8.1% respectively.

[11] In Yorkshire & Humberside, UKIP's share of the vote fell by 13.4 % points to 2.6% and the Tory share of the vote increased by 7.8 points to 40.5%. (Labour's vote increased by 9.9 points to 49%, giving a 1% swing to Labour from the Tories.)

Tory swings has, over a number of years, obscured the more important political factor of nationalism and Brexit emerging as proxies for dissatisfaction with neo-liberal austerity, blamed in different ways by the SNP and UKIP on a 'Westminster elite.'

Appendix 4

Labour's narrative

The Labour Party Manifesto 2017

Foreword

A big part of being the leader of a political party is that you meet people across the country and hear a wide range of views and ideas about the future. For me, it's been a reminder that our country is a place of dynamic, generous and creative people with massive potential.

But I've also heard something far less positive, something which motivates us in the Labour Party to work for the kind of real change set out in this manifesto. It is a growing sense of anxiety and frustration.

Faced with falling living standards, growing job insecurity and shrinking public services, people are under increasing strain. Young people are held back by debt and the cost of housing. Whole families are being held back from the life they have worked towards.

I'm constantly told of these pressures in the workplace. Faced with constant cuts and interference, our police, nurses, doctors, teachers and council staff are held back from delivering the public services they signed up to.

Workers are held back by falling real pay and job security. Our entrepreneurs and managers are being held back from growing their business. If you are increasingly asked to do more with less, then you are not alone.

Every election is a choice. What makes this election different is that the choice is starker than ever before. You can choose more of the same: the rich getting richer, more children in poverty, our NHS failing and our schools and social care in crisis. Or you can vote for the party that has a plan to change all of this – The Labour Party.

Britain is the fifth richest country in the world. But that means little when many people don't share in that wealth. Many feel the system is rigged against them. And this manifesto sets out exactly what can be done about it.

Britain needs to negotiate a Brexit deal that puts our economy and living standards first. That won't be achieved by empty slogans and posturing. We cannot put at risk our links with our largest trading partner. Instead we need a jobs-first Brexit that allows us to upgrade our economy for the 21st century.

Labour will invest in the cutting-edge jobs and industries of the future that can improve everybody's lives. Which is why this manifesto outlines a fully costed programme to upgrade our economy. From childcare to transport, housing to lifelong learning, Labour understands how a successful economy depends on services that support us all.

So yes, this election is about what sort of country we want to be after Brexit. Is it one where the majority are held back by the sheer struggle of getting by? That isn't the Britain Labour is determined to create.

So let's build a fairer Britain where no one is held back. A country where everybody is able to get on in life, to have security at work and at home, to be decently paid for the work they do, and to live their lives with the dignity they deserve.

Let's build a country where we invest our wealth to give everyone the best chance. That means building the homes we need to rent and buy, keeping our communities safe with more police officers, giving our children's schools the funding they badly need, and restoring the NHS to its place as the envy of the world.

Don't let the Conservatives hold Britain back.

Let's build a Britain that works for the many, not the few.

Jeremy Corbyn

Leader of the Labour Party

Appendix 5

<u>The Tory attack on Diane Abbott analysed</u>

The Tories produced a video attacking Diane by extracting just 52 of her words from the 2,500 in an interview with Andrew Marr on Sunday May 28. Because the average viewing time for online videos of this kind is usually not much more than ten seconds, the passage we were most concerned about was the one the Tories edited to open the video. The effect was to give the false impression that Diane had specifically opposed the banning of Al Qaeda in 2001 (when the issue was the blanket proscription of 21 organisations, some of which she thought could be considered dissident rather than terrorist groups).

The following is the full text of that passage with the words the Tories <u>left out</u> in italics:

Marr: *Let me come onto your bit, you said, nobody votes against these kinds of things without a lot of thought.* Shortly before 9/11 you voted against proscribing Al Qaeda as an organisation. *That was a huge mistake on your part was it not?*
Diane: *Have you actually read the legislation we were voting on?*
Marr: *I have read the legislation and I've looked at the addendums as well*
Diane: *And what* the legislation brought forward was a whole list of...
Marr: Which I have here.

Diane: Organisations, *some of which some people would argue were not terrorist organisations but dissident organisations. And to say that because I.....*

Marr: *Which ones, because I've got the list here.* Al Qaeda, Egyptian Islamic Jihad, the Armed Islamic Group, Harakat Mujahideen, the Liberation Tigers of Tamil, the Palestinian Islamic Jihad, *Islamic Army of Aden, the Abu Nidal organisation, the Kurdistan Workers Party,* which of these should not be proscribed?

Diane: *Titles are one thing, but the reality of some of those groups (was) that they were dissidents in their country of origin, and that's why some of us were not — had they taken Al Qaeda as one thing, that would have been something. But you know....*

Marr then continues to press Diane on which organisations she was against proscribing and puts the list in front of her saying: "*I'm just wondering which ones you think are okay.*" To this she replies: "*it's not that I thought they were okay — I thought that they were dissident organisations.*"

Putting it round the other way, here is the attack video transcript, i.e. the above without the words in italics. It starts with the voice of *BBC* presenter Andrew Marr, who is out-of-vision, saying: "Shortly before 9/11...." Then Marr comes into view with the words, 'you voted against proscribing Al Qaeda as an organisation.'

The sequence continues:

Diane: The legislation brought forward was a whole list

of...

Marr: Which I have here.

Diane: Organisations.

Marr: Al Qaeda, Egyptian Islamic Jihad, the Armed Islamic Group, Harakat Mujahideen, the Liberation Tigers of Tamil, the Palestinian Islamic Jihad... Which of these should not be proscribed?

Then a black-on-white graphic comes up with: 'She would be in charge of tackling terrorism.'

The unedited passage from the interview lasts about 90 seconds. The Tory extracts last just over 15 seconds. The claim that Diane had 'voted against banning Al Qaeda just before 9/11' is established in the opening seconds and only 10 of Diane's words are used.

344

Acknowledgments

This is a purely personal account of a dramatic campaign that produced countless stories. I have tried to cover most of the major ones. No doubt others will enrich the picture of a game changing election with their own perspective on events.

My account of what happened is based on how things looked from the engine room, Labour's head office in Westminster. I did not spend much time in the constituencies, nor did I go on the road with Jeremy. I did, however, have an over-view of the whole campaign. I was part of the strategy group that shaped it, and I worked closely with Jeremy, John McDonnell, and the other key politicians who led it.

Where there were gaps in my knowledge because of the need for a division of labour between colleagues, I have checked the details with those directly involved. I am grateful for their help, but responsibility for what's written here is entirely mine. If there are any mistakes, I would be pleased to hear about them. If you disagree with my analysis, I am open to debate.

The book is unashamedly partisan. I make no secret of what I think as the story unfolds. But partisanship should not be at the expense of truth. I have therefore restricted myself to first-hand knowledge and verifiable facts. Unlike some of the accounts from people claiming to be independent, I have not relied on hearsay and gossip or quoted anonymous sources.

In the editing process, my two official task masters were James Stewart and Tony O'Shaughnessy, who both teach broadcast journalism to postgraduates at Cardiff

University. Appointed by the publisher, they are also old friends and former colleagues at *BBC Wales*. I knew they would be rigorous and frank, and I was not disappointed.

The first draft was also read by my Freshwater colleague John Underwood, who had a spell as Labour's director of communications in the early 1990s and knows the party well. John and I were active in student politics together at Sheffield University in the 1970s when he was editor of *Darts* and I held various union and NUS posts. Another Freshwater colleague and Labour party member, Angharad Neagle, was a sounding board for my thoughts on digital strategy and read those sections of the book at draft stage. My thanks to both of them.

The photographs in the book are mainly snaps I took with my phone. Their quality is mixed, but they do give a feel for what was going on behind the scenes. I am pleased to say they have been supplemented by some photographs supplied by Sian Jones, LOTO's head of media, Jennifer Larbie, LOTO's head of international policy, and Steve Hoselitz, my former boss at the South Wales Argus who worked on the campaign.

The writing of *Game Changer* involved much more work than I expected – unlike my novel, *Over The Line*, I couldn't make things up! On delivering the manuscript, I felt a huge sense of achievement and relief. But I also knew that the journey was unfinished: a book has to be attractively produced and properly promoted. I am therefore immensely grateful for all the support I have had from Accent Press and Freshwater.

At Freshwater, Hannah Jones, Simon John, Louise Harris and Ann Rees have helped with everything from updating my website and issuing press releases to distributing signed copies and organising an events programme.

At Accent, Hazel Cushion and her team have been unstinting in their support. Hazel knows the publishing world inside out and worked wonders in getting her trade contacts excited about *Game Changer* at an early stage, ably assisted by Katrin Lloyd.

This book, and the experience on which it is based, could not have happened, of course, without the subject on which it is based: Jeremy Corbyn and the game changing movement that has transformed British politics. I could not believe my luck when, at 63, I was given an opportunity by Seumas and Karie to be part of Jeremy's team.

I hope this book will, in a small way, help carry forward what was achieved by collective effort in the campaign. And I look forward to continuing to support Jeremy and my brilliant former colleagues in whatever ways I can from a different place in the movement.

My personal and political soulmate in all this has been Kim, who I met at Sheffield University when collecting money for striking steelworkers and she persuaded her friends to give some. Forty years on, we were equally united in wanting to see Jeremy's leadership succeed; and when the call to work for him came, she had no hesitation in putting our other plans on hold and helping to make it possible for me to work mainly in London when my home was still in Cardiff.

Steve Howell

Index

After running a successful PR consultancy for twenty years, Steve Howell had half an eye on retirement when 'the call' came – would he like to work for Jeremy Corbyn? As a long-standing Labour party member, it was an irresistible opportunity. Howell took the job but had barely been cleared for a parliamentary pass when Theresa May called a snap election. Suddenly, as deputy director of strategy and communications, he was at the centre of what Corbyn would called 'the fight of our lives.'

Howell was born in Wallasey and grew up in north London. After studying at Sheffield University and working as an anti-apartheid campaigner and journalist, he founded his own communications business in 1997. By the start of 2017, he had handed over much of the day to day running of Freshwater - now employing more than fifty people - to colleagues and was working on his second novel. But his writing plans were put on hold to join the real-life drama unfolding in British politics.

OVER THE LINE
by Steve Howell

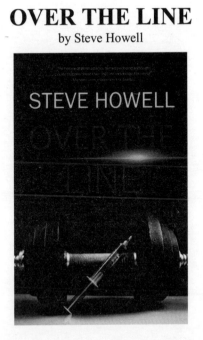

Olympic athlete Megan Tomos goes into hiding a week before the Rio Games after detectives reopen their investigation into the suspicious death of her childhood friend.

Back in her home town of Newport, Megan reconnects with Will, her rugby-playing ex-boyfriend who failed a drugs test. Her coach, Liam, doesn't know what to think - he wants to believe in her, but she doesn't make it easy for him as pressure grows from the police and media.

Set in the steroid underworld of South Wales, *Over The Line* exposes the overlapping epidemic of drug abuse for appearance-enhancing body-building.

'The heroine of British athletics, tainted by doping and death. Couldn't happen? Read *Over The Line* and decide. Absorbing.'
- Michael Calvin, Independent.